JOHN HENRY NEWMAN

GARLAND REFERENCE LIBRARY
OF THE HUMANITIES
(VOL. 1475)

JOHN HENRY NEWMAN
Theology and Reform

edited by
Michael E. Allsopp
and
Ronald R. Burke

LONDON AND NEW YORK

First published 1992 by Garland Publishing, Inc.

2 Park Square, Milton Park, Abingdon, Oxfordshire OX14 4RN
52 Vanderbilt Avenue, New York, NY 10017

Routledge is an imprint of the Taylor & Francis Group, an informa business

First issued in paperback 2018

Copyright © 1992 Michael E. Allsopp
and Ronald R. Burke

All rights reserved. No part of this book may be reprinted or reproduced or utilised in any form or by any electronic, mechanical, or other means, now known or hereafter invented, including photocopying and recording, or in any information storage or retrieval system, without permission in writing from the publishers.

Notice:
Product or corporate names may be trademarks or registered trademarks, and are used only for identification and explanation without intent to infringe.

Library of Congress Cataloging-in-Publication Data

John Henry Newman : theology and reform / edited by Michael E.
  Allsopp and Ronald R. Burke
    p.   cm. — (Garland reference library of the humanities ; vol. 1475)
  "...papers presented originally at the...Newman Centennial Conference, held at Creighton University, 18-20 October 1990"—Preface.
  Includes bibliographical references and indexes.
  ISBN 0-8153-0384-X (alk. paper)
  1. Newman, John Henry, 1801-1890—Congresses. 2. Theology, Doctrinal—History—19th century—Congresses. 3. Catholic Church—Doctrines—Congresses. I. Allsopp, Michael E. II. Burke, Ronald R. III. Series.
BX4705.N5J635   1992
230'.2'092—dc20   92-21667
                                                        CIP

ISBN 13: 978-0-8153-0384-8 (hbk)
ISBN 13: 978-1-138-87333-9 (pbk)

Dedication

In Memory of

Rev. Anthony P. Weber, S.J.

(1921-1990)

* * *

"Give me your love and your grace,

for this is sufficient for me."

CONTENTS

Preface ix

Acknowledgments xi

Introduction xiii

Madeleine Kisner, A.S.C.
NEWMAN, THE CHAMPION OF TRUTH 3

Ronald Burke
NEWMAN, LINDBECK AND MODELS OF DOCTRINE ... 19

Edward E. Kelly
ATHEISM OR CATHOLICISM:
Stark Disjunction From Complex Newman 45

David G. Schultenover, S.J.
GEORGE TYRRELL:
Devout Disciple of Newman 57

Philip C. Rule, S.J.
GROWTH THE ONLY EVIDENCE OF LIFE:
Development of Doctrine and
The Idea of a University 87

Paul G. Crowley, S.J.
THE *SENSUS FIDELIUM* AND CATHOLICITY:
Newman's Legacy in the Age of Inculturation 109

Bernard J. Mahoney
NEWMAN'S CONSCIENCE:
A Teleological Argument 131

Francesco Turvasi
THE DEVELOPMENT OF DOCTRINE IN
JOHN CARDINAL NEWMAN AND ALFRED LOISY 145

Martin X. Moleski, S.J.
ILLATIVE SENSE AND TACIT KNOWLEDGE:
A Comparison of the Epistemologies of
John Henry Newman and Michael Polanyi 189

John R. Connolly
NEWMAN ON THE CRITICIZABILITY
OF CATHOLIC FAITH 225

Gerard Magill
IMAGINATIVE DISCERNMENT:
Newman's Safeguard of Faith and Morals 241

Contributors 257

Index 259

PREFACE

This collection of papers grew out of a concern of several at Creighton University for the perduring nature of the thought of John Henry Cardinal Newman. Although Cardinal Newman died some one hundred years ago, his influence on today's thinking is still strong. Like Sir Thomas More with his *Utopia*, Newman put forward an ideal of society and life which has a recognizable relation to the lasting possibilities open to humankind.

Whether Newman is seen variously as a reformer, or a mind fundamentally Catholic and constitutionally Protestant, or one thrown among strangers, or even a point of reference in a troubled world, there is no doubt that he was not only alive to the problems of his age in Church and society, but that he continues to inspire, to uplift and to enlighten us today. The editors and paper contributors of this volume have been brought together by a common interest in a man for whom the continual search for truth is paramount.

Cultivation of the intellect, which Newman considered to be the necessary and sufficient end of education, was also the critical ability needed to be able to withstand the spread of opinions and values he believed to be greatly inadequate to the human condition. It is that critical ability that gives his analyses an uncanny contemporary relevance to issues of faith and life and their public significance, and what many contemporaries call the "privatizing" of religion.

Following Newman, Jan Walgrave, O.P., has said that the proper excellence that a good intellectual training should impart to the mind is a keen and subtle power of openness, flexibility, and comprehension. To be able to enter into a different pattern of thought, to understand its point of view, to distinguish its principles, to see its consequences, to judge its lack of consistency within the perspective of its own view, to criticize it from within, to identify with its spirit and method without losing a sense of objective distance, is the basis of real dialogue. Indeed, one gets the impression that Newman did not fear the encounter of another, nor did he ever fear to encounter another. To such courage were joined an evangelical patience and wonderful modesty. For he knew that he was only cooperating in what was, after all, God's work.

He not only stood firm for a certain intellectual integrity, but also for a freedom of mind, which would not neglect that superior capacity to understand all that is human, which is the prime condition of intellectual culture. Few championed the full rights of conscience as he did. Few pleaded so persuasively on behalf of its authority and liberty. Yet he never allowed any trace of subjectivism or relativism to taint his teaching. "Conscience has its rights because it has its duties."

As Dean of Creighton College of Arts and Sciences, I am most pleased that thanks to Garland Publishing Inc., the editors and paper contributors, a wider audience will now be able to enjoy this volume of papers presented originally at the College's Newman Centennial Conference, held at Creighton University, 18-20 October 1990.

"Lead, kindly light, among the encircling gloom."

Michael Proterra, S.J.
Easter 1991
Omaha

ACKNOWLEDGMENTS

A book does not come about by spontaneous generation. This book owes its existence to the efforts of a number of friends and colleagues.

First, we must thank the contributors not only for their willingness to allow their papers to be published in this volume but also for their active collaboration in the editorial work. Also our thanks to Michael Proterra, S.J., for writing the volume's preface.

We are indebted to the editors of the *Heythrop Journal*, and the journal's publisher, Basil Blackwell, for permission to include the essays by David Schultenover, "George Tyrrell: 'Devout Disciple of Newman'," and Paul Crowley, "Catholicity, Inculturation and Newman's *Sensus Fidelium*," both of which have appeared in the *Heythrop Journal* in revised versions.

To Paula Ladenburg and Phyllis Korper, Garland Publishing, Inc., we owe special debts for their support of this project, and their professional advice.

We are grateful to colleagues in our universities and to members of our departments, in particular the secretaries, for their interest and assistance.

For her professional assistance in completing the text, we are indebted to Jean Stillmock, Creighton University.

Finally, our thanks to John Franklin, Creighton University, without whom this book would not have been published.

INTRODUCTION

Political realities were the decisive influence upon Roman Catholic theology in the nineteenth century. Revolutionary developments in European political life brought reactionary responses from officials who "controlled" theology in the Roman church. Because of this control, Roman Catholic thought was turned toward a more conservative and medieval kind of theology called "scholasticism." The basis of authority in this theology was insistence upon the authority of the pope ("ultramontanism").[1]

In the following pages I wish to introduce John Henry Newman in terms of the positions he took amidst this general political and theological transition. I want to indicate: 1) the nineteenth-century political developments that threatened the Roman Catholic church; 2) reasons for the Catholic selection of scholasticism and ultramontanism as the best "reaction" to these developments; and 3) the ways in which nineteenth-century popes implemented this reaction. Then I will review Newman's own life and writings. He combined "modern" virtues of historical consciousness, Protestant conscience, and limits to papal authority with an uncompromising love of the Roman church and pope. He united the new with the old and was almost condemned. He is now a candidate for sainthood who has challenged the Catholic church to face squarely the strengths and diversity of modern times.

Revolution

The age of revolution was a time of significant demographic growth in Europe. The continent's population more than doubled in the nineteenth century, from 187 million persons at the time of the French Revolution to 401 million at the beginning of the twentieth century.[2] This population explosion resulted in part from scientific discoveries and industrial developments. These developments brought better hygiene and medicine (including purification of water and the use of vaccinations), as well as improvements in methods of agriculture, in availability of power, speed of transportation, and means of communication. Together, these changes in science and industry eliminated the plagues and hungers that had previously—and with regularity—decimated the populations of European cities.[3]

These technological successes contributed also to the new and "liberal" spirit in Europe. Nourished by the success of science and industry, many persons were ready to experiment with political structures. This readiness for change reflected a new reliance upon *internal authority* rather than *external authority*, a trust in the creative imagination of the human subject. Along with the simple fact of a greatly increased population, the readiness for experimentation diminished the authority of popes, traditions, and kings, while investing the individual with new rights and freedoms. It led away from the Old Regime of monarchy and toward the new world of liberalism and democracy.

For many persons, however, the emphasis upon individual freedoms and new experimentation was synonymous with the debacle of the French Revolution. Liberty and change inherently implied the death of kings and the collapse of the authority of the church. For these conservatives, any theology that followed such a "modern" and "inward-turning" kind of method, placing authority in the thought and experience of the human subject, was conspirator with the Revolution. It had to be condemned.

The French Revolution of 1789 was an illustration of the modern cultural forces in Europe which, in a long century, would terminate the church's military and political power. The Revolution was followed in 1793 by the Reign of Terror, then by an alternation between Napoleonic emperors, restored kings, and republican democracies. In the Revolution, however, it was especially the liberal spirit that was given indelible European expression. In defiance of monarchy and papal authority, new emphasis was given to the rights and freedoms of the people, especially the middle class. Serfdom, privileges of birth, and control by the church over departments of the state were permanently abolished.

The decline in monarchial and papal authority continued, with many reversals and progressions, through the many democratic revolutions of 1848 (France, Italy, Austria-Hungary, and Germany) and through the pope's loss of the (Italian) Papal States in 1870. The long century of secularization culminated in France with the 1905 *Law of Separation of Church and State*, which guaranteed freedom of worship for Catholics, but which permanently disestablished the Roman Church from secular power in France and removed from it all state support.

Reaction

In reaction against liberalism and the "de-throning" of its political power, the official Catholic church of the nineteenth-century glorified the past. The policy of the church was an effort to restore a past prominence to the papacy.[4] The church's glorification was in some ways successful. Romantics such as Chateaubriand and Schlegel extolled the church's emphasis upon hierarchial authority, tradition, and immutable truth. Missionary expansion ran parallel to Europe's colonial expansion and combined with Catholic immigration to the New World to increase the number of Catholics and Catholic dioceses around the globe. Popular support made funds available for new Catholic churches in rural areas and in new urban centers. New dogmas reflected intensified Catholic faith among the laity. Pro-Catholic political parties were founded and new rights were accorded Catholics in non-Catholic countries such as England and the Netherlands.[5]

This "successful" glorification of the past had questionable theological consequences. It led to the indiscriminate condemnation of many newer theological positions.[6] Not trusting "modern" theologies, all of which gave increased attention to the thought and experience of the human subject, the official church increasingly demanded conformity with the more "traditional" scholastic theology. This kind of theology relied conservatively upon the authority of the hierarchal church.

Theology and Scholasticism

Many individuals introduced new and modern theologies to make sense of Catholic faith in the language and philosophies of the day ("*fides querens intellectum*"). This was especially true in the period of modern Catholic thought from 1790-1840 in Germany.[7] Such modern theology was found in the work of Frederich Schlegel (1772-1829), George Hermes (1775-1831), J.S. Drey (1777-1853), Ignaz von Dollinger (1799-1890), Felicite de Lamennais (1782-1854), Anton Gunther (1783-1863), Antonio Rosmini (1797-1855), Jakob Frohschammer (1821-1893), Herman Schell (1850-1906), and (later) the Roman Catholic modernists.[8] All of these theologies were specifically put on the *Index of Forbidden Books* or more generally condemned.

One result of such condemnations and the general theological control by the magisterial church was a consistently decreasing diversity in Roman Catholic theology.[9] In the early years of the century, many different theologies were taught in Catholic seminaries, not only in Germany but in Rome itself. Some of these were based on teachings of modern philosophers, such as Kant, Hegel, and (most commonly) Descartes. Although these theologies often had only a few references to the Bible and little reference to the authority of the hierarchial church, they did attempt to find consistencies between modern philosophy and traditional faith. As the century progressed, and such theologies were condemned, the only acceptable form of theology came to be scholasticism.[10]

Why was it that this particular theological method was advocated? It was not simply because it had been dominant in the middle ages and hence had been used longer than other methods. Philosophically it was, in fact, embarrassingly outdated, with a propensity for generalizing on the basis of so-called "universals," not attending to historical criticism, and not investigating the biases or ideologies of its sources.

What the scholastic method did quite consistently emphasize, however, was the authority of the hierarchical Catholic church. Standard scholastic "manuals" of theology were strongly encouraged in seminaries of the nineteenth century and these clearly championed the authority of Rome in a brief syllogism: 1) revelation is possible; 2) revelation's occurrence can be demonstrated by certain signs, such as miracles; 3) miracles prove Jesus Christ had special authority as sent by God; 4) Jesus Christ handed on his authority *to the Church* which he founded, including custody of the divine truths he had taught.

The Church, then, had authority from God in Christ. Its authority included not only the determination of official doctrines. It included also the authority to declare the character and range of its own authority! Hence scholastic theology, with nothing in the way of critical historical study, "proved" the authority of the Church and made autocratic rule legitimate. *Quod erat demonstratum.*

Such "acceptable" theology did not find basis for its claims in human experience (which was not to be trusted), in modern or transcendental philosophies (which were summarily condemned), in the careful study of history (which was not yet acceptable), or finally in the Bible. The Bible was seen primarily to direct authority on to Rome and the church. Authority was to be found in *traditional teaching*, under the guardianship of the church. By the end of the century, however, the authority was vested even more in the *guardian* than it was in the *teachings themselves*.

It was this specific character of scholasticism, the way in which it established authority for the hierarchy of the church, which made it most attractive. To the beleaguered papacy in an age of revolution, it was much more attractive than all other theologies of the day. It was not the intellectual excellence of scholasticism so much as the institutional power of Rome which was decisive to scholasticism's "success" in the latter half of the nineteenth-century.[11]

Nineteenth-Century Popes

The persons who led and exemplified the church's glorification of the past against the new and liberal spirit of the age were the powerful and conservative popes of the nineteenth century. Pius VII (1800-1823) restored the Society of Jesus (the Jesuits) in 1814, with their special vow of obedience to the pope.[12] He also restored the Office of the Inquisition and the *Index of Forbidden Books*.

Leo XII (1823-1829) helped bring considerable emancipation to Catholics in England. Gregory XVI (1831-1846), in his encyclicals *Mirari vos* (1832) and *singulari nos* (1834), expressed strongly his opposition to liberal Catholicism, especially as it developed in France. He spoke against freedom of conscience, freedom of speech, and freedom of the press. With words of strident hostility, he condemned in *Dum acerbissimas* (1835) the work of George Hermes and his constructive response to Kant.

Pius IX (1846-1878), longest reigning of the century's popes, was himself originally quite liberal. He allowed Jews to live outside the ghetto; laws of censorship of the press were softened; and a constitution was finally granted to the papal states. He turned radically conservative, however, in the wake of the 1848 democratic revolutions, especially the one in Italy. The three major themes of his pontificate were an emphasis upon scholastic thought; a centralizing and strengthening of the magisterium in Rome; and an opposition to experimentation in both theology and politics.[13] In 1849, he put Rosmini's work on the *Index of Forbidden Books* and in his *Eximiam tuam* (1857) he condemned Gunther for questioning the "perennial immutability" of faith.

An important symbol of Pius IX's papacy was the *Syllabus of Errors*, an appendage to his 1864 encyclical, *Quanta Cura*. This was occasioned by two International Congresses of liberal Catholics, at Malines and Munich, convened in 1863. These Congresses encouraged democracy, religious toleration, and academic freedom. The second Congress especially attempted to balance the rights of scholars and scientists in their disciplines with the authority of the church. Comprised primarily of the laity, these Congresses seemed to the pope to go too far in *disseminating* the authority which he sought to *centralize*. A short time later he sent a public letter, the "Munich Brief," to the Archbishop of Munich. In it he demanded from all Catholics proper deference to church authority and final submission in all matters to the decisions of the magisterium.

The "Munich Brief" was followed in December of 1864 by the *Syllabus of Errors*, which was sent to all Catholic bishops. It was structured as a list of condemnations. Among the condemned ideas were these:

1. non-Catholics might be saved;
2. the Pope's temporal power might clash with his spiritual power;
3. the church should not use force in religious matters;
4. church and state should be separate from each other;
5. Catholicism did not have to be the only religion in the state;
6. the Pope should reconcile himself to progress, liberalism, and modern civilization.[14]

No previous document in modern times had more sharply exemplified a cultural disparity between Catholics and non-Catholics. Whereas many Roman Catholics embraced the propriety of the *Syllabus*, many secular newspapers ridiculed it as the most unreasonable document in the history of the papacy. They lampooned Pius IX as a senile old woman, incompetent, medieval, vindictive, bitter, and attempting only to preserve (in general) the "old ways" and (in particular) his dwindling political and military power.[15]

Pius IX also promulgated the dogma of the Immaculate Conception of Mary (1854) and convened in 1869-1870 the (First) Vatican Council, which declared popes infallible—before its meetings were suspended by the victories of the Italian nationalists and the prospects of the Franco-Prussian war. By the time of the pope's

Introduction

death, he was a contradictory figure: seen by some as a saint repelling the "modern" assaults of the devil; seen by others as a conceited autocrat, manipulated like a puppet by a clique of diehard reactionaries.[16]

Leo XIII (1878-1903), last of the nineteenth-century pontiffs, is most famous as a more liberal advocate of social justice. He was also, however, quite conservative in teaching the inerrancy of Scripture (*Providentissimus Dei*, 1891), and in directing Catholic theology to that of St. Thomas Aquinas (*Aeterni Patris*, 1879).

The "success" of this century-long campaign of defensive conservatism and self-glorification was only temporary and superficial. Rather than investigating the various possibilities opened by the ground-swell of European liberalism (which had been symbolized and in some was distorted by the violence of the French Revolution), officials of the church chose grandly and indiscriminately to condemn it. The popes controlled the shape of Catholic theology, but did so not by influencing its spirit so much as by stifling its expression.

Ultramontanism

Especially in the time of Pius IX, the office of pope came to be venerated as the supreme locus of Catholic authority. Although by the final years of his reign many were unhappy with his thundering denunciations of liberalism, he was seen by many others as worthy of veneration. Threatened by secular and political revolutions in general; threatened specifically by Italian nationalism and the forced termination of papal temporal rule; describing himself finally as a "prisoner in the Vatican," surrounded by Italian nationalists; the pope was seen by many Catholics as the most holy of persons. This personal popularity was coupled with the scholastic theology which assigned to him the highest possible authority. The result was an impressive basis for "ultramontanism" in reaction to anti-Catholic forces.[17]

"Ultramontanism" was an insistence upon papal power. The name was a label put upon certain supporters of the papacy by their opponents. These opponents claimed the supporters asserted that the pope had temporal as well as spiritual power, and not just power in the papal states of Italy. His power extended "beyond the mountains" (the Alps), into Europe and the rest of the world.

There were in fact at least two very different kinds of ultramontanism in the eighteenth and nineteenth centuries. The earlier ultramontanism contested the power of kings; a later ultramontanism contested even more the authority of the people.

In the eighteenth century, ultramontanism was a liberal and intellectual movement to defend the rights of the pope in a church threatened by kings. Ultramontanists opposed the excessive power of kings in nations such as France. There, in alliance with local bishops, the king had been able to control the church's theology, its episcopal appointments, and its very life. This power of the French king (and "conservative" French bishops) was known as "Gallicanism" and those who opposed it were seen as "liberals" as well as ultramontanists.[18]

With the success of the French Revolution, however, the enemy of the original ultramontanism (the king) was dead. Nonetheless, a new threat to papal power and the church was perceived: the very spirit of the revolution and its call to the rights, freedoms, and self-determination of the people. Against this new spirit of political liberalism a second ultramontanism arose, one that was more hierarchical, romantic and reactionary, as well as more clerical and anti-democratic. It extolled the pope as royal guardian of beauty, tradition, and of truth.[19]

The new ultramontanism was not supported by liberals, those who advocated authority in the people, the expansion of individual rights and freedoms, and readiness for change. Rather than championing the pope's authority to *balance* that of kings, the new ultramontanism seemed dedicated to preserving the past by giving autocratic power to the pope, demeaning the power of individuals, and standing strong against all change.

Ultramontanism, in reaction to the revolution(s), polarized the church. It became the party of political conservatives and of the pope. By this group it was identified with orthodoxy itself. Its opponents were derisively labelled as "liberals" and opponents of the Catholic tradition.

Newman in England

Amidst this century of revolution and ultramontanism, a special tale of Roman Catholicism was told in England. From the time of 1688 and William of Orange, the Catholic church in England was *constitutionally* English (or "Anglican"), not Roman. It was in this

Introduction

Anglican church that John Henry Newman was born and raised, not converting to Roman Catholicism until he was forty-five years of age. Despite spending the first half of his life in a different communion; despite "polarities" within his own theology; and despite the suspicion with which he was viewed by officials of the Roman church; Newman became one of the most important influences in the church of the twentieth century.

There was a proud tradition in the English church—including elements of fear, disgust, and hate—which separated the English people from the foreign rule and religion of the Roman popes. The belief was widespread in England that Roman Catholics were superstitious, idolatrous, and morally corrupt. This belief seemed confirmed in the nineteenth century by the *Syllabus of Errors* (1864) and the definition of papal infallibility (1870).[29] There were in fact laws against Roman Catholics in England: marriages in front of Roman priests were not valid and resulting children were legally bastards; Roman Catholics did not have the right to vote or hold office; and Roman Catholics could not serve in the military.[21]

Against this background, however, the shock-wave of the French Revolution initiated among the English a new benevolence toward Roman Catholics. The death of French royalty and the attack upon the Catholic church in France were seen as threats to civilization itself. There was a sense that Christian nations (and monarchies!) had to band together to protect their traditions and beliefs. In that situation, not only were seven thousand French Roman Catholics welcomed to England, there were also new laws of toleration passed which enlarged the rights of Roman Catholics on English soil.

Nonetheless, the true church of England was and remained the Anglican, the English Catholic church. Even after the Catholic Emancipation Act of 1829, "Popery continued its traditional role of red-rag to John Bull."[22]

John Henry Newman

It was in this same English Catholic church that John Henry Newman (1801-1890) was born and raised. The young Newman was sometimes characterized as a withdrawn scholar; sometimes as a more aggressive reformer; and quite consistently as a controversialist and a supporter of the underdog. Before he joined the Roman Catholic church, Newman had experienced his father's fall toward bankruptcy; received a kind of "religious awakening" from an evangelical mentor; was ordained an Anglican priest; taught (primarily seminarians) at Oxford; was pastor to a poor church near the university; began publishing details of his historical knowledge and love of the ancient Catholic church; became well-known as an Anglican preacher; and led what became famous as the "Tractarian" or "Oxford Movement," an effort to re-instill ancient and authentic Catholic Faith in members of the English Catholic church.

Newman was an exceptional individual. His talents were wide and deep. He was not only an educator, a philosopher, a preacher, and a theologian. He was also a true master of English composition, with a controversialist's gifts for levels of meaning, rhetoric and satire. His best known novel was *Loss and Gain: the Story of a Convert* (1848) and his longest poem was "The Dream of Gerontius" (1865).

Talent and Criticism

Ian Ker proposes that Newman's talents have been under-recognized. He claims his literary achievements are comparatively unperceived; his philosophical achievements not sufficiently appreciated; his legendary fame in his own day as a preacher remarkably unexamined; and the main thrust of his position on liberal education, in *The Idea of a University*, surprisingly misunderstood.[23]

Despite all of his talents, Newman has received numerous criticisms. Some have complained, for instance, that despite all his training and work as an historian of early Christianity, he never developed a critical historical method in regard to Scripture. In fact—and this is often a second criticism—he seemed to substitute for such a method a pre-emptive emphasis upon the authority of the magisterial church. Indeed, after hearing that he marshalled a defense for exclusive national churches and one for the Roman Catholic church's crimes of the Inquisitions, his love of the church does sometimes seem excessive!

Further, as Terrence Merrigan has pointed out, he was also "theologically backward" in some of his views. He spoke uncritically of the "unpardonable sin" of the Jews, for instance, something more recently seen as grossly inappropriate.[24]

More personally, Newman had peculiarities of character. His degree of introversion; his emphasis upon other-worldliness; his

Introduction

extreme monasticism; and, most of all, his seriously distressed relationships with the members of his own family—these factors and others in his life make him an interesting "case study" and together with his talents cause some ambiguity regarding his sickness and his health.[25]

Notable beyond every other talent and flaw, however, was Newman's theology. His writings were consistently quite foreign from the orthodox mold of scholasticism. In his early years as a Roman Catholic he may have received some special allowances because he was such a "prize catch" from the English Catholic church. For many years his works teetered at the edge of being put on the *Index of Forbidden Books*. And yet by the time of the centenary of his death (1990), his writings in various theological areas had become more important than those of any other nineteenth century author.

The Newman Riddle

Before looking briefly at some of those areas of Newman's special importance, one final point needs to be made. Beyond all criticism and praise, Newman has been known as a "riddle" in Catholic theology since at least 1908.[26] The riddle revolves around classifying him as a conservative or as a liberal. Paul Sobry and J.H. Walgrave have attempted to resolve the riddle by saying that he is both: there are health "polarities" and a consistent "balance" in Newman's thought. Ian Ker makes the same point, with strong praise, when he writes:

> The mind of Newman, I argue, is characterized not by contradictions but by complementary strengths, so that he may be called, without inconsistency, both conservative and liberal, progressive and traditional, cautious and radical, dogmatic yet pragmatic, idealistic but realistic.[27]

Newman did represent two different worlds. He had, on the one hand, a deep-seated piety, a thoroughly loving dependency upon the church—which he explicitly refers to as a nurturing mother. On the other hand, he had a kind of "Protestant pride," a critical independence of conscience which included a more historical view of the church.

The distinction between conservative and liberal is important in efforts to identify the whole Newman. Yet the distinction can also be overdone. As Marvin R. O'Connell has written, "A liberal is someone who wants to correct things that are wrong and a conservative is one who wants to preserve things that are right."[28] Newman wanted both. He wished always to protect the church which he revered. At the same time, he keenly recognized that the church was an historical entity, one which had experienced substantial change from its ancient past and needed to continue in change to complete its mission in the future. In his view, the identity of the church was something to be maintained through the "tension between the conservative and innovative elements in the Church."[29]

Newman was himself both conservative and innovative. The most important "novelties" he brought to Roman Catholicism were 1) an historical realism; 2) a Protestant conscience; and 3) modern limits to papal authority. All of these liberal novelties challenged the adequacy of "official" scholastic theology. Yet Newman blended and enriched these novelties with a relentless love of the church and the papacy. After introducing this relentless love, we will review the novelties he blended with it.

Love of Church and Pope

Newman's love for the Roman Catholic church and its authority was massive and filled his sermons and his writings. To many, by modern standards, it would seem excessive. He was himself born in the pale of the French Revolution and he reacted like so many others by becoming "anti-liberal." As Philip Griffin has pointed out, like other English theologians of his day, he wanted to preserve "at all cost, the authority . . . of the church."[30]

The church was to Newman the practical source of revelation and faith. It was like the mother upon whom the infant depended for life and nurture. The church was the guide, intended by Christ, to help the Christian understand the teaching of scripture and revelation. Christians must have "a faith in the church," he wrote, which is

> submission of the reason and will towards God, wistful and loving meditation upon the message, and childlike reliance on *the guide* which is ordained by Him to be the interpreter of it. The Church Catholic [the guide] is our *mother*; if we attend to this figure, we shall have little practical difficulty in the matter

before us.[31] I will accept her doctrines and her rites, and her Bible—not one, and not the other, but all.[32]

Griffin found Newman completely faithful to this authority. "It is a measure of his faithfulness and docility to the Catholic Church that—from conversion to deathbed—there is no recorded instance of ever wishing to teach any doctrine which would be against her *magisterium.*"[33]

In Newman's view, Protestantism was but a temporary "historical bubble." Its members had inverted the proper authority and priority of faith, putting Scripture before church. He insisted that the church had to be first, as it always had been. Early conversions to the church came before the New Testament was written and it was the authority of the church itself which had *introduced* Scripture as an aid to faith and future conversion.[34] The proof of the authority of Scripture, until the time of the Reformation, "rested on the testimony borne to it by the existing Church."[35]

For Paul, Newman wrote, the church was a "pillar and ground of the truth." It was nothing less than that for him. He listed Scriptural references which testified to the main aspects of the church: its existence, organization, order, ordination, rules, and discipline.[36]

In addition to this commitment to the church, Newman also pledged his fealty to the pope. One might have supposed that Newman was so English and so natively anti-Roman that affection for the papacy would be impossible. Yet that misses how deeply devoted Newman became to the early church during his studies and in the Oxford Movement. When he finally joined the Roman Catholic church it was not with reservations regarding the pope.

Yet there was some development, some mellowing, in Newman's own view of the papacy. He chose the authority of the pope over what he saw as the fleetingness of every other source of authority in the world. In an address he delivered as the first Rector of the (new) Catholic University in Ireland, Newman said:

> Deeply do I feel, ever will I protest, for I can appeal to the ample testimony of history to bear me out, that in questions of right and wrong, there is nothing really strong in the whole world, nothing decisive and operative, but the voice of him to whom have been committed the keys of the kingdom and the oversight of Christ's flock. The voice of Peter is now, as it

> ever has been a real authority, infallible when it teaches, prosperous when it commands, ever taking the lead wisely and distinctly in its own province, adding certainty to what is probable, and persuasion to what is certain. Before it speaks, the most saintly may mistake; and after it has spoken, the most gifted must obey.[37]

Sincere words such as these from Newman make him sound like a complete and total ultramontanist. There were signs of that throughout his life.[38] And yet when the pope failed, over a four-year period (1854-58), to give him the support he required in establishing Ireland's university, his trust in the papacy's worldly wisdom was diminished. He wrote:

> A sentiment which history has impressed upon me, and impresses still, has been very considerably weakened as far as the present Pope is concerned . . . I cannot help thinking in particular, that, if he had known more of the state of things in Ireland . . . then at least he would have abstained from decreeing a Catholic University. . . . I am led to think it not rash to say that I knew as much about Ireland as he did.[39]

Newman had extreme respect for the pope, but it did not remain without qualification throughout his life.

Before giving further consideration to Newman's view of the papacy, let us now review some of the landmark works in which he introduced to Roman Catholic thought the "modern" ideas of historical realism, Protestant conscience, and limits to papal authority.

Historical Realism

In *An Essay on the Development of Doctrine* (1845), Newman brought historical realism to Roman Catholics. He did this by bringing to them at least a sharpened—if not an entirely new—recognition of historical changes in the doctrines of their church. This new recognition was quite exceptional in a church which officially emphasized the "perennial *immutability*" of the faith. Newman outlined significant changes between the ancient church and the church of the nineteenth century. He claimed to see, nonetheless, a kind of "congruency" between the two and asked if others could not also see the underlying likeness in the two dissimilar pictures.

This suggestion of historical continuity despite historical dissimilarity was for Newman the answer to a question. It suggested how changes between the ancient and the nineteenth-century churches could be explained as growth and development, and not necessarily as loss of identity and truth. Yet to officials of the Roman Catholic church, the historical model was threatening. It contradicted the dominant view which emphasized eternal, a-historical sameness in the church. In this view, there had been in the time of the apostles a "deposit of faith," comprised of timeless propositions. This deposit was guarded and explained through the centuries by the scholastic theology of the Catholic hierarchy. This scholastic model had no place for historical change and Newman's historical model had little place for scholastic theology.

For Newman, the deposit was a living and growing "idea," one which influenced every dimension of Christianity (rites, music, theology, morality, art, philosophy, etc.) and not simply doctrine. The "idea" was intended forever to develop in the community of the church's minds (which included laity as well as priests and bishops).[40] To live was to change and to be perfect was to have changed much.[41]

Newman was not trained in Roman scholasticism. He had psychological and intellectual discomfort with its a-historical and abstract syllogisms. And so he refused to use it. He replaced it with a more concrete, historical, and inductive approach, one which gave attention to the uniqueness of each object (rather than generalizing about "essences") and of each experience (rather than avoiding human subjects). His method did accommodate history and human affections. To scholasticism, the whole method was impermissibly "subjective." Yet in spite of the subjectivity, Newman seemed always to arrive at impeccably orthodox and "objective" conclusions. As Gabriel Daly has written, "No wonder Rome did not quite know what to make of him."[42]

Protestant Conscience

A second work of major significance was his *Essay in Aid of a Grammar of Assent* (1870). In it he turned to the human subject, the turn that nineteenth-century popes had so often condemned. He explored the interior of the mind, the multi-dimensional dynamics of the human journey toward faith. In this exploration, Newman affirmed what he called the "illative sense," a kind of mental "shortcut" by which persons could proceed from data to conclusions without complex theories or complicated processes of deduction. This was a kind of logic of the heart, of conscience and imagination—and it was a gift shared by fisherman and peasant, scholar and businessman alike. The peasant, for instance, could look at the clouds and know that soon it would rain. A scholar might review the history of the church and be certain that Jesus Christ was Lord.

Newman was convinced that this illative sense was of fundamental importance to everyday life. It meant that a person could come to a kind of practical certitude in matters of faith without technically sufficient proofs.[43]

This kind of thinking implicitly demeaned the "assistance" of scholasticism, with its essences and proofs. It lay more in the tradition of Augustine and Pascal than of Aristotle, Thomas, and the scholastics. Unfortunately, the former was a tradition which the narrowing of Catholic theology in the nineteenth century did not accommodate. Yet many Catholics embraced this work by Newman because of the way it resonated with their own experience. Others, of course, were dismayed because to scholastic ears it sounded like the abandonment of intellectual responsibility and the loss of objective truth.[44]

Another work, again suggesting Newman's distinctive method, was the book most famous in Newman's own time, his *Apologia pro vita sua* (1864). Sheridan Gilley calls it "one of the most moving autobiographies in the language."[45] In that work he stated the case for Roman Catholicism, the case that had brought him to leave family and friends behind (in fact, many converted with him) and to accept a new baptism, a new communion, and a new ordination in the Roman Catholic church.

What Newman really defended were the rights of his own conscience. He was convinced that he had neither been deceived nor been dishonest. Even in his conversion, he followed principles that had been with him since infancy, slowly played out in a kind of journey of self-discovery. Again, it was not traditional arguments, not a scholastic logic, and not external authorities which had brought him to faith. It was much more the feelings of the heart. As Gilley summarizes it:

> The whole of Newman's thought lies between the poles of two God-given popes, the private preemptory if fallible *pope of conscience*, the witness to the God within, creating that hunger for God which is satisfied and fulfilled by *the public pope* of the external revelation of God in Scripture and Tradition, as upheld in the witness of the infallible Church.[46]

In Newman's embracing view, the Roman Catholic faith has place for both the private and the public pope, for conscience and the papacy in Rome. Both are essential. The public pope is the reliable guide of faith. And in the application of the moral law, if conscience were to "come into collision with the word of a Pope, it [conscience] is to be followed in spite of that word."[47]

Limits to Papal Authority

In the revolutionary nineteenth century, the most difficult question for Roman Catholicism was the extent of papal authority. To what degree was the pope an absolute monarch? Was his autocracy a link to a better and happier past? Was he in some sense an exclusive and divinely-appointed channel which connected humanity to God? Newman offered a response to these questions which proved satisfactory to persons who previously had proposed conflicting answers. He deftly assigned limits to papal and hierarchical authority without diminishing the exterior manifestations of his love for pope and church. He did this in regard to three separate questions: (a) the *importance of the laity*; (b) the *temporal authority* of the pope; and (c) the claim of *papal infallibility*.

(a) In the work, *On Consulting the Faithful in Matters of Doctrine* (1859), Newman argued from history that the laity were an important part of the entire church and, as such, they played a role in determining what doctrines and beliefs were binding upon church members. As an example, he proposed it was the laity in the fourth century (and not the hierarchy) which had preserved the church from reducing the doctrine of the divinity of Christ to a kind of Arianism ("Christ is almost divine"). One conservative English bishop was so appalled by the book that he related it to Rome. It was this book, more than anything else that Newman wrote, that put a "cloud of suspicion" over his head. When Newman explained his position, it was accepted. But because of "negligence" on the part of certain members of the English Roman Catholic hierarchy, the explanation was slow to reach Rome and the cloud remained over Newman's head for at least seven years.

(b) On the feast of the Rosary, October 7, in 1866, in an emotional setting and a sermon entitled "The Pope and the Revolution," Newman confronted the question of papal temporal power.[48] The army of the Piedmontese king was approaching Rome at the time, and only the presence of a friendly French garrison kept the Piedmontese from immediately taking the city from the Pope. For many Catholics, especially in England, the litmus test of orthodoxy was denunciation of the aggressive acts of the king of Piedmont and affirmation of the temporal power of the Pope. What position did Newman take?

He passed the test. He condemned the Piedmontese action, praised the pope, and prayed his subjects might retain him as the king of Rome. In Newman's view, the papacy was an authentic part of the Catholic church, with authority dating from most ancient days, and for some time it had held considerable temporal power.[49]

Yet what was Newman's final word in the sermon regarding the temporal power of the pope in the face of revolution? He did not take the position that I would call a "hyper-ultramontane." He clearly disagreed with those who wanted to make the pope's temporal powers a *de fide* doctrine, required of all members of the church. And it was with his ready familiarity with history that he could explain his point.

Newman knew well there was a time in the past when temporal powers were not yet given to the pope and so he was not horrified that there might be a time in the future when they were taken away:

> Let us suppose that the Pope loses his temporal power, and returns to the condition of St. Sylvester, St. Julius, St. Innocent, and other great Popes of early times? Are we therefore to suppose that he and the Church will come to nought? God Forbid! To say that church can fail, or the See of St. Peter can fail, is to deny the faithfulness of Almighty God to His word. "Thou art Peter and upon this rock will I build My Church, and the gates of hell shall not prevail against it." . . . The Church is not the creature of times and places, of secular politics or popular caprice. Our Lord maintains her by means of this world, but these means are necessary to her only while He gives them; when He takes them away they are no longer necessary. He works by means, but He is not bound to means.[50]

Introduction

In these few words, and with a marvelous balance, Newman both praised the papacy and belittled its temporal power! He suggested that better ways than temporal power might be in God's providential plan for the church in modern times. Ways of the past should not be presumed to limit the freedom of God or the future of the church. His words were not those of a simple conservative or ultramontane!

(c) Finally, there is his famous position on infallibility. As we have already suggested, Newman was in many eyes as infatuated with the authority of the Roman church as with its pope. He supported unquestioningly the indefectability of the church and almost as strongly the notion of the infallibility of the pope. Yet he was not, like England's Cardinal Manning, the kind of "hyper-ultramontane" that wanted to claim that no pope could ever make any kind of mistake in anything that he said or did. Newman knew such a claim was blatantly fallacious from the facts of papal history and he had more than enough examples which he was ready to offer.[51] Further, in the midst of revolutions and Catholic reactions, he did not think the time was opportune for defining such a claim.

Nonetheless, the pope's infallibility was officially declared at the First Vatican Council (1870). There was controversy in England regarding whether there was an implied division of loyalty for English subjects between pope and king. William Gladstone, Prime Minister of England (who was defeated in re-election at this time), published a strong criticism of papal infallibility as a threat to English patriotism. Newman replied with a *Letter to the Duke of Norfolk on Occasion of Mr. Gladstone's Recent Expostulations* (1875).

What Newman did was clarify the limits of the conciliar definition. Gladstone was mistaken when he claimed infallibility applied to political decisions by the pope, Newman argued. Infallibility implied neither the pope's general impeccability nor the guarantee of truth in all he said. It applied only to those rare times when the pope spoke officially (*ex cathedra*) and then only when he was speaking in regard to faith and morals for the whole church.

Newman's position united the Roman Catholics of England. Their polarization was healed and there was a new pride in their faith.[52] Newman's explanation has since become the standard Roman Catholic interpretation of papal infallibility. He stood in support of infallibility, but at a great distance from the understanding of it that some had encouraged (such as Manning) and others had attacked (such as Gladstone).

A New Model

In all of this balance between an uncompromising love of the church and an introduction of things that were new, Newman was exceptional. He embodied a different model for theology and Catholic thought, one that applauded church authority and yet functioned to correct its abuses. He was devoted to the authority of the pope, but also to the freedom required for the dogged pursuit of truth; to the dignity of the individual and his conscience; to historical awareness; and to alternatives to the scholastic method. Standing on this inclusive middle ground, Newman was subjected to criticism from either side. Neither simply conservative nor simply liberal, he was subject to opposition from all those who were.[53]

Lingering Clouds

In his own autobiographical writings Newman explained that he always felt somewhat "under a cloud."[54] It was not until he was made a cardinal by Pope Leo XIII in 1879 that he felt the cloud was finally lifted and all the stories destroyed which had suggested he was "a liberal, only half a Catholic, and someone not to be trusted."[55]

Even after his death, however, there was debate on Newman's orthodoxy.[56] The theology of Roman Catholic "modernism" was condemned in 1907 by Pope Pius X (1903-1914) in his encyclical, *Ascendi dominici gregis*. The condemnation came seventeen years after Newman's last breath, but there was immediately a brawl of opinions regarding whether Newman himself had been condemned. Could there be toleration for his ideas of historical change, personal conscience, and limits to papal power?

"Modernist" George Tyrrell judged that Newman must have been condemned. Even though Newman personally despised it, he was the "progenitor," Tyrrell said, of modernism's condemned "doctrinal liberalism."[57] It was Newman who put into the hands of the modernists the weapons of historical research and personal introspection.

Ignaz von Dollinger suggested Newman was *not* condemned, but only because the popes could not read English![58] English journalist Robert Dell said that if Pius X did not intend to condemn Newman then he must have signed an encyclical which he did not understand![59]

Introduction   *xxxiii*

Newman's affirmation by the official church was confirmed, however, on 10 August 1908, in a letter from none other than Pius X himself.[60] Pius said Newman's works were as valuable to him as they had been to the Pope who made him a cardinal (Leo XIII). Newman was one of the "best and wisest" of men, one whose thought had "nothing to do with Modernism."

Despite this superlative praise from the highest official in the church, Newman's standing *still* retained some degree of ambiguity. Although innumerable Catholic centers on college campuses were named after him, his true "rehabilitation" in Catholic theology did not begin until the second half of the twentieth century. His currency increased asymptomatically with the Second Vatican Council (1961-65).[61] Since that time he has been reaffirmed by Popes Paul VI and John Paul II.[62] It was this lingering suspicion, however, that brought comparative neglect to Newman's important works and allowed less than explicit appreciation of his contribution to the church.

Permeating the Church

Despite the lingering clouds of suspicion, Newman has had great influence upon the Catholic theology of the twentieth century. His influence has sometimes been hard to perceive, since he wrote in the shadow of the Catholic condemnation of revolutions and its glorification of a scholastic past. But it has also been pervasive. As Baron Friedrich von Hugel said of Newman's influence shortly after his death: "the results have been and are too general and far-reaching, too secret and deep to be thus tangible and self-evident to a generation bathed in and penetrated by them."[63]

Not only the nineteenth but even more the twentieth century is bathed in and penetrated by Newman's influence. As Paul Misner has pointed out in his excellent study of Newman, few today would challenge what was then a startling hypothesis, that some kind of change is inherent in the very longevity of Christianity, without necessarily entailing any loss of identity.[64]

Similarly, more than one hundred years after the pope's loss of temporal power, who doubts that it is more a benefit than an injury to the religion of Roman Catholicism? Who doubts the limits

Newman assigned to papal infallibility? Who contests his call to accommodate the rights of laity and of personal conscience? Finally, who today would even think conceivable, let alone advantageous, an end to pluralism and a return exclusively to scholasticism? Even the conservative Vatican Secretary of State, Joseph Ratzinger, has looked back with criticism upon what he called "the prison of the Roman school system."

Other instances of Newman's influence are no less tangible and concrete. Outside the restrictions of Roman scholasticism, twentieth-century giants like Bernard Lonergan show signs of Newman's influence in their own explanations of a kind of "illative sense."[65] Similarly, Karl Rahner's twentieth-century magnitude was rooted in his dedication to conscience, introspection, and the history of the early church.

Today Newman is close to canonization as a saint.[66] This may be due in part to the fact that he lived astride two separate eras in the history of the church. Even though he died long before the new era was born, he struggled against what was worst in the old and helped to carry into the church some principles that were best in the new.

One of the most definitive and revealing stands that Newman took in his whole career was "anti-Novatian." Novatianism he saw as the ancient heresy which had encouraged the church to be sectarian, to look only to its own tradition, and speak only its inherited language. It was Novatianism that emerged again in the reactionary Catholic response to Protestantism, revolutions, and modern times. This reactionary response colored Catholicism from the Council of Trent in the middle of the sixteenth century until the Second Vatican Council in the last third of the twentieth.

Novatianism, Newman emphasized, was appropriately condemned. He stood for a world-wide church, one that sought to expand its arena of influence, one that opposed narrowing its lines of communion. It was this anti-Novatianism that explains why Newman was not so much a theologian of the nineteenth century as of the twentieth. He did not advocate the narrowing of theologies back to medieval scholasticism. He represented the even older and more recent effort to mount the dangerous courage to speak boldly Christian faith to all the world. He did not support the effort to inflate the Pope's sectarian power simply because his secular power was in collapse. He sought rather to see the waxing and waning of papal power in the perspective of God's continuing plan. In ways

Introduction

such as these, Newman was a harbinger, if not a cause in Catholic thought, of more recent theological reform. From him we have much to learn. Toward such learning, these essays are a new beginning.

Ronald Burke
University of Nebraska at Omaha

NOTES

1. James A. Weisheiple, *Encyclopedia of Religion*, vol. 13, 188 (New York: Macmillan Publishing Company, 1987).
2. See Jean-Loup Saban, "European Christianity Confronts the Modern Age," 425-599 in *Christianity: A Social and Cultural History*, by Howard Clark Kee, *et al.* (New York: Macmillan Publishing Company, 1991), 553.
3. See William H. McNeil, *Plagues and People* (New York: Doubleday, 1977).
4. See Richard P. McBrien, *Catholicism* (Minneapolis: Winston Press, Inc., 1981) 434.
5. Saban, *op. cit.*, 575.
6. See Joseph Fitzer, "J.S. Drey and the Search for a Catholic Philosophy of Religion," in *Papers of the Nineteenth-Century Theology Working Group*, ed. by Joseph Fitzer and Richard Crouter (Duplicated at Berkeley: Graduate Theological Union, 1981).
7. See Thomas O'Meara, *Romantic Idealism and Roman Catholicism* (Notre Dame: University of Notre Dame Press, 1982). O'Meara claims that there was at this time a Catholic spirit which "understood how to be faithful to tradition while fashioning a theology that spoke to a particular age," 9.
8. Thomas Loome organized extensive data to show historical continuity between the three theological movements in his title, *Liberal Catholicism, Reform Catholicism, Modernism* (Mainz: Mathias-Grunwald-Verlag, 1979).
9. Gerard A. McCool, *Catholic Theology in the Nineteenth-Century: the Quest for a Unitary Method* (New York: Seabury Press, 1977).
10. See Gabriel Daly, *Immanence and Transcendence* (Oxford: Clarendon Press, 1980), 8-25.
11. See Francis Fiorenza, "Catholic Nineteenth-Century Theology: Selectivity and Interpretation," in *Papers of the Nineteenth-Century Theology Working Group*, eds. Joseph A. Bracken and Claude Welch (Duplicated at Berkeley: Graduate Theological Union, 1985).
12. The Jesuits had been banned in 1773 by Pope Clement XIV, largely because of fear and jealousy regarding their world-wide success. See John Clayton, "Schelling, Romanticism, and Roman Catholic Theology in Nineteenth-Century Germany," in *Papers of the Nineteenth-Century Theology Working Group*, eds. Peter

Hodgson and Darrell Jodock (Duplicated at Berkeley: Graduate Theological Union, 1984).
13. Saban, *op. cit.*, 576-9.
14. See J. Derek Holmes, *More Roman than Rome: English Catholicism in the Nineteenth Century* (London: Burns & Oates, 1978), 127-9.
15. *Ibid.*, 127-9.
16. See Roger Aubert, "Three Popes: Pius IX, Leo XIII, Pius X," in *The Christian Centuries*, vol. 5, *The Church in a Secularized Society* by Roger Aubert, *et al.* (New York: Paulist Press, 1978).
17. *Ibid.*
18. For some important distinctions on ultramontanism and liberalism, see James C. Livington, *Modern Christian Thought* (New York: Macmillan Company, 1971), 271-75.
19. Holmes, *op. cit.*, 111.
20. *Ibid.*, 44.
21. *Ibid.*, 13-26.
22. Quoted by Holmes, *op. cit.*, 43.
23. Ian Ker, *The Achievement of John Henry Newman* (Notre Dame: University of Notre Dame Press, 1990), ix. Works like the present one are an effort to explain why that under-appreciation has occurred; it is intended also to help correct the situation.
24. Terrence Merrigan, "'One Momentous Doctrine which enters into My Reasoning'," in *Downside Review* 108, 373 (October, 1990), 254-281, esp. 276.
25. See Ronald Burke, "John Henry Newman: the Man Behind the Cloud," delivered 2 December 1990, at St. Louis University, Newman Centenary Conference, Gerard Magill, Director.
26. Charles Sarolea, *Cardinal Newman and His Influence on Religious Life and Thought* (Edinburgh: T. & T. Clark, 1908).
27. Ian Ker, *John Henry Newman* (Oxford: Clarendon Press, 1988), viii.
28. Marvin R. O'Connell, "Newman and Liberalism," in *Newman Today: Proceedings of the 1988 Wethersfield Institute* (San Francisco: Ignatius Press, 1989).
29. Quoted by Terrence Merrigan in his "Newman the Theologian," 103-118 in *Louvain Studies*, Summer/Fall, 1990, 107.
30. See Philip Griffin, "Newman's Thought on Church and Scripture," *Irish Theological Quarterly*, 56, 5 (1990), 287-307. Griffin does a very nice job of showing that it is the church,

more than Scripture, tradition, reason, or experience, that is the highest possible authority for Newman.

31. *Ibid.*, 296, my italics; from the *Via Media*, uniform edition, I. 257.
32. *Ibid.*, 288, from *Discussions and Arguments on Various Subjects*, 1872, 252.3.
33. *Ibid.*, 298.
34. *Ibid.*, 291. *Letters and Diaries*, XXV, 109.
35. *Ibid.*, 295, *Tracts*, I, no. 45, 1-2. Published 1834.
36. *Tracts*, I, no. 11, 7-8.
37. This was part of an address Newman delivered as Rector of the Catholic University of Ireland (1854), posthumously published in *My Campaign in Ireland. Part I. Catholic University Reports and Other Papers*. Private Circulation (Aberdeen: A. King & Co.), 211-4.
38. In a sermon delivered on October 7, 1866, he wrote: "to follow him [the pope] whither he goes, and never to desert him, however we may be tried, but to defend him at all hazards, and against all comers, as a son would a father, and as a wife a husband, know that his cause is the cause of God." *Sermons Preached on Various Occasions*. 3rd ed. London: Burns & Oates, 1870, 269.
39. See *Autobiographical Writings*, ed. Henry Tristam (New York: Sheed and Ward), 1957, 320. For some of the political maneuverings which surrounded the opening of the University, see Louis McRedmond, *Thrown Among Strangers. John Henry Newman in Ireland* (Dublin: Veritas Publications, 1990).
40. Avery Dulles, "From Images to Truth: Newman on Revelation and Faith," *Theological Studies* 51 (1990), 252-67, esp. 253-5.
41. Ian Ker, *The Achievement of John Henry Newman* (Notre Dame: University of Notre Dame Press, 1990), 113.
42. See Gabriel Daly, "Newman and Modernism: A Theological Reflection," 185-207 in *Newman and the Modernists*, ed. Mary Jo Weaver (Latham, MD: University Press of America, 1985), 186.
43. See John Coulson, *Religion and Imagination* (Oxford: Clarendon Press, 1981), 46-78. See also Mary Kenny, "Preaching of the Converted," 26-7, in *The Listener*, August 9, 1990.
44. Gabriel Daly, *Transcendence and Immanence* (Oxford: Clarendon Press, 1980), 23.

Introduction

45. Sheridan Gilley, *Newman and his Age* (London: Darton, Longman and Todd, 1990), 2. This book by Gilley is outstanding. Not so much an introduction, it is a great aid to those seeking a deeper and more contextual understanding of Newman.
46. *Ibid.*, 362.
47. *Ibid.*, 375.
48. *Sermons Preached on Various Occasions* (London: Longman, 1921), 282-313.
49. *Ibid.*
50. *Ibid.*
51. Gilley, *op. cit.*, 376.
52. *Ibid.*, 385.
53. See James Livingston regarding criticism of Newman from traditionalists and liberals alike in *Modern Christian Thought* (New York: Macmillan Publishing Company, 1971), 276.
54. John T. Ford, "Newman Studies: Whence and Whither?", 11-16 in *Papers of the Nineteenth-Century Theology Working Group*, ed. Paul Misner and Robert F. Streetman (Duplicated at Berkeley: Graduate Theological Union, 1980).
55. Marvin R. O'Connell, "Newman and Liberalism," 79-93 in *Newman Today: Proceedings of the 1988 Wethersfield Institute* (San Francisco: Ignatius Press, 1989), 87.
56. See Gary Lease, "Newman: The Roman View," 161-75 in *Newman and the Modernists* (Lanham, MD: University Press of America, 1985).
57. See Tyrrell's introduction to the English translation (by C.C. Corrance) of Henri Bremond's *The Mystery of Newman* (London: Williams and Norgate, 1907), xv.
58. *Letters and Diaries of John Henry Newman*, ed. Charles Dessain, vol. 29, (Oxford: Clarendon Press, 1976) 132.
59. Letter to *The Times*, 13 November 1907, 19.
60. *Acta Sancta Sedis* 41 (1908), 200-202. For an English translation, see *The Times*, 23 March 1908, 4.
61. See John T. Ford, "Newman Studies: Whence and Whither?", *op. cit.*, 11-26.
62. See Lease, *op. cit.*
63. See R.K. Browne, "Newman and von Hugel: A Record of an Early Meeting," *The Month* 212 (July, 1961), 32-33. Quoted by Daly, *op. cit.*, 204.

64. Paul Misner, "Newman's Significance: A Sketch," 1-10 in *Papers of the Nineteenth Century Theology Working Group*, ed. Paul Misner and Robert F. Streetman (Duplicated at the Berkeley Graduate Theological Union, 1980).
65. Misner, *op. cit.*, 7.
66. Vincent F. Blehl, "Prelude to the Making of a Saint," *America* 160, 9 (March 11, 1989), 213-16.

John Henry Newman

NEWMAN, THE CHAMPION OF TRUTH

Madeleine Kisner, A.S.C.

At the end of 1863, a severe blow was aimed at Newman. Perhaps it was the culmination of his troubles which had gathered over the past few years. Newman was sent the January 1864 copy of *MacMillan's Magazine*, containing a written attack on Newman by Charles Kingsley. This was the beginning of the controversy that led to the writing of the *Apologia Pro Vita Sua*. In a letter to MacMillan and Co., on December 30, 1863, Newman pointed out that the accusation was not substantiated by evidence, ". . . the January number has been sent to me . . . with a pencil mark calling my attention to page 217. There, apropos of Queen Elizabeth I, I read as follows: 'Truth, for its own sake, had never been a virtue with the Roman clergy. Father Newman informs us that it need not, and on the whole ought not to be; that cunning is the weapon which Heaven has given the saints wherewith to withstand the brute male force of the wicked world which marries and is given in marriage. . . .'" Newman merely wanted to draw the company's attention "to a grave and gratuitous slander . . ." (*A Packet* #97, 146-7).

Unable to prove his charge apart from reference to one of Newman's Anglican sermons, Kingsley offered a flimsy apology. In February, 1864, Newman published a pamphlet, *Mr. Kingsley and Mr. Newman* about the affair and added a couple of pages of his own reflections. Even though this pamphlet was a literary sensation, Newman had to be careful in the acknowledgments to his supporters. He feared he might offend the London Ultramontane (papal extremists) who held power and authority.

Kingsley was still not satisfied with Newman's answer and published his violent and biased pamphlet, *What Then Does Dr. Newman Mean?* In a letter dated March 31, 1864, to his friend William Copeland, Newman wrote that, so far as he understood, the strength of what Kingsley said, to the popular mind, "lies in the antecedent prejudice that *I was a Papist while I was an Anglican.* Mr. Kingsley *implies this.* The only way in which I can destroy this is to give my history, and the history of my mind, from 1822 or earlier, down to 1845. I wish I had my papers properly about me" (Martin 115). This was exactly what Newman did in writing the *Apologia Pro Vita Sua.* Newman set out to collect as many letters as he could from friends in order to give himself a check on his facts. Newman wrote to Rev. R. William Church, one of his earlier friends, who did not correspond with him after his conversion. It was William Copeland who encouraged Newman to write to Church which he did on April 23, 1864. He says, "I am in one of the most painful trials in which I have ever been in my life and I think you can help me." Newman continues, "It has always been on mind that perhaps someday I should be called on to defend my honesty in the Church of England." Newman realized that there had been many "hits" against him in newspapers and articles—all anonymous. He writes, "But I have considered that, if anyone with his name made an elaborate charge on me, I was bound to speak. . . . Now, when the call comes on me, I am quite unprepared to meet it. I know well that Kingsley is a furious foolish fellow—but he has a name— . . . now he comes out with a pamphlet bringing together a hodge-podge of charges against me all about dishonesty" (Eds. Stanford and Spark, *Letters* #83, 206-7). Newman could not afford to allow these slanders to be known to those who knew him in the town of Birmingham. He, therefore, asked the Rev. Church to help him check facts. He writes, "I have little more to trust than my memory. There are matters in which no one can help me . . . those which have gone on in my mind, [he had his own papers organized only up to 1863] but there is also a great abundance of public facts, or again, facts witnessed by persons close to me, which I may have forgotten. I fear of making mistakes in dates, though I have a good memory for them, and still more of making bold generalizations without suspicion that they are not to the letter tenable." Because Church was so much with Newman from 1840 to 1843 or even 1845 Newman asked him in the letter "to correct any fault of fact which you found in my statement. Also, you might have letters of mine to throw light on my state of mind, and this by means of contemporaneous authority" (Eds. Stanford and Spark, *Letters* #83, 207). These were the matters that Newman requested of Church. Already the Longman Company was pressuring Newman to release his work without delay. Between April 21 and June 2, 1864, Newman put out his *Apologia* in weekly installments. A year later in May, 1865, he published the finished edition of the *History of My Religious Opinions*, a book of over five hundred pages. Newman's influence was never greater: the *Apologia* was a notable success making him popular both at home and abroad. People from all over wanted to meet Newman. His reputation both in the Church and in the world was secure.

What is there in the *Apologia* that can enlist our attention and concern in our treatise on Newman, the Champion of Truth?

Let us examine Newman's *Apologia*, a somewhat autobiographical account of half his life, to ascertain his final Truth-seeking victory. Brian Martin says that in its final form, the *Apologia* is, in a sense, "an exercise in self-justification. . . ." He continues saying that it is:

> . . . a masterpiece of moving prose, which embodies all of Newman's gifts, certainly his personality and powerful charm . . . . In it he refuted Kingsley's ill-founded accusations, and seized the opportunity to justify himself to all those who suspected his honesty of motive in embracing Roman Catholicism (146).

The publication of the *Apologia* and the warmth of its reception began to bring about a change in Newman's position. Bouyer notes that it looked as if the dawn was breaking and the tide was beginning to turn in Newman's favor. Not only was the ever-growing neglect he had suffered at last made up for, but it soon became clear that, in Newman, the Church had one of the most gifted, and perhaps one of the most saintly of her children (363).

Some very difficult struggles still lay ahead, but the steadily deepening oblivion, the unfriendly indifference which had been his lot, were now episodes of the past. Bouyer says, "When you could not agree with him, there was nothing for it but to do battle with him. And there was no doubt on which side the victory would lie" (363).

Newman was, above all, a man of prayer and of total devotion to truth. When accused of untruth and of its defense, he would write an *Apologia* for his whole life—his *Apologia Pro Vita Sua*—to state from the beginning to the end his strategies that affected the true history of his religious opinions. This was an arduous task, a baring of oneself. But for the sake of truth he would face his attacker. In the *Apologia*, Newman writes:

> It is not pleasant to reveal to high and low, young and old, what has gone on within me from my early years. It is not pleasant to be giving to every shallow or flippant disputant the advantage over me of knowing my most private thoughts, I might even say the intercourse between myself and my Maker. But I do not like to be called to my face a liar and a knave; nor should I be doing my duty to my faith or to my name if I were to suffer it (*Apologia* 28).

Newman's whole life history shows his total devotion to faith and to truth. Newman had no personal bitterness toward Kingsley: he saw Kingsley had simply made some awkward slips. Newman says in his *Apologia*, that "in these pages, out of the thousand and one which my accuser directs upon me, I mean to confine myself to one, for there is only one about which I much care—the charge of untruthfulness" (*Apologia* 15). Thus, in the *Apologia*, having "loved honesty better than name, and Truth better than dear friends" (*Apologia* 14), Newman unravelled as best he could the complex and affecting story of his change. After all, Newman's honor, as well as that of the Church, was at stake. Pressures were upon him as he sent out installments of the *Apologia* in serial form. He wrote to Sister M. Gabriel Du Boulay, a Dominican who was earlier received into the Church by Newman, June 25, 1864:

> When I was at Oxford, I have twice written a pamphlet in a night, and once in a day—but now I had writing and printing upon me at once, and I have done a book of 562 pages, all at a heat; but with so much suffering, such profuse crying, such long spells of work, sometimes 16 hours, once 22 hours at once, that it is a prodigious awful marvel that I have got through it, and that I am not simply knocked up by it. I am sure it is the prayers of my friends, which have sustained me, and you must go on praying that I may not feel the bad effects of such a strain on me afterwards (*A Packet* #100, 150).

The structure of the *Apologia* reveals the changing status of Newman's mind as he progressed towards the Roman Catholic Church. According to Thomas Vargish, for Newman there was only one source of truth. He was led to it in his individual way. But he was *led* to it, *led* by what he believed was Divine guidance. Vargish maintains that in tracing the development of his own mind, Newman set forth on a theological as well as personal odyssey. His *Apologia* offers the history of his own religious opinions, but this properly understood is nothing less than the history of the action of God's will and guidance upon his intellectual development. Vargish holds that "Introspection and the perception of divinity are almost simultaneous or synonymous acts" (Vargish 184).

Newman's early "History of his Religious Opinions" (Part III and IV) in the *Apologia* were written he says, "as no romantic story to tell; but I wrote them because it is my duty to tell things as they took place" (*Apologia* 57). Throughout the writing of the *Tracts*, Newman spoke with firm confidence in his position about his battle with liberalism, the anti-dogmatic principle and its developments. For Newman the main principle of the Movement was just as dear to him as it ever was. He says, "From the age of fifteen, dogma has been the fundamental principle of my religion: I know no other religion. . . . What I held in 1816, I held in 1833, and I hold in 1864" (*Apologia* 67). Then, too, Newman was confident of a certain definite religious teaching, based upon his foundation of dogma. He held that there was a visible church with sacraments and rites which were the channels of invisible grace. His readings and writings supported his belief in the doctrine of Scripture, of the early Church, and of the Anglican Church. "My bishop," he says, "was my pope; I knew no other; the successor of the apostles, the vicar of Christ" (*Apologia* 69).

When Newman announced his conversion in 1845, he wrote to Wiseman saying that he would obey the Pope as he had obeyed his own Anglican bishop (*Apologia* 69). Moreover, in his view of the Church of Rome Newman frankly says that when he was young, and after he was grown up, he thought the Pope to be Antichrist (*Apologia* 70). Later, during the Tract Movement, he thought the essence of her offense consisted in the honor given to the Blessed Virgin and the saints (*Apologia* 70). From Hurrel Froude, with whom Newman traveled to Sicily, Newman learned to admire the great medieval pontiffs, the Councils, particularly the Council of Trent which, for Newman, was "the turning-point of the history of Christian Rome" (*Apologia* 71). In spite of the arguments against and the pleas in favor of the Church of Rome, Newman says that, "My judgement was against her [the Church], when viewed as an institution, as truly as it ever had been" (*Apologia* 71).

From the time that Newman was public tutor at his college, when his doctrinal views were very different from what they were in 1841, he had thought strongly about commenting on the Articles. The opportunity and actual cause of putting his thoughts on paper came with the restlessness of those who neither liked the *Via Media* nor Newman's strong judgement against Rome. Enjoined by his bishop "to keep these men straight" who had a difficulty subscribing to the Articles, that were "directly against Rome," Newman set forth in the main thesis of *Tract 90*, that "the Articles do not oppose Catholic teaching; they but partially oppose Roman dogma; they for the most part oppose the dominant errors of Rome" (*Apologia* 91). His problem was to draw the line as to what they allowed and what they condemned. In the universal storm of indignation with which the *Tract 90* was received, Newman says, "I was quite unprepared for the outbreak, and was startled at its violence. I do not think I had any fear. . . . I am not sure that it was not in one point of view a relief to me" (*Apologia* 99). It seemed now, the truth had set him free. He was asked to withdraw the *Tract* but refused to do so "for the sake of those who were unsettled or in danger of unsettlement." Then, too, "he would not do so for his own sake." How could he give in to a "mere Protestant interpretation of the Articles" or how could he "range himself among the professors of a theology of which it put his teeth on edge even to hear the sound?" (*Apologia* 99-100). He wrote to the Bishop of Oxford and resigned his place in the Movement saying, "I have acted because others did not act, and have sacrificed a quiet which I prized. . . . May God be with me in time to come . . . and He will be, if I can but keep my hand clean and my heart pure . . . so that I am preserved from betraying sacred interests, which the Lord of grace and power has given into my charge" (*Apologia* 100).

In the *History of Newman's Religious Opinions—1839-1841* (Part V) Newman said he was "on his deathbed" as regards the membership with the Anglican Church. By the summer of 1841, Newman found himself at Littlemore, determined to translate St. Athanasius, when several blows turned the tide of his thinking. His readings in the Arian history gave him perspectives; the bishops directed charges against Newman regarding his *Tract 90* but Newman remained adamant about reasserting his essay. He would speak out, if the bishops spoke (*Apologia* 140). It was plain that members of the group would be persuaded to either give up those principles he advocated or to give up the Church. The affair of the Jerusalem bishopric brought a protest from Newman. The project sought to have the Archbishop of Canterbury appoint and consecrate a bishop for Jerusalem. This experiment, if it failed, was too far away to pose any harm on the susceptibilities of any party at home. If the project succeeded, it raised the status of Protestantism in the East, which, in association with the Monophysite or Jacobite and the Nestorian bodies, formed a political instrument for England, parallel to that which Russia had in the Greek Church, and France in the Latin (*Apologia* 141). Newman made a solemn protest and sent it to the Archbishop of Canterbury, as well as a letter to his own bishop maintaining that "as to the project of a Jerusalem bishopric, I never heard of any good or harm it has ever done, except what it has done for me; which many think a great misfortune, and I one of the greatest mercies. It brought me on to the beginning of the end" (*Apologia* 146) of his search for Truth.

Newman made a long statement of the state of his mind and conscience in a letter addressed to John Keble, June 8, 1844. He says, in part, speaking of the time after Keble's 1833 sermon on "National Apostasy" that sparked the Oxford Movement:

> And now at the end of eleven years from that time, what is my own state? Why, that for the last five years (almost) of it, I have had a strong feeling, often rising to an habitual conviction. . . . very active now for two years and a half . . . growing more urgent and imperative continually, that the Roman Communion is the only true Church--and this conviction came upon me while I was reading the Fathers and from the Fathers--and when I was reading them theologically, not ecclesiastically, in that particular line of study, that of the ancient heresies, to which circumstances, external to myself, had led me fourteen years ago, before the movement began (*A Packet* #42, 64).

Thus, in 1841-45, Newman's membership with the Anglican Church was precarious, the Jerusalem bishopric condemned the old theory of the *Via Media* which for Newman posed an abnormal state for the Anglican Church, and then, too, there was trouble over *Tract 90*. In his letter to J.W. Bowden, March 15, 1841, Newman says, "The

Heads . . . have said that my interpretation of the articles is an evasion . . . you see no doctrine is censured . . . the articles are to be interpreted, not according to the meaning of the writer, but . . . according to the sense of the Catholic Church" (*A Packet* #35, 52).

Feeling that he could do more good for his people in Littlemore, Newman proposed to live there because he had a resident curate in Oxford. A temporary retirement from St. Mary's Church seemed to be expedient for him under the prevailing excitement of his choice to live a more regulated life at Littlemore. Some of his friends joined him there as he says, "I made Littlemore a place of retirement for myself, so did I offer it to others" (*Apologia* 170). With the unexpected conversion of one of the young men, Newman felt it was impossible to remain in Littlemore. He begged of his Bishop of Oxford in a letter, September 6, 1843, "to resign the living of St. Mary's. . . . so many Bishops have said things of me, and no one has taken my part in respect to that interpretation of the articles under which alone I can subscribe them" (*A Packet* #40, 59-60).

Still, not positive about his position in the Roman Catholic Church, Newman the Truth-seeker retired into lay communion holding "not indeed being a Catholic, in my convictions, but in a state of serious doubt, and with the probable prospect of becoming some day, what as yet I was not" (*Apologia* 175). He gave up his duties, his trip to Rome, his living and for two years before his conversion, he took no clerical duty. Newman's last sermon was in September 1843; then he remained at Littlemore in quiet for two years (*Apologia* 175). In all of this, however, Newman was made a subject of reproach because he did not leave the Anglican Church sooner. During this time, Newman was engaged in writing his *Essay on Development* in favor of the Roman Church, and indirectly against the English. He says, "but even then, till it was finished, I had not absolutely intended to publish it, wishing to reserve to myself the chance of changing my mind when the argumentative views which were actuating me had been distinctly brought out before me in writing" (*Apologia* 176-177).

In 1843, Newman made a formal retraction of the hard things he had said against the Catholic Church. Moreover, he resigned the living both at St. Mary's and at Littlemore. Newman concludes in the *Apologia*, "And now I have brought almost to an end, as far as the sketch has to treat them, the history both of my opinions, and of the public acts which they involved" (198). He had only one more advance of mind to make; and that was "to be *certain* of what I had hitherto anticipated, concluded and believed; and this was close upon my submission to the Catholic Church. . . . I had only one more act to perform, and that was the act of submission itself" (*Apologia* 198).

In November, 1845, shortly after his being received into the Church, Newman sent John Keble a message of gratitude and a farewell saying, "To you I owe . . . what and where I am. Others have helped me in various ways, but no one can I name but you . . . who has had any part in setting my face in that special direction which has led me to my present inestimable gain" (*A Packet* #48, 73).

Later, Dr. Nicholas Wiseman, in whose vicarate Oxford lay, called Newman to Oscott. Afterwards he sent him to Rome and finally placed him in Birmingham. Newman left Oxford for good on February 23, 1846. He says in the closing lines of the *Apologia*, "I have never seen Oxford since, excepting its spires, as they are seen from the railway" (214).

From the time he became a Catholic, Newman had no further history of his religious opinions to narrate.

In his general answer to Mr. Kingsley, Newman says, "I have been in perfect peace and contentment. . . . I was not conscious of firmer faith in the fundamental truths of revelation, or of more self-command; . . . it was like coming into port after a rough sea; and my happiness on that score remains to this day without interruption" (*Apologia* 215).

Thus, we note that the *Apologia* assuredly was written as Newman's defense in his personal life and decisions. After the appearance of the article, "On Consulting the Faithful," Newman fell under a shadow. His orthodoxy was suspected by some of the Hierarchy. His subsequent projects for Catholic lay-education were actively opposed by Cardinals Wiseman and Manning. In a letter to Wiseman on January 19, 1860, Newman writes in regard to his article, "On Consulting":—"I marvel. . . . after many years of patient and self-denying labour in the cause of Catholicity, the one appropriate acknowledgement in my old age should be considered to consist in taking advantage against me of what is at worst a slip of pen in an anonymous untheological paper . . ." (*A Packet* #83, 121). Newman, who professed not only the rights of truth, but also the necessity for opportune truth in the Christian family, judged his research would only aggravate an already tense environment. He reluctantly abandoned this research on the *Rambler* and, in 1870, began to write in the silence and peacefulness of the Oratory's country house at Rednal. After he had finished, he felt he had aged. Wilfrid Ward records that Newman wrote about his *A Grammar of Assent*, "It is my last work" (Ward II 268). In a letter to Aubrey de Vere, August 31, 1870, Newman considered his *A Grammar of Assent* "a subject that has teased me for 20 or 30 years. I felt I had something to say upon it, yet, whenever I attempted, the sight I saw vanished, plunged into a thicket, curled itself up like a hedgehog, or changed colours like a chameleon." In an inner need to express himself and his deepest intuitions, Newman says, "I have a succession of commencements, perhaps a dozen, each different from the other, and in a different year, which came to nothing" (*A Packet* #125, 183-184). He continues that about four years previous (1866), when he was up at Glion, over the Lake of Geneva, he received an inspiration, the "Open Sesame" of the whole subject. He wrote it down immediately and "pursued it about the Lake of Lucerne." Then, when he returned home, he began in earnest and have "slowly got through it" (*A Packet* #83, 184).

In writing *A Grammar of Assent* Newman says, "I could not help feeling that I had something to give it, whatever its worth, and I felt haunted with a sort of responsibility, and almost a weight on my conscience, if I did not speak of it . . ." (*A Packet* #83, 184).

In the opening of his *A Grammar*, Newman sets the tone for much of his work. According to Rev. Thomas Norris in his book *Newman and His Theological Method,* Newman does not adhere to a very rational plan or strict outline. Structurally, his work is more pedagogical in tone and spirit than logical in its development. But this is what Newman set out to do. Faithful to his principles, he felt that one stumbles across the truth, discovering a point here, a vein there, sometimes by design, but more often accidentally. There are many roads that lead to the discovery of the whole truth (Norris 29). According to Norris, Newman understood the problems that William Froude confessed to him about how the demands of scientific investigations and the rigorous standards of evidence were moving him further and further into skepticism and agnosticism (24). Then, too, J.M. Capes, the founder of *The Rambler,* had a similar problem to Froude's. He, too, held that "the teaching of the Church could . . . be only probable, for certainty was impossible and confined to the province of mathematico—scientific demonstration" (Norris 24). Thus, Newman set out to justify the "assent of every believer, simple or cultivated, to the truth of the Catholic Religion." Newman's essay begins with refuting the fallacies of those who contend that "we cannot believe what we cannot understand" (Norris 27). *A Grammar of Assent* proceeds to "to justify certitude as exercised upon accumulation of proofs, short of demonstration separately" (*G.A.* 383).

For all practical purposes the philosophy of *A Grammar* is according to Charles Dessain, "that of common sense, of the plain man, of the philosopher when he is not philosophizing, but occupied with the ordinary affairs of life" (Dessain 154). Dessain also holds that Newman wanted to find the answer to a crucial problem. He wished to justify men's right to be certain, and especially their right to certitude in matters of religion (148).

Concerned with the cardinal errors of the liberal theologians, Newman wrote *A Grammar* as an "argumentative work in defence of my Creed." Thus, in his theological method he sets up his process of investigation in what he refers to as his mode of Phenomenological investigation or "Organum Investigandi, the self-appropriation of this structure given us for gaining religious truth" (*G.A.* 386).

Norris holds that the key to *A Grammar* is the "grasp of the vital distinction between inference and assent. Formal inference was held up by the liberals as the unique and only way to arrive at certitude that was deserving of one's acceptance. Scientific investigation was the only means of gaining truth." Norris maintains that Newman contends that "true judgment or assent is another and more universal means of arriving at truth" (Norris 29-30).

In Part I of *A Grammar*, Newman is not directly concerned with the problem of certitude but with showing, against Evangelicals, the importance and value of doctrinal statements in religion. Dessain says that Newman defends theology, and shows that so far from being antagonistic to vital religion, there can be no sound Christianity without it. Even though it is an abstract, logical science, it clarifies for us the truths on which our religion must rest. Dessain continues saying that theology can be a merely intellectual science without the life of religion, but it doesn't need to be. What is real is particular, and theology deals with general notions. It only holds a truth in the intellect, but faith gives a real assent to a concrete reality, which is appropriated by the imagination and the heart. Newman then proceeds to show how, setting aside Revelation, one can give a vivid assent to the being of God stronger than one can give to a mere notion of the intellect. Dessain says that Newman argues from one's sense of moral obligation and emphasizes the importance of the conscience as the connecting principle between the creature and his Creator. It brings us into His presence as a Living Person. These pages in *A Grammar* are Newman's clearest exposition of his basic theme: how, by means of one's conscience, one comes to acknowledge the fact that there is One Personal and Present God (Dessain 149).

Newman insists in his *A Grammar of Assent* (1909 ed.) that the proposition, "There is a God," when really apprehended, "is the object of a strong energetic adhesion, which works a revolution in the mind; but when held merely as a notion, it requires but a cold and ineffective acceptance, though it be held ever so unconditionally" (*G.A.* 126).

In a similar way, Newman maintains that the doctrine of the Holy Trinity, professed in the Creeds, does not deal with abstractions but with realities. He concludes the first part by saying that "theology has to do with the Dogma of the Holy Trinity as a whole made up of many propositions; but Religion has to do with each of those separate propositions which compose it, and lives and thrives in the contemplation of them" (*G.A.* 140).

In Part II of *A Grammar of Assent*, Newman deals with his basic problem, certitude, and, above all, certitude in matters of religion. Dessain says that Newman was writing to counter rationalism, and to explain how faith, whether in the realm of religion or of ordinary life, was a reasonable act even when not based on strictly scientific demonstration (Dessain 151). He had in mind both the educated agnostics, as well as the great majority of humankind, who believed truths that they were incapable of explaining satisfactorily or defending logically. Newman maintains that in the latter case, it was also necessary that they were justified in believing what they could not absolutely prove (Dessain 151-152). Newman set out, then, to vindicate the right of the simple, unlearned, ordinary person to assent and to have certitude about truths which he never had, and probably never could demonstrate. Newman specifies in *A Grammar*:

> Abstract argument is always dangerous. . . . I prefer to go by facts. . . . We are in a world of facts, and we use them; for there is nothing else to use. . . . If I may not assume that I exist, and in a particular way, that is, with a particular mental constitution, I have nothing to speculate about and had better let speculation alone. . . . We act according to our nature, by means of ourselves, when we remember or reason. We are as little able to accept or reject our mental constitution as our being (*G.A.* 346-7; 61).

Newman continues to distinguish between explicit and implicit reasoning called formal and informal inference. Formal inference is that verbal logic, with many limitations, that enables one to argue with others. Insisting in the 1909 edition that "Logic does not really prove ... it suggests ideas ... but for genuine proof in concrete matter we require an *organon* more delicate ... than verbal argumentation" (*G.A.* 271), Newman, then, arrives through the processes of reasoning "which ... lead to assent, to action, to certitude ... only in subordination to a higher logic" (*G.A.* 303). This higher logic is informal and natural inference. According to Newman, "our most natural mode of reasoning is, not from propositions, ... but from wholes to wholes" (*G.A.* 330). His position is that there is an implicit intellectual process, not opposed to conceptual reasoning, which gives complete and legitimate evidence, prior to any conceptual proof. It is the mind itself which controls its own reasonings, its informal and natural inferences, and not any technical apparatus of words and propositions. According to Dessain, this power or faculty of judging and concluding, when perfected by experience, Newman called the *illative sense*. He continues, saying Newman compared this sense with the moral sense, which enables a person to decide what is right or wrong for one in given circumstances. An ethical system must be applied in a particular case. Referring to Newman's *A Grammar*, Dessain says, "The illative sense is simply one's intellect, or reason, sharpened by experience, working unconsciously, and arriving at its conclusions in an intellectual and reasonable manner" (157). Newman, in *A Grammar* (1909 ed.), called the illative sense a solemn word for an ordinary thing. He says, "the sole and final judgement on the validity of an inference in concrete matter is committed to the personal action of the ratiocinative faculty, the perfection or virtue of which I have called the Illative Sense, a use of the word 'sense' parallel to our use of it in 'good sense,' 'common sense,' a 'sense of beauty,' ..." (*G.A.* 345). Dessain says an exercise of the judgement in coming to a conclusion, as distinct from the passive attention, which is all that is required in following a rigidly scientific proof, is an exercise of the illative sense. The illative sense is a purely intellectual faculty. Dessain clarifies this by offering a simple illustration of its working in Willa Cather's novel about French Canada, *Shadows on the Rock*:

> "When there is no sun, I can tell directions like the Indians." Here Auclair interrupted him, "And how is that Antoine?" Frichette smiled and shrugged, "It is hard to explain, by many

things. The limbs of the trees are generally bigger on the south side, for example. The moss on the trunks is clean and dry on the north side—on the south side it is softer and maybe a little rotten. There are many little signs; put them all together and they point you right" (157).

According to Dessain, this heaping together of tiny indications, little facts, none of which, by itself, is conclusive, is what produces certitude in one's mind. He also says that those whose minds have been disciplined by a strict and rigorous scientific and syllogistic method of ratiocination, find great difficulty in accepting this view (157). These people argue that probabilities can only lead to probabilities, and a thousand probable arguments cannot produce certitude. More than a mere quantitative heaping up of probabilities is involved here. At a certain point there is a qualitative change. The indications corroborate each other, and produce something greater than themselves (158).

Newman concluded *A Grammar of Assent* (1909 ed.) by applying his principles, and giving his outline of the evidences for Natural and Revealed Religion. Hence, he began by laying down that "egotism is true modesty." In religious inquiry a man can only speak for himself. "He knows what has satisfied and satisfies himself; if it satisfies him it is likely to satisfy others" (*G.A.* 384-5). According to Dessain, Newman, in his final chapters, illustrates his own fundamental principles, the necessity of moral dispositions for the search after truth, the importance of antecedent probability as the instrument of conviction, and the value of converging probabilities in building up a proof (159). Newman's aim in *A Grammar* (1909 ed.) was to show, as he says, that the Christian Revelation "is a definite message from God to man distinctly conveyed by his chosen instruments, and to be received as such a message . . . not as probably true, or partially true, but as absolutely certain knowledge" (*G.A.* 387).

Upon finishing his *An Essay in Aid of A Grammar of Assent*, Newman concludes in his letter to Aubrey de Vere that "it is the greatest possible relief, at length to have it (the Essay) off my mind. . . . and thus I feel as if I could die happier, now that I have no *Essay on Assent* to write, and I think I shall never write another work, meaning by work something which is an anxiety and a labour" (*A Packet* #125, 184). As Dessain holds, Newman wanted Catholics to come out of the ghetto and take their place in the world, to adapt themselves, to enlarge their minds in the confidence that truth could never contradict truth, and to be guided like responsible people by the enlightened consciences. His views on faith, on open discussion, on the Church as a Communion, on the role of the laity whether in the Church or the world, are now appreciated, as are his return to the source of Revelation and his effort to make real the spiritual teaching of the New Testament. Newman had supreme trust in the power of truth, yet his defense was humble, and did not give in to intellectualism at the expense of mystery. His entire life was a sacrifice for the truth. In all respects, Newman was the champion of Truth. He was the apologist *par excellence* of the Church, who gave up so much he loved in the English Church, only to face misunderstanding and opposition in the Catholic Church. All through this turmoil, Newman was buoyed up by his trust in Providence. Before he was sixteen he had come to realize that God was truly personal and always present. The Presence and Providence of God was perhaps the lesson on which this Champion of Revealed Religion insisted most. Although the unseen world was quite vivid to him, he yet knew the limitations of Revelation, and asked to have inscribed on his memorial table the words, "Out of shadows and images into the truth" (Dessain 168-9).

WORKS CITED

1. Bouyer, Louis. *Newman, His Life and Spirituality*. London: Burns and Oates, 1958.
2. Dessain, Charles S. *John Henry Newman*. New Jersey: Thomas Nelson and Sons, 1966.
3. Martin, Brian. *John Henry Newman, His Life and Work*. London: Chatto and Windus, 1982.
4. Newman, John H. *Apologia Pro Vita Sua*. New York: E.P. Dutton, 1930.
5. Newman, John Henry Cardinal. *An Essay in Aid of a Grammar of Assent*. New York: Longmans, Green, 1909.
6. Newman, John Henry. *An Essay in Aid of a Grammar of Assent*. New York: Doubleday (Image Book), 1955.
7. Newman, John Henry. *Letters of John H. Newman*. Eds. Derek Stanford and Muriel Spark. London: Peter Owen Ltd., 1957.
8. Newman, John Henry. *A Packet of Letters*. Edited with Introduction by Joyce Sugg. New York: Oxford University Press, 1983.
9. Norris, Thomas V., Rev. *Newman and His Theological Method: A Guide for the Theologian Today*. Leiden: E.J. Brill, 1977.
10. Vargish, Thomas. *Newman, the Contemplation of Mind*. New York: Oxford University Press, 1970.
11. Ward, Wilfrid. *The Life of John Henry Cardinal Newman*. 2 vols. New York: Longmans, Green, 1912.

NEWMAN, LINDBECK AND MODELS OF DOCTRINE

Ronald Burke

At an International Symposium in Rome, held in honor of the centenary of the death of John Henry Newman (11 August 1890), Pope John Paul II referred to the "special place in the history of the Church" held by "the great English Cardinal."[1] Newman's theology and memory have been highly honored by a great variety of Roman Catholics, not only in papal praise and academic symposia, but also in such events as the official declaration, in August of 1990, of his "holiness," the step immediately preceding his consideration for canonization.[2]

Despite the almost total unanimity of praise Newman has received,[3] there have been differences amounting to contradictions in the ways his greatness is understood. Liberals or progressives in the Roman church have claimed him as the progenitor of Catholic modernism and as ancestor to the changes promulgated at the Second Vatican Council.[4] More conservative persons in the church have described him as a champion of conservatism.[5] Newman himself said, upon receipt of the Cardinal's hat in 1879, that his entire life had been a "struggle against liberalism."[6]

Newman was in simple terms neither "liberal" nor "conservative." He was in fact a theologian of great "equilibrium."[7] He was a defender of traditional Catholic faith against the dangers of modernity. Avoiding a reactionary traditionalism, however, Newman did not simply condemn these modern dangers. Rather, with his gift for equilibrium, he attempted to understand and hold what was best about modernity in juxtaposition with important themes of the Catholic tradition.

Newman can legitimately be seen as *both* "progressive" *and* "traditional," each in ways that do not preclude the other. He attempted to *hold together* themes representative of both positions. Illuminating in regard to his greatness, his gift for "equilibrium," and his contribution to the history of Roman Catholic thought is the model he introduced to explain the development of Catholic doctrine.

In presenting the model of development, Newman was insightful if not also revolutionary. The greatest flaw in his model was its incompleteness. While presenting a modern notion of doctrine's *development*, he did not adequately examine or revise the standard, traditional notion of *doctrine* itself. This inadequacy is suggested in his own discussion of doctrinal development. After looking at the problems Newman faced and the model of development he introduced, we will look at a notion of doctrine more consistant with development in the recent writings of George Lindbeck.

Part One
John Henry Newman

Modernity

Modernity was part of the world in which Newman was raised. It was "new" and "different" enough to be seen as a threat to traditional Catholic faith. Two primary themes of modernity suggest some of the dangers and the possible strengths it presented to the Catholic tradition.

First of all, "modernity" included an *individualism* that has become so much a part of how westerners think that it is difficult to isolate and define. Some of its most important themes were dramatically represented in the personal stand of Martin Luther against the excesses of the medieval Roman Catholic church. Luther championed the freedom and authority of the individual. Even outside the institutional Roman church, he claimed, the individual has the free authority personally to interpret Scripture and to develop a faithful relation to God. Such an emphasis upon the rights and responsibilities of the individual was not at all a part of medieval culture but has become a hallmark of modern western thought.

Besides this emphasis upon the individual, modernity also included a new appreciation for *cultural specificity*. Since the time of the Italian renaissance, there was a growing recognition that persons in different cultures saw and dealt with "reality" in significantly different ways. Careful historical examination of art and literature from ancient times or from foreign parts of the globe encouraged in modern times new recognition of cultural differences. These differences gave some persons a self-reflective recognition of the interdependence of thought and culture. Not only are cultures slowly shaped by human thought; in subtle and encompassing ways, human thought itself is largely shaped by the thinker's surrounding culture.

In the midst of a particular modern culture, John Henry Newman did his theology. Raised an Anglican and educated at Oxford, he was in no sense a cloistered Roman Catholic. As an educated English Catholic, he did landmark study of the history (and culture) of the early Catholic church.[8] He revered the example of the early church and it was some of its signal strengths that he found sadly lacking from the church of his day. From among those strengths it was especially an *appreciation of doctrine* that he wanted to retrieve for his own Anglican church.

Doctrine in Modern Times

It was doctrine's absence from favor in the Anglican church which was a major factor in Newman's decision, in 1833, to begin the reforms of the Oxford Movement.[9] Many Anglicans seemed to Newman excessively set upon absorbing modern freedoms. They viewed religion as primarily a personal sentiment, including some widely-accepted ethical and political positions, but without any significant doctrine. It was this kind of religion that Newman always opposed as "liberalism." He saw such religion as only "a dream and a mockery."[10] Such liberalism suggested a wish to preclude from history anything transcendent and lasting. It was a sign of secularism and unbelief.[11] Looking back on his own life since the time of his semester-long religious experience at fifteen years of age, Newman took doctrine to be the "fundamental principle" of his religion.[12] He did not want doctrine without feelings. But neither did he want feelings without doctrine.

Doctrine did seem to be in direct conflict with themes of modernity. It was the explicit summary of beliefs contained in a particular religious tradition. This summary was not simply to be an historical *description* of what members of a religious tradition had believed *in the past*. It also was seen to be a *prescription* of what members must believe *in the present*. It provided in propositional form a kind of "definition" of the invisible world that lies beyond ordinary human perception. To these definitions the members of a religion were required to subscribe.

Newman did not directly challenge this standard view of doctrine, though he did perceive that it did not perfectly match the notion of development he later introduced.

Themes of modernity were in conflict with these *prescriptive and definitive* roles of doctrine. Scientific discoveries and historical studies rendered less credible the literal correspondence with reality of many doctrines (such as creation). The pervasive modern emphasis upon the freedom of the individual made people less willing to accept for the sake of membership any outside authority which told them what they had to believe. This attitude was compounded by the second modern emphasis: heightened modern consciousness of cultural specificity. Modern persons became more agnostic. They were less ready completely to subscribe to any particular culture's or religion's system of thought—at least if they had no personal experience of that system's benefit or legitimacy.

Roman Catholicism and Change

In his efforts to overcome such obstacles and return doctrine to greater acceptance in the Anglican religion, Newman did not try to revise the notion of doctrine itself. He tried more to share a celebration of the poetic and mystical value of ancient doctrinal understandings. He wrote twenty-nine "Tracts for the Times" and, in 1837, a work entitled *Lecture on the Prophetical Office of the Church Viewed Relatively to Romanism and Popular Protestantism*. This work included harsh criticism of Roman Catholicism because it had allowed too much innovation and change in the history of doctrine.

By the summer of 1839 Newman began to see how difficult it was to reform Anglican views of religion and doctrine.[13] He also saw that doctrine had greater currency in the Roman Catholic church than in the English Catholic church to which he belonged. Hence he began to feel that if any of the early Church Fathers were to be alive again in the nineteenth century, it would be the Roman church that they would recognize as their own.

Newman finally took a year off from teaching and ministry to explore his new perceptions. In that year, 1844-45, he produced the book titled *An Essay on the Development of Christian Doctrine*.[14] Just prior to the completion of the book he was baptized into the Roman Catholic communion.

The Development of Doctrine is a book filled with a host of insights and presuppositions. A primary perception of its author is often overlooked in commentaries. Unlike the case in Anglicanism, Newman saw that doctrine was neither demeaned nor neglected in Roman Catholicism. It may have been because the Roman church was still comparatively more "medieval," and correspondingly less "modern," but in that church doctrine's instructions and implications were still cherished and debated. In Roman Catholicism, Newman would not have so great a struggle to find a popular appreciation for doctrine.

Yet there was still a problem for Newman in the Roman Catholic treatment of doctrine. It was the same one he had articulated in his *Lecture on the Prophetical Office*. It was clear to him that there had been *substantial changes* in doctrine between the time of the early church and the Roman Catholic church of the nineteenth century. Any such changes would seem to risk greater separation from the sacred and original revelation upon which doctrine was based. It would also seem to risk contamination from the human culture in which the change was articulated. Yet he also saw that these were the same sort of changes as had occurred between the time of the apostles themselves and the time when many doctrines were first defined by the early church (which he so revered.) Was *later* change absolutely evil if *earlier* change had been proper and appropriate? This was the question which perplexed him.

At some point between 1839 and 1844, Newman began to recognize that "change" in doctrine was *not* universally and inherently evil. That recognition, combined with his appreciation for doctrine's importance and for its continued prominence in the Roman Catholic communion, led him to struggle in his book for "an hypothesis to account for the difficulty" of doctrine's Roman Catholic changes. He needed a theory, a model, for the history of doctrine that could accommodate change without forsaking doctrine's enduring value. In a comparatively "conservative" way, Newman wanted to preserve the importance of doctrine. In a more "liberal" fashion, he was ready to accept the propriety of significant doctrinal change. He found a way to connect these disparate positions in the notion, or model, of "development."

The concept of "development" was new in nineteenth-century Roman Catholicism. Written twelve years before Darwin's *Origin of the Species*, Newman's book on doctrine's "development" accomplished two things. It provided both an apology for the changes in Roman Catholic doctrine (which he had so harshly criticized as excessive) and also, less directly, an explanation of his own change in denominational affiliation.

Doctrinal Problems: Words, Change, and Revelation

In addition to his reverence for doctrine, his allowances for change, and his appreciation of Roman Catholicism, Newman's book on *Development* included three insights that conflicted with the standard, propositional view of doctrine. These insights had to do with the frailty of human words, a greater appreciation for change, and a holistic understanding of revelation.

Newman developed the first insight, involving the *frailty of human words*, in his Oxford University Sermons. There he described, while still an Anglican, human language: a fragile instrument, commonly misinterpreted, replete with weaknesses, dependent upon cultures and history. Only by an act of mercy comparable to the Incarnation itself, Newman proposed, had God in revelation "condescended to speak to us so far as human thought and language will admit, by approximations."[15]

Newman focused upon the fact that (doctrinal) words could be no more than an approximation of the transcendent reality described. He emphasized the disparity between God's revelation and the human words in which it was not so much "contained" as "approximated." He presented an example of the point in his definitive work on the Arian controversy, in words regarding the Trinity.[16] Words of the trinitarian formulae were like a kind of "shadow" in a foreign medium, beset with inconsistencies, mystery, and incompleteness. The term "Son" did not pertain literally or materially to the Second Person of the Trinity. Nor was it, however, merely a metaphor. Based upon an intense and accurate "idea," it was an instance of language reaching beyond its grasp.

Such recognition of the limitations of language before the mysteries of God was not unique to Newman, but neither was it prominent in the Roman Catholic church of his day. It was common in the more mystical "negative theology" of the Catholic tradition and reminiscent of the legendary story regarding the great mystic and systematician, Thomas Aquinas. Thomas is said to have exclaimed at his death-bed that: "all my words are straw!" before the mystery of God. In the nineteenth century, however, the Roman Catholic church was attempting to respond to threats from modernity: rationalism, the French Revolution, Napoleon, democracy, and—even yet—the Protestant Reformation. The official church was the counter-reformation church: defensive, ultramontane, and more anxious to assert the infallibility of its doctrines (as it did in 1870) than to admit the limitations of its words.[17] Newman saw clearly doctrine's inherent frailty and did not abandon his perception. But neither did he replace the standard, propositional notion of doctrine.

Newman's second insight was a modern and history-conscious *appreciation of cultural change*. During and after his religious experience of 1815, he had been fascinated with the importance of a maxim found in the evangelical writings of Thomas Scott: "Growth the only evidence of life." His development of this insight is reflected in his own revolutionary axiom regarding doctrine's development: "In a higher world it is otherwise, but here below to live is to change, and to be perfect is to have changed often."[18] Such words were quite extraordinary for a man who so revered the early church, its life, and its doctrine. They were also extraordinary in a conservative or reactionary church whose official leaders had sought to preserve the power of kings, emphasized the power of popes, and sanctified the notion of "always the same" (*semper eadem*). They were the words of a man who was very much an historian. In the words of Lord Acton, one of Newman's Roman Catholic contemporaries, Newman's *Development* "did more than any other book of his time to make his countrymen think historically."[19]

Previous Catholic apologists, like Bossuet, were more systematicians and less historians. They minimized the significance of changes in the doctrines of the Church.[20] Bossuet had claimed that there was a "deposit of faith" that remained *unchanged* and that later doctrine was but the clearer explanation of things already contained in the original gospel. This view fit nicely with the traditional, propositional understanding of doctrine.

Newman agreed with a portion of the understanding. As a theologian, he knew there was an enduring sameness or identity in doctrine. As an historian, however, he also recognized that doctrine's developments were not simply logical extrapolations. The changes were more substantial than Bossuet and logic could allow. If doctrines were propositional bearers of ontological truth, how could such change be explained? Appreciating the value of sameness, Newman also embraced the necessity and propriety of change.

Newman's third insight which conflicted with traditional views of doctrine was his *holistic understanding of revelation*. Newman's idea of revelation was also developed while still an Anglican in his Oxford University Sermons, between 1826 and 1843.[21] The idea was in some ways idiosyncratic to Newman. It lies close to the foundation of his whole theological position. He certainly did not have a "propositionalist view" of revelation, seeing it simply as a collection of propositional truths delivered from God to man. Revelation would better be categorized in his holistic view as a "confrontation" or "invitation." Newman sometimes called it an "impression" made on the mind, an "idea" God gives of himself.[22] It was not so much an idea that the mind possessed. It was more an idea that possessed the mind.[23]

Revelation was the source behind *all* authentic expressions of Christianity: not only its doctrine, but its whole life and worship, its ethics and government, its sacred stories and artistic expressions, etc. Doctrine itself was a human effort to provide, in intellectually consistent and propositional form, a "list" of what revelation included. Newman recognized that this traditional doctrinal effort was both *valuable and impossible*.

Doctrine was *valuable* because the "translation" of revelation into doctrinal "truths" was prerequisite to human reflection, judgment, and action. As Newman said, "The human mind cannot reflect upon (revelation) except piecemeal, cannot use it in its oneness and entireness, nor without resolving it into a series of aspects and relations."[24]

Yet the effort to translate revelation into intellectual terms was inherently *impossible*. This was not only because of the frailty of human words, discussed above. Newman recognized that revelation was *more than an intellectual reality*. The "translation," necessary as it was for thoughtful human consideration, involved a kind of improper "reduction." Revelation was something more than a collection of propositions. There was something "mystical" and transcendent about it which was impossible for doctrinal propositions to contain. That was why Newman went to some lengths in the essay on *Development* to emphasize that a "mystical interpretation" of Scripture was the very badge of Catholic orthodoxy.[25] Although he did not use the phrase, it was as if he saw revelation as a kind of "performative utterance." A curse or a friendly greeting "accomplishes" more than the intellectual content it contains. It influences attitudes, it alters perceptions, it builds or threatens the relationship between a speaker and a hearer. Revelation, likewise, is not just intellectual. It is a multi-dimensional communication. It shapes a relationship and the identities of the persons involved.[26] Newman perceived and emphasized this holistic, multi-dimensional character of revelation. Yet he did not develop a notion of doctrine that was more fully compatible with it.

Newman's insights regarding the insufficiency of doctrinal words, the more-than-logical character of doctrinal change, and the multi-dimensional character of revelation all were in conflict with the traditional notion of doctrine. They were especially mismatched with Bossuet's notion of doctrinal change being a matter of logical "clarification." Newman did not, however, work directly toward a new model of doctrine. He worked only for a new model of doctrinal change.

Development as Model

Newman brought together in his conversion a host of interesting insights and complexities. (1) He saw that doctrines had changed substantially in the history of Roman Catholicism and that they were still cherished and debated in that church. (2) He saw that doctrines were a sacred intellectual summation given to revelation, but that they were frail approximations in a human medium that but dimly reflected the Mystery which they bespoke. (3) He saw that doctrines were not purely intellectual but were to reflect and inspire appropriate perceptions, feelings, and action. Finally, (4) and most "revolutionary," he saw that change might be a positive, rather than a negative, process.

Newman struggled for the right model to explain this combination of perceptions. It was to be the "hypothesis to account for the difficulty" of change. The basic model he chose was that of the "development of ideas," through time, in a society. Over a period of generations, he proposed, an influential idea makes a mark on history by impressing itself on many minds in a changing community.[27] In this community the idea develops, complete with stops and starts, advances and failures, confusions and clarifications, anger and appreciation. Other models he used were easier to grasp, but were not as complex and appropriate: the development of an individual; the organic development of plants and animals from seed to maturity; and development in a tripolar dialectic between theology, church order, and the worshipping life of the local community. All of the models had value. Each emphasized an enduring identity amidst considerable change. In them he tried to show that development might have great size and variety, might be cumulative, linear, episodic, or dialectic, and yet it might be a process that was natural and "preservative" to the reality involved. It might indeed be the divinely intended character of doctrine and revelation. Not to develop might be to die.

Newman was both liberal and conservative. He used the *modern* concept of "development" to retain the *traditional* importance of doctrine. In this equilibrium he wanted to show that change was not inherently destructive, that it was in fact quite natural, and that it had occurred earlier in the history of the church. He wanted at least to suggest that change was co-extensive with life and that development was integral to a living faith.

Conclusion

An important problem remained in Newman's new view of doctrinal change. In what sense could words and propositions be sufficient to convey the mystery of revelation? Newman alluded to this difficulty in his own talk about the frailty of words, a history of substantive doctrinal change, and the more-than-intellectual character of revelation. He reflected the same tension in speaking of how doctrine should be somewhat mystical, evoking not only thought, but also emotions, feelings, decisions, and actions. Yet his model for doctrinal change—the notion of the historical development of an "idea" in the minds of a community—did not provide an alternative view of doctrine. The model of *doctrinal change* was exclusively a model of *change* and not a new model of *doctrine*.

Newman's was a great improvement over the classical and traditional Catholic model of doctrinal change: the notion of a logical "unfolding" from an unchanging text or deposit. It did at least suggest that doctrine was not simply a collection of propositions which somehow defined a hidden reality. The fact that Newman was talking about something else was perhaps most clear when he talked of revelation possessing the mind, rather than the mind possessing revelation. Yet the explanation of how this more-than-propositional reality was related to doctrine remained indistinct. I want to propose that the direction Newman began has been carried to a new stage in the recent writings of George Lindbeck. I believe that here is found a new understanding of *doctrine* which complements Newman's idea of *development*.

Part Two
George Lindbeck

Lutheran scholar and theologian George Lindbeck has proposed a forceful new model of doctrine in his book on *The Nature of Doctrine*.[28] The model is especially interesting in light of Newman's notion of development. Although he has referred to the significance of Newman's work, Lindbeck did not begin with Newman's problems nor conclude with his notion of change. He began by examining doctrine itself and how it functions in a religion. He came to questions regarding doctrinal change from a background of problems in ecumenical discussions. Like Newman, he wanted to legitimate certain changes in doctrine, but not (particularly) the changes in the history of Roman Catholicism. He sought a way to explain the propriety of doctrinal change in the future: the kind of changes that are prerequisite to the possibility of explicit ecumenical reconciliation.

Lindbeck lamented the inadequacy of standard models of doctrine, which he classified as either "classical" or "modern."[29] He reported that these models encumbered ecumenical discussion. He proposed they were inadequate because with them one could not seriously entertain "the possibility of doctrinal reconciliation without capitulation."[30] Classical and modern models of doctrine did not allow for the possibility of change without foregoing all claim to significant truth. Lindbeck outlined a model that he proposed could.

In the classical model, doctrines are conceived as "informative propositions or truth claims about objective realities."[31] In such a classical or "propositional" model, doctrines are seen as authoritative because they correspond to the objective realities they represent.

In a more liberal or modern model, doctrines are regarded as "noninformative and nondiscursive symbols of inner feelings, attitudes, or existential orientations."[32] In this modern or "experiential-expressivist" model, doctrines are viewed as authoritative to the degree that they articulate the *living experience* of individuals in the church, discerned or constructed by theologically talented members.

Neither of these models can combine claims that doctrines are significantly true and also subject to significant change. The classical, propositional model is "pre-modern," with no sense of the cultural inter-dependence of thought and words. In this model, the meaning of doctrine is *invariable*, for it purports to describe unchanging, eternal, ontological reality. The principle of contradiction precludes the reconciliation of differing doctrinal propositions.

By the same token, the experiential-expressive model is modern, with such an appreciation of the individual and of cultural specificity that the meaning of doctrine is *limitlessly variable*. Doctrinal reconciliation is uncomplicated but vacuous. The only "truth" involved is the accuracy with which a particular "depth experience" is described.

A Rule-Model of Doctrine

In this situation of radically opposed models, Lindbeck proposed something significantly different: a "functional" or "regulative" model of doctrine. This model offered a path between the Scylla of classical absolutism and the Charybdis of modern relativism. The model was developed from what Lindbeck characterized as a "cultural-linguistic" perspective, a perspective which has become popular in many other disciplines, such as history, sociology, anthropology, and philosophy.

This cultural-linguistic perspective recognizes the influence of cultural history upon systems of thought. Yet it does not downgrade the significance of such thought. Hence Lindbeck claimed the model might accomplish the impossible: it would allow for variability in the doctrines of faith without compromising the transcendent value those doctrines purport to contain.[33]

In this cultural-linguistic view, religions are understood to function analogously to languages and cultures. They constitute broad "systems of meaning" which are constructed and taught. They provide "patterns" or "idioms" for the construing of reality and for the living of life. These "patterns" are conveyed by religions in narratives, doctrines, rituals, myths, ethics, and art. The patterns encourage particular existential self-understandings. As persons interiorize what is broadly seen as their religion's "language" or "grammar," they become reliable representatives of that religion.

This cultural-linguistic view of religion is the foundation of Lindbeck's regulative model of doctrine.[34] Doctrines here are not presumed to present ontological truth-claims (as they must in the classical model) nor to contain only subjective symbols and experiences (as they do in the modern model.) Doctrines are seen, rather, as "communally authoritative *rules* of discourse, attitude, and action."[35]

> The novelty of rule theory . . . is that it does not locate the abiding and doctrinally significant aspect of religion in propositionally formulated truths, much less in inner experiences, but *in the story* it tells and *in the grammar* that informs the way the story is told and used . . . (here) religion is first of all a comprehensive interpretive medium or categorial framework with which one has certain kinds of experiences and makes certain kinds of affirmations. In the case of Christianity, the framework is supplied by the biblical narratives interrelated in certain specified ways (e.g., by Christ as center).[36]

In this "rule theory" view of religion, doctrine is guardian of the story a religion tells. It delimits the story and relates the grammar with which the story is conveyed. Doctrine defines the "categorical framework" of the biblical narratives and the "certain specified ways" in which they are "interrelated . . . (e.g. by Christ as center)."

Making this role of doctrine more specific, Lindbeck explained how doctrines provide lexical, syntactical, and semantic rules for the Christian narrative. He illuminated his explanation with the example of a particular doctrine:

> The doctrine that Jesus is the Messiah, for example, functions *lexically* as the warrant for adding the New Testament literature to the canon [of the Bible], *syntactically* as a hermeneutical rule that Jesus Christ be interpreted as the fulfillment of the Old Testament promises (and the Old Testament as pointing toward him), and *semantically* as a rule regarding the referring use of such titles as "Messiah."[37]

Doctrines in this view are an integral part of guiding the nurture and instruction by which a religion *shapes* members of a community into a particular identity, a particular way of seeing and dealing with reality.

Sources of Personhood and of Experience

This regulative model of doctrine involves a revised (or reclaimed) view of *personal identity* and of the relationship between *words and experience*. In regard to the person, selfhood is not so much a "given" as a goal. Modernity has created what Lindbeck called the "myth of the transcendental ego," suggesting that selfhood precedes social interaction and that it is to be found by a kind of archaeological penetration into one's own "inner depths." In the cultural-linguistic perspective, this individualistic view of human selfhood is an illusion. Selfhood is something that can only be achieved through interaction with society.[38]

Similarly, in the regulative view, a commonly mistaken understanding of the relation between words and experience is corrected. Words do not emerge so much from experience as experiences emerge from words. Lindbeck's view is articulated in his criticism of Karl Rahner (1904-1984). According to Lindbeck, Rahner was mistaken in his argument that there is a universal "prereflective, inarticulate *experience* of the divine" which is (later) developed into humanity's practice of religion and the *words* of the Christian gospel.[39]

Lindbeck opposed the sequence of experience preceding words and the notion of a pre-reflective experience of the gospel. In his counter-position, he gave *priority to words* and attached more importance to the public dimension than to the private dimension of religion. He emphasized the importance of audibly *hearing* the word of God rather than the supposedly prior, interior, and *pre-reflective experience* of God.

This emphasis upon the public dimension is more compatible with the methodology of anthropologists and cultural-linguists. It reflects their fundamental view of religion. But what does all this imply for theology and doctrine? Let me paraphrase Lindbeck's words:

> For cultural-linguists, religions are not *expressions* of the transcendental heights and depths of human *experience*. They are, rather, *patterns of behavior*: patterns of ritual, myth, belief, and conduct. These patterns do not result from a people's existential self-understanding. To the contrary, *the self-understanding results from these informative, nurturing patterns*.
>
> What does this revolution in understanding mean for Christian theology? It means that theology must recognize that just as an individual becomes human by learning a language, so he or she begins to become a new creature, a Christian, through hearing and interiorizing the language that speaks of Christ.[40]

In other words, a person's identity is not a given that *precedes* social interaction. Identity, self-hood, and the "heights and depths of experience" are realities obtained only *through* language and social interaction.

In such a cultural-linguistic perspective, "language" and "doctrine" are the *source*, and *not the result*, of distinctively human experience. Doctrines are no longer propositions that define a hidden reality, at least not primarily and necessarily. They are "rules" or "second-order propositions." They speak not so much of "how reality is" but of "how a Christian talks."[41] The same sentences might be used for both purposes, but in this rule-theory, doctrines *primarily* inform one of "how the Christian story is to be told and used." Doctrine shapes Christian perception and nurtures Christian identity.

The story and its correct narration are very important. The story evokes certain kinds of experiences, affects the "shape" a particular society gives to reality, influences judgments, elicits actions, and encourages affirmations. The language or story is integral to the identity of the people. Doctrines are guardians of the story. The norm for truth is no longer a *correspondence* between language and ontological reality. It is more a matter of *consistency* or coherence between particular statements and the rest of the Christian story.[42]

The Contextual Possibility of Change

It may begin to seem that doctrines, in this regulative view, could *never* change. The Christian story would seem properly to remain always the same. But that interpretation misreads how the rule theory describes the "patterns" that are shaped by the Christian story. The story is not itself a worldview that is always to be the same. It is more the framework or the partner in a dialogue between religion and culture. It influences the way that a culture's worldview is altered or adjusted by persons in a Christian community.

As views of the world change, what doctrine preserves is the "framework of the biblical narrative." The worldview of contemporary western culture is not the same as that of Greek philosophy, nor is either one of these the same as the worldview of the ancient Near East. Yet through all these changes in worldviews, the biblical narrative has remained. This narrative has "Christianized" the various world pictures and their distinct definitions of the good, the real, the divine, and the human. Doctrines do not define a society's worldview, but they do interact with it by reminding a Christian people of the biblical narrative that is particularly theirs.

The real point of the rule theory, then, is not that doctrines must remain always the same. Doctrine is seen to depend upon story and context. As long as the context in which the Christian story is being told remains the same, doctrine does not change. But doctrine lives in history as part of the interaction between a religion and a culture. An essential part of a Christian community is the cultural context in which it lives. It is the changing cultural context which explains why the "grammar" in which the Christian story is told, the doctrine which is its guard, must change for the story to stay the same.

> The meaning of rites and utterances depends on contexts. To [merely] *replicate* the old forms in new situations frequently loses the original meaning, the original spirit. Just as the only way to love parents, spouses, children, and neighbors (as they age) is to behave toward each in a distinctive (and changing) fashion, so often the only way to convey the same message (in different times or places) is to proclaim it differently. Everyone knows this intuitively, but the fear of relativistic anomie at times leads religious groups to a rigidity that gravely impairs their loyalty to a past they profess to revere.[43]

Lindbeck gave an example of this need for doctrines to *change* in order *to stay the same* in terms of the doctrine of creation. The words in which this story is told change according to the cultural context of the story: Babylonian myth, Platonic philosophy, or contemporary science. Similarly, in different contexts of description, Jesus may best be called "messiah," "logos," or "Man for Others." Changes in the doctrinal words can be seen not as *destroying* the story but as fusing the self-identical story with new worlds in which it is retold.[44]

Lindbeck offered as another example the doctrine of the immortality of the soul.[45] This doctrine is *eternally* true—crucial to the biblical story of Christianity—within the context of classical soul-body dualism. It is, by that very qualification, *historically* true as well—and not necessarily part of the Christian story in an historical context which does *not* include such classical dualism. Such non-dualistic contexts would include the world of ancient Hebraic thought and a post-classical, modern perspective.

The cultural-linguistic view places doctrinal truth-claims into a cultural context without demeaning the possibly transcendent value of the truth-claims. Whenever such and such a condition or context applies, then the doctrine is "true," as integral to the Christian story. When the condition does not apply, however, the doctrine is not necessarily "true" and it does not define how the Christian story is properly told. The doctrine is conditionally permanent and permanently conditional, and in these senses *both* permanent and conditional, eternal and historical. Its truthfulness is contextual. Most important, however, these qualifications make no judgment upon the transcendence of doctrine's origin or the ontological truthfulness of its claims.[46]

The New Model of Doctrine

The important implication for ecumenism is that there can be an appreciation for cultural contexts and cultural change. Different Christian doctrines can apply in different circumstances, with different domains, priorities, and use. A parallel might be shown in conflicting rules for driving. One rule requires driving on the right side of the road and another requires driving on the left. Here there is obvious and inescapable contradiction, but disastrous conflict is avoidable if all drivers recognize that each rule applies only in its specific domain, whether it be England, Japan, the United States, or the Soviet Union.

Similarly, different contexts explain the Eucharist in different ways, some with and some against the language of transubstantiation. It is possible that such differences, which once were irresolvable conflicts, might now be harmonized by appropriate specifications of their respective priorities, uses, and domains. "To the degree that doctrines function as rules, there is no logical problem in understanding how historically opposed positions can in some, even if not all, cases be reconciled while remaining in themselves unchanged. Contrary to what happens when doctrines are construed as propositions or expressive symbols, doctrinal reconciliation without capitulation is a coherent notion."[47]

This, of course, was the whole task that Lindbeck had set for himself: removing from ecumenical discussion the encumbrance of doctrinal models which (falsely) made impossible the thought of doctrinal reconciliation without capitulation. Lindbeck made the notion coherent not by compromising doctrines or by eliminating their claim to a transcendent source. He did it by examining carefully what doctrines actually do. The result was the functional model. The first thing doctrines "do" is to teach members of a religion how they are to "speak," defining the sacred story and explaining how the story is to be told. In this they fashion the distinctively Christian identity of the religion's members. All this can be accomplished prior to and independent of any philosophical debate about the ontological truthfulness or correspondence of the story. Hence differences between denominations need not escalate into denominational wars. They can be "tamed" and seen for what they are: historical differences between denominations. From this new model, doctrinal reconciliation, without capitulation, is more feasible and realistic.

Conclusion

Lindbeck's struggle to facilitate ecumenical reconciliation has added significantly to Newman's invaluable model of doctrinal development. Where Newman's model was focused on *development*, Lindbeck's model was focused on *doctrine*. His "regulative model" placed doctrine in a (changing) cultural context, as guardian of a sacred story. The appreciation for cultural context was distinctively ("post-") modern. And yet the model also resolved many of the problems suggested in Newman's own writings. The problem of doctrinal "frailty of words" is resolved because the model's truth-claim is less a correlation to a hidden reality and more a coherence with a tradition's central story. The problem of why doctrine might change when a culture changes is directly addressed by claiming that in the changed words the same story can be "fused" with a new worldview. And, finally, the more-than-intellectual character of revelation is accommodated in the sense that doctrine, as the grammar with which a story is presented, is indeed intended to influence holistically the way new members of a community are shaped, nurtured, and initiated into a particular religious tradition.

In these ways Lindbeck's view may indeed be more radical than Newman's own revolution. Lindbeck has analyzed more rigorously the role of doctrine in a religious community and has applied new perspectives upon "religion" and "truth." It might be argued, however, that Lindbeck's understanding of how doctrine changes is surprisingly similar to what Newman proposed. The similarity is suggested by perceiving the equation between Newman's "idea" and Lindbeck's "story." What Lindbeck does is make more tangible Newman's notion that an idea (or story) takes possession of minds rather than minds taking possession of the story (or idea). The idea "makes a mark" on a community of minds *in the particular cultural context or community*. The idea is received and handed on. As the community lives and the context changes, the doctrine or "grammar" in which the idea (or story) is framed also changes. Newman proposed that revelation (and its resulting doctrine) is not so much possessed by minds as it is in fact a reality that possesses them. Similarly, for Lindbeck, members of Christianity do not shape their story: the story of Christianity shapes the identity of its members.

Newman and Lindbeck were both concerned to retain the importance of doctrine and to accommodate the finest strengths of modern times. With comparable kinds of equilibrium, both persons were progressive and traditional, in ways by which neither precluded the other.

NOTES

1. "Newman Centenary," *The Pope Speaks*, 34: 4 (July/August, 1990), 309-12. The Pope's address was delivered on 27 April 1990.
2. See Vincent F. Blehl, S.J., "Prelude to the Making of a Saint," *America*, 160: 9 (March 11, 1989), 213-6 and the article by Robert Roberts, released by the Catholic News Service on 10 August 1990.
3. There have been instances of opposition amounting to vindictiveness against Newman, both inside and outside the Roman Catholic church, but amazingly little in the last half-century. Among the classic examples is that by Newman's own brother, Francis, soon after John Henry died. He claimed John Henry was sly and deceitful, disdained others, had a fanatical love of authority, and was secretly a Papist prior to his 1845 conversion. See Francis William Newman, *Contributions Chiefly to the Early History of the Late Cardinal Newman* (London: Kegan Paul, Trech, Trubner and Co., Ltd., 1891). Similarly, Edwin Abbott described Newman as an egotist who despised humanity and was so driven by self-doubt that he sought security in the dogmatism of the Roman church. See Edwin Abbott, *Philomythus: An Antidote Against Credulity; A Discussion of Cardinal Newman's Essay on Ecclesiastical Miracles* (second edition; London: Macmillan and Co., 1891), ix. In a slightly more nuanced criticism, Gaius Atkins proposed Newman was afraid of the revolutionary hopes of modern times and was driven toward intolerance and absolutism by a personal, subjective need. See Gaius Atkins, *Life of Cardinal Newman* (Creative Lives, Harold E. B. Speight, editor; New York: Harper and Brothers Publishers, 1931), 288-289.

    Official Roman Catholic opposition was so strong for part of his lifetime that for almost nine years (1858-67) Newman was unable to publish. The official fear was that he was too Protestant and accorded too much authority to the people. See the *Rambler* controversy, *On Consulting the Faithful in Matters of Doctrine*, ed. John Coulson (New York: Sheed and Ward, 1961).
4. Claims of Newman's link to Roman Catholic Modernism have shown significant endurance. The legitimacy of such claims was discussed in *Newman and the Modernists*, ed. Mary Jo Weaver

(New York: University of America Press, 1985). The theme dates back to one of the foremost Modernists, George Tyrrell, who himself called Newman the "unwitting father of the Modernist movement." Tyrrell also wrote: "The solidarity of Newman with Modernism cannot be denied. Newman might have shuddered at this progeny; it is none the less his." See "The Prospects of Modernism," in *The Hibbert Journal*, VI (January, 1908), 243. What loomed large in Tyrrell's view of Newman was the latter's recognition of the frailty of human (dogmatic) words and the "probabilities" (rather than the "proof") of faith. He did not see how these modernist traits could be eliminated by a love of tradition and authority. He knew, however, that Newman called himself the opponent of liberalism and hence he wrote: "Newman's incontestable abhorrence of doctrinal liberalism does not at once prove that he may not be the progenitor of it." See his "Introduction," to *The Mystery of Newman*, by Henri Bremond, trans. H. C. Corrance (London: Williams and Norgate, 1907), xvii.

5. See, for example, some of the articles in the 1979 symposium, *John Henry Newman: Theologian and Cardinal* (Rome: Urbiana University Press, 1981), especially the articles by Vincent Blehl (17-32), John F. Crosby (99-126), and Giovanni Velloci (131-54).

6. "For thirty, forty, fifty years I have resisted to the best of my powers the spirit of Liberalism in religion." See "The Biblietto Speech," in *A Newman Reader*, ed. F.X. Connolly (New York: Doubleday and Co., 1964), 384.

7. See Jan-Hendrik Walgrave, O.P., *Newman the Theologian. The Nature of Belief and Doctrine* (London: Geoffrey Chapman, 1960) and his "A Psychological Portrait of Newman," in *John Henry Newman: Theologian and Cardinal. op. cit.*, 155-71.

8. Among his most notable works are *The Arians of the Fourth Century* (London: Longmans, Green, 1895 [1833]); *Lectures on the Doctrine of Justification* (Westminster, MD: Christian Classics, 1966 [1838]); and *Select Treatises of St. Athanasius in Controversy with the Arians*, 2 vols. (1841, 1844).

9. As we will see below, this absence may have also been very significant in his eventual decision to join the Roman Catholic church.

10. *Apologia*, 54.

11. See his critique of Milman's *History of Christianity*, in *Essays Critical and Historical*, vol. II (London: Longmans, Green, 1885 [1817]), 186-248, esp. 193-96.
12. *Apologia*, 54.
13. Newman gave first expression to troublesome feelings in the summer of 1839. That fear receded and then returned in the summer of 1841. See his *Apologia*, 115, 118, and 148. See also *The Letters and Correspondence of John Henry Newman During his Life in the English Church*, vol. 1, Ed. by Anne Mozley (London: Longmans, Green and Co., 1891), 445.
14. The original edition of the book was in 1845. Because changes in it are small and because the later book has had greatest circulation, I have used the third, revised edition of 1878 (London: Longmans, Green, 1906). Hereafter: *Development*. References will be to chapter, section, and subsection numbers.
15. See *Newman's University Sermons: Fifteen Sermons Preached before the University of Oxford 1826-1843*, third edition, ed. by D.M. MacKinnon and J. D. Holmes (London: SPCK, 1970), 269. Hereafter: *OUS*.
16. *The Arians of the Fourth Century*, op. cit.
17. Newman thought the Roman Catholic church was the one most successful in preserving revelation's message amidst the pitfalls of history. Yet he also saw that revelation was not something written in stone. In this he was precursor of what was best and most important in many of the Catholic Modernists: "the distinction between what is revealed and how it is described, defined, and spoken of." See John Coulson, *Religion and Imagination: 'In Aid of a Grammar of Assent'* (Oxford: Clarendon Press, 1981), 73. These Modernists, like Newman, affirmed the transcendent origin of revelation. Unlike many pastorally-minded or defensive officials of the church, however, they also admitted the frailty of its human expression.
18. *Development*, I, 1, 7.
19. The words are quoted by Nicholas Lash in his *Newman on Development: The Search for an Explanation in History* (London: Sheed and Ward, 1975), 54. His source is the Cambridge University Library, Additional Manuscripts, MSS 4987.60.
20. On this topic, see Owen Chadwick, *From Bossuet to Newman: The Idea of Doctrinal Development* (Cambridge: University Press, 1957), especially chapters 1 and 2.

21. Credit for alerting me to the importance of the *OUS* goes to conversation with Avery Dulles and to his article, "From Images to Truth: Newman on Revelation and Faith," in *Theological Studies*, 51:2 (June, 1990), 252-67.
22. *OUS*, 320-24. Despite the time devoted to the holistic concept of revelation, Newman did not develop how it was to be explained as the "transcendent source" of doctrine.
23. *Ibid.*, 317.
24. *OUS*, 331-2.
25. *Development*, 336-42.
26. Doctrines, Newman proposed, like revelation itself, must be able to "kindle devotion, rouse the passions, and attach the affections." *An Essay in Aid of a Grammar of Assent*, ed. Ian T. Ker (Oxford: Clarendon Press, 1985 [1870]), 64. They must be able to excite in people "feelings of humility, love and devotion." They are to be the support "of all religious minds whatever, in the case of a child, or a peasant, as well as a philosopher." *Grammar, op. cit.*, 129-31. Doctrines were not to be simply membership cards in a kind of gnostic society of "right belief." They were to build a perspective and encourage a particular type of feeling and action. As was said before in his complaint about Anglicanism, he did not seek feelings without doctrines, but neither did he seek doctrines without feeling.
27. See Nicholas Lash, *Newman on Development, op.cit.*, 46-51.
28. *The Nature of Doctrine. Religion and Theology in a Postliberal Age* (Hereafter: *Doctrine*), by George A. Lindbeck (Philadelphia: Westminster Press, 1984). A large number of commentaries have been written on this ground-breaking work. See, for example, John D'Arcy May, "Integral Ecumenism," in *Journal of Ecumenical Studies*, 25:4 (Fall, 1988), 573-91 and Owen C. Thomas, "On Stepping Twice into the Same Church: Essence, Development, and Pluralism," in *Anglican Theological Review*, LXX:4 (1989), 293-306.
29. *Doctrine*, 16. He mentioned that there have also been efforts to combine the two types but that "for our purposes" the hybrid could be included under the first type.
30. *Doctrine*, 16.
31. *Ibid.*
32. *Ibid.* Lindbeck proposed that Kant "cleared the ground" for the emergence of this experiential-expressive model of doctrine. He demolished "the metaphysical and epistemological foundations" of

the classical model. Scientific developments then rendered less credible literalistic propositional interpretations of many doctrines (*e.g.*, creation) and historical studies had similar effect by implying "the time-conditioned relativity" of all doctrines. Kant defended religious belief on the basis of God being the necessary, transcendental condition of morality, but this seemed to leave religion sorely (and emotionally) impoverished. Schleiermacher "filled the breach" by charting a course which suggested religion and doctrine to be based upon prereflective, internal experience. See *Doctrine*, 20-1. For Lindbeck's opposition to this "modern" view of doctrine and religion, see below.

33. *Doctrine*, 17.
34. Two qualifications are necessary. First, Lindbeck himself does not abandon the effort to examine the "objective truthfulness" of Christian doctrine, which is a primary responsibility of someone operating within the ambit of the classical model. He emphasized that his new model does not *require* such an abandonment. He thinks, however, that the abstract search for truth has led theologians away from a concern for rules and life—rules regarding how Christians are to live.

    Second, he recognizes the popularity of the symbolic (a la Tillich) interpretation of doctrine and admits it will continue to have considerable sway. But he also fears that it is more of a compromise with culture than reaffirmation of authentic Christian identity.
35. *Doctrine*, 18.
36. *Doctrine*, 80 (italics added).
37. *Doctrine*, 81 (italics added).
38. *Doctrine*, 126.
39. *Doctrine*, 56 and 61.
40. *Doctrine*, 62 (paraphrased).
41. Lindbeck liked the early church practice of how converts are trained into Christianity. He wrote: "Pagan converts to the Catholic mainstream did not, for the most part, first understand the faith and then decide to become Christians; rather, the process was reversed: they first decided and then they understood. They were first attracted by the Christian community and form of life . . . They submitted themselves to prolonged catechetical instruction in which they practiced new modes of behavior and learned the stories of Israel and their fulfillment in Christ. Only

after they had acquired proficiency in the alien Christian language and form of life were they deemed able intelligently and responsibly to profess the faith, to be baptized." (*Doctrine*, 132.)
42. *Doctrine*, 64-9.
43. *Doctrine*, 79. I have made parenthetical changes in this text to preserve and extend its meaning.
44. *Doctrine*, 82.
45. *Doctrine*, 86-7.
46. Lindbeck argues that Thomas Kuhn (*the Structure of Scientific Revolutions*, 2nd ed. [University of Chicago Press, 1970]) and others show that "reasonableness in religion and theology, as in other domains, has something of that aesthetic character, that quality of unformalizable skill, which we usually associate with the artist or the linguistically competent. If so, basic religious and theological positions, like Kuhn's scientific paradigms, are invulnerable to definitive refutation (as well as confirmation) but can nevertheless be tested and argued about in various ways, and these tests and arguments in the long run make a difference. Reason places constraints on religious as well as on scientific options even though these constraints are too flexible and informal to be spelled out in either foundational theology or a general theory of science." *Doctrine*, 130-1. This is probably the best norm of "objective" truth Lindbeck's model offers in regard to doctrine.
47. *Doctrine*, 18.

ATHEISM OR CATHOLICISM:
Stark Disjunction From Complex Newman

Edward E. Kelly

Born in 1801, Newman was inevitably part of the Romantic Age, though, of course, he lived right through the partially reactionary Victorian Age, dying in 1890. Some Newman scholars resist acknowledgment of Newman's romanticism and are uncomfortable with his ready expression of emotions, sensitivity, and individualism. But more important, and now more generally admitted, are similarities between Newman's epistemological views and those of other Romantics. Walter Jost has recently written that "Newman's epistemology is thoroughly interpretive, predicated on the indeterminacy of the concrete and the mediatorial role of mind and language. As such, it was a scandal, more or less, for those not yet habituated by romanticism to the importance of 'imagination' and 'self'" (Jost, 54). Newman philosophized at length on this matter in the *Grammar of Assent* in 1870, but a passage from a letter of 1828 is especially romantically expressed: "I agree with you too in feeling the incommensurability (so to speak) of the human mind—we cannot gauge and measure by any common rule the varieties of thought and opinion. We all look at things with our own eyes—and invest the whole face of nature with colors of our own. Each mind pursues its own course and is actuated in that course by ten thousand indescribable incommunicable feelings and imaginings." (L, II, 60)

The tide has turned and the problem now is to accept and realize the more rationalistic (and seemingly unecumenical) side of Newman. He made it abundantly clear that his lifelong work was to oppose the Rationalism or Liberalism which he felt was threatening Christianity and basic theistic faith. And his attacks on logic in the *Apologia* and *Grammar of Assent* are almost as fierce as those of Carlyle. But at the same time, Newman often insisted that reason was the true instrument of controversy and should be employed in religious questions and in arriving at the truth of Catholicism. In the same work in which he warned that reason as used even by theologians in a Catholic university tends naturally towards heresy, he also claimed categorically that "Reason rightly exercised, leads the mind to the Catholic Faith" (Idea, 157). In the *Apologia* he again reasoned to the Church's infallibility precisely as a remedy for the defectiveness of human reason (Chapter V).

Perhaps Newman's strongest defense of reason—in fact, its most scientific form, logic—is found in his oft-repeated disjunction between atheism and Catholicism: there is "no medium, in true philosophy" between them, he claims, and he concludes that a "perfectly consistent mind . . . must embrace either the one or the other" (*Apologia*, 179-80). Much of the *Apologia* is Newman's illustration of his own logically consistent mind that reached Catholicism in 1845. He writes in that work of the "logical connexion of Theism with Catholicism," (180) and he wrote to R.H. Hutton while engaged in the *Apologia* that "I am both logically and morally right in being a Catholic" (L, XXI, 90).

Newman seemed partially aware that his shocking disjunction and his insistence on logic would appear to be a trick of false rhetoric designed to frighten or force others to a decision for Catholicism. We are certainly more aware today that Newman was a thoroughly rhetorical writer and preacher. Cicero was the subject of his first scholarly publication and a clear influence on Newman's prose style. He once called himself the "Rhetorician" of the Oxford Movement (L, V, 225) and at other times identified himself, not as theologian or literary man, but as "controversialist" (*Apologia*, 236, L, XXII, 157). Newman seemed at times to enjoy logical exercises and controversial warfare as ends in themselves, and his mind had a natural tendency to develop ideas by way of antithetical positions, paradoxes, and challenging disjunctions. He admitted to using "false" rhetoric at times and that in the early years of the Oxford Movement he was a controversial snob, condemning the controversial position of the Low Church and even playing for sport with dull opponents: "I was not unwilling to draw an opponent on step by step, by virtue of his own opinions, to the brink of some intellectual absurdity, and to leave him to get back as he could" (*Apologia*, 51).

It is good to remember some of Newman's other disjunctions. In the *Apologia*, for example, he claimed that "there was no alternative between silence altogether, and forming a theory and attacking the Roman system" (187). In Newman's novel, *Loss and Gain*, his hero Charles Reding remarks: "Either there is no prophet of the truth on earth, or the Church of Rome is that prophet" (157). In the same novel a priest on the train with Charles insists that "either we believed the whole revealed message, or really we believed no part of it" (261). There are similar disjunctions in Newman's other novel, *Callista* (61, 174) and in the *Grammar of Assent* (335).

It is also important to remember that other nineteenth-century writers were also seriously struggling with radically-opposed religious positions. Carlyle dramatized a striking ascent from an Everlasting No to an Everlasting Yea in *Sartor Resartus*. Arnold was less hopeful in portraying nineteenth-century man as "Wandering between two worlds, one dead,/The other powerless to be born" ("Stanzas from the Grande Chartreuse"). Coleridge once wrote against Deism as a viable theistic position as challengingly as Newman ever did: "The utter rejection of all present and living communion with the Universal Spirit impoverishes Deism itself, and renders it as cheerless as Atheism, from which indeed it would differ only by an obscure impersonation of what the Atheist receives unpersonified, under the name of Fate or Nature" (Coleridge, 50). John Newton, an Evangelical whose work the young Newman admired, categorically announced that there was "no medium between holding [Calvinistic doctrines] and not holding them" (Brown, 245-6). And even Charles Kingsley in a wild moment wrote his fiancee that ". . . there is no middle course. Either Deism, or the highest and most monarchial system of Catholicism" (Chitty, 59). Finally, the momentous "Either/Or" of Kierkegaard, Newman's Danish contemporary, can be profitably compared to Newman's radical disjunction between atheism and Catholicism.

Newman was moving from an early age towards disjunctive thinking in religious matters. Jean Guy Saint-Arnaud has pointed to the radical religious choices required in the New Testament, especially by St. Luke, as a source for Newman's later disjunction between atheism and Catholicism (273). As analogue, Scripture probably was a kind of source, but Newman did not, to my knowledge, ever apply any Scriptural texts as analogues to his disjunction. Butler's *Analogy of Religion* was undoubtedly a partial source of Newman's later more developed disjunction, but Newman's manner of expressing alternatives began before he read this work in 1823. Calvinism is a more likely source for Newman's disjunctive thinking. Its classic polarities of God and creation, the Elect and the Reprobate, took hold of the fifteen-year-old Newman, and a certain residue of Calvinistic ethos remained with him even in his Catholic years, as David Newsome has pointed out (26-30). Newman's father warned his twenty-one-year-old son against religious extremism. His religious temper in 1822, according to his father, could lead to "something alarming"; and he was cautioned against doing anything "ultra," for "strong minds are easily carried into infidelity" (L, I, 117). It is interesting for this paper to note that in a letter of 1853 Newman acknowledged that if his theory of doctrinal development did not solve his problems with Rome, it would tend "to throw me back out of the Church of England Towards infidelity *quite as logically*" (L, XV, 373).

Newman read the skeptical and atheistic views of writers like Paine, Hume, Gibbon, and Voltaire, and he knew more immediately the religious Liberalism of Oxford; but perhaps the most telling proof for him of the descent into infidelity and atheism from false logical thinking came from his two brothers. John Henry wrote long and fierce letters to his brother Charles in 1825 about the consequences of his picking and choosing Scriptural teachings for rationalistic or emotional reasons. He insisted to his brother that the contents of revelation may not be measured "by any preconceived standard or morals or philosophy"; in fact, if the contents are made a test of its genuineness, no revelation could be made us (L, I, 226, 219, 253). Thus, while it is certainly only an inchoate form, an important part of Newman's final religious disjunction was formulated as early as 1825.

Newman watched more seriously the religious descent of his other brother, Frank, over a longer period of time: from zealous Evangelical Christianity to Unitarianism to a so-called moral theism. According to William Robbins, Frank, who had a "rigorously logical mind," was comfortable with atheists "provided they were men of moral goodness" (67). John Henry would have agreed with Frank's Evangelical critics that his book, *Phases of Faith* of 1850, might more properly be titled "Phases of Unbelief." For he wrote a friend after its publication that he was not surprised that Frank was denying Scripture and dogmatic truth: "he must, with his independent mind, work out his principles, and they tend to atheism" (L, XIII, 415). In 1854, John Henry did question Frank's theism when he humorously but tellingly remarked that Frank's vow not to cut his beard was absurd: "to whom is it made?—to what god or devil?" (L, XVI, 307). And in 1860, John Henry wrote to Frank himself a form of his great religious disjunction. Frank had written that George Holyoake, an atheist, was a great admirer of John and his writings. John responded: "my Creed leads me to feel less surprise at an Atheist than a Protestant feels. In truth, I think that *logically* there is *no* middle point *between* Catholicism and Atheism" (L, XIX, 286).

> Let us return to the disjunctive conclusion that Newman claimed he arrived at in 1842 and still held in 1864: that there was no medium, in true philosophy, between Atheism and Catholicity, and that a perfectly consistent mind, under those circumstances in which it finds itself here below, must embrace either the one or the other (*Apologia*, 179-180).

Both Catholic and non-Catholic readers were disturbed by this disjunction and inevitably some of them misunderstood it, which resulted in Newman's trying to clarify it in private notes, personal letters, in a new appendix to the 1880 edition of the *Grammar of Assent*, and almost at the end of his life in his controversy with Fairbairn in the *Contemporary Review* (1885-1886). In the rest of this article I will offer some basic explanations of the intellectual makeup of Newman's disjunction, some of the many expressions of it in his writings, and, finally, I will indicate some more nineteenth- and twentieth-century forms of it. I do not intend to justify or even suggest the exact syllogistic form of the alleged logical foundation of the disjunction. Newman never did.

Newman did note that there is an ascending logical movement towards Catholicism and a descending movement towards atheism, with Anglicanism and Liberalism as half-way houses but not logically intermediate positions (*Apologia*, 179, 185). Newman's conversion story in the *Apologia* is meant to be a kind of illustration of the way in which a consistent mind moved gradually but logically to Catholicism. His religious journey began with the early religious experience of a personal God in conscience. And so, added to his disjunction is the insistence: "I am a Catholic by virtue of my believing in a God" (180). He further maintains that "of all points of faith, the being of a God is, to my own apprehension, encompassed with most difficulty" (215). Then, as if to shock his readers all the more, he describes a world and human history that contain "no reflection" of God, and he suggests that if he did not know God from his conscience, he himself would be an atheist (216). In a letter of 1862 he wrote: "I think there are fewer objections to the divine origin of the Roman communion than there are to the being of a God" (L, XX, 304n).

Pre-Catholic, partial forms of Newman's great disjunction appeared in some of his most significant works of the 1830's and 1840's. His anxiety in the *Oxford University Sermons* with the erosions of faith caused by Liberalism is well known. Using rather extreme language, he maintained in "The Usurptions of Reason" that "on religious subjects we may prove anything or overthrow anything and can arrive at truth but accidentally, if we merely investigate by what is commonly called Reason" (OUS, 55). In another sermon he insisted that no religious position is safe: not the least doctrinal forms of Christianity, nor even those of the Unitarians, who "(to be consistent), should find a difficulty in the doctrine of an Unity of Person, as well as of a Trinity; and having ceased to be Athanasians, should not stop till they become Pantheists" (OUS, 32).

In Tract 85 of 1838, "Holy Scripture in its Relation to the Catholic Creed," Newman developed a position that was critical to his ultimate conversion to Roman Catholicism. He demanded, as logically necessary, a true church, and not the Bible, as the definitive source of the Christian creed. The church is not yet the Roman Catholic Church, but Newman's logic will move him further in a few years to it. This tract illustrates his unrelenting drive to arrive at the exact and the whole truth and his probing mind that is willing to follow where logic leads him. He admitted that his approach is an unsettling "kill-or-cure remedy": "if you are reasonable in believing the other. . . . You ought not to stand where you are; you ought to go further one way or the other" (Tract, 112). If a person denies the Apostolical Succession, to be consistent, he ought to deny the divinity of the Holy Ghost. All Bible-Protestants are in the same difficulty; their escape is either "by falling back into utter skepticism and latitudinarianism, or, on the other hand, by going on to Rome" (Tract, 144). Even in 1838, then, Newman's famous disjunction was all but complete: either skepticism or Rome.

In many of his Anglican writings, then, Newman expressed a logical need to go forward and a warning about going backwards religiously. In 1845 he tested the logic of going to Rome for himself in his *Essay on the Development of Christian Doctrine*. A key sentence is given there to express the final part of his ascending logic: "A revelation is not given, if there be no authority to decide what it is that is given" (89). Revelation demands Rome, and doubts about Rome must be extended back to the very idea of a divine revelation and ultimately to God Himself.

As we have seen, Newman formally expressed his full disjunction between atheism and Catholicism in many of his Catholic publications. His private letters after his conversion in 1845 also contain many versions of it. It is simply one of his major apologetic and pastoral instruments for persuading correspondents to accept Catholicism or to remain in it. Exactly one month after his conversion, Newman wrote a stranger who inquired about the reasons for his conversion: "I had no alternative but to leave [the Church of England], unless I gave up the Fathers, nay all revealed religion" (L, XI, 27). In his long correspondence with the then unconverted Henry Wilberforce, Newman often reverted to various elements of his disjunction. For example, in 1846: "I hold it *impossible* that you should remain in this half and half position, believing one thing on the same ground, on which you reject another. You must go one way or the other" (L, XI, 175). Almost three years later he wrote bluntly to Wilberforce again: "Alas! there is no alternative between Catholicity and infidelity to the clear thinker" (L, XIII, 78). To Lady Chatterton in 1863, he felt it sufficient simply to confront "three momentous questions": "1. is there a God?; 2. has He spoken to us?; 3. through whom has He spoken?" (L, XX, 465). Of course, if she answered these questions logically for Newman, she would easily arrive at Catholicism. Newman was also very brief even in answering Pusey in 1864. When Pusey wrote of his difficulties with Indulgences, Newman replied with a very oblique form of his disjunction: "How I view 'Indulgences' is thus: are there any grounds, theological, of historical fact, or in reason, of *sufficient strength* to hinder men from giving credit to the word of the Church which is 'the pillar and ground of the Truth?' I know of none" (L, XXI, 361). One of Newman's latest statements of his disjunction is also one of his most important for this article, since it rejects false rhetoric as its motive. To George Edwards in 1886 he wrote that "viewed abstractly by the intellect only there is no alternative between belief in the Catholic Church and infidelity though I should never tell a man to become a Catholic *in order* to crush his doubts" (L, XXXI, 120).

Perhaps the most challenging test of the logic of Newman's disjunction involved the doctrine of Hell. Many people lost their faith over it or else simply denied the necessity of believing it. Newman himself often ventured to make the doctrine more reasonable and less crude. "Is it more probable," he wrote to J.M. Capes, "that eternal punishment should be true, or that there should be no God; for *if there be a God, there is eternal punishment, (a posteriori)*" (L, XIII, 318-319). And to Lord Blachford in 1886 Newman wrote: "to relinquish the doctrine of future punishment was to unravel the web of Revelation" (L, XXI, 114).

From the foregoing discussion, it seems clear that Newman usually invoked his disjunction between atheism and Catholicism as a notional principle to be confronted by formal logic. This comes as a surprise, as I indicated in the first section of this article, but such a controversial tool could be effective only if it was part of communicative logic. When Newman learned that Archbishop Manning criticized him for equivalently denying that there is logical proof of a God, Newman answered in a personal memorandum: "what I *really say* is that the *same bad logic* which leads to the rejection of Catholicism necessarily leads also to the rejection of Theism" (L, XXI, 324n). Manning was worried about Newman's logic, however, and published a pamphlet claiming that Deism, not Atheism, is the logical alternative to Catholicism. Since Theism is both natural and moral, Manning wrote, "it would be both intellectually and morally impossible to propose to any one the alternative of Catholicism or Atheism" (Manning, 109).

Some of the reviewers of Newman's *Apologia* did not mistake his serious logical claims. In the High Church weekly magazine, *John Bull*, Newman is described as "too essentially a logician, . . . to rest satisfied with that practical compromise which is after all the predominant characteristic of the Church of England" (July 23, 1864). On the other hand, the reviewer in *The Clerical Journal* wrote that Newman "displays the same ignorance of the nature of a true logical inference, as has been the cause of all his previous eccentricities" (July 7, 1864). A writer in a London paper complained in 1880 that Newman's disjunction between atheism and Catholicism was unreasonable and an unfair threat. Newman responded in a note added to his *Grammar of Assent* that the same sophistry which denies Catholicism may deny God. On the other hand, if one has a real assent to the being of God, he is "already three-fourths of the way towards Catholicism" (500).

Was Newman's great disjunction and its accompanying logic known to his contemporary world and to the twentieth century? I will conclude this study with some interesting examples to show that it was, though expression of it of course varied. Gerard Manley Hopkins was received into the Catholic Church by Newman and influenced by his writings. It is not surprising, therefore, to read in one of his letters to his father in 1866 (two years after Newman's *Apologia*) that he cannot delay his conversion to Catholicism because God calls him to it and because he already believes in Catholic doctrine, especially in the Real Presence. "When I doubted it," he writes, "I should become an atheist the next day." It would be a "gross superstition unless guaranteed by infallibility . . . [but] I should go on believing this doctrine as long as I believed in God" (Hopkins, 165). Most of Newman's disjunction is at least indirectly involved in these sentences. Thomas Huxley was more direct. He agreed that there were only two alternatives (unbelief and Catholicism) but he exclaimed: "Newman chooses one, I the other" (Ward, 350). Newman's own brother, Francis, maintained that people throughout history chose forms of theism without being illogical. He wrote sarcastically of his brother's "avowal that there is no logical standing-point *between* Romanism and Atheism, but whatever is between is gliding down into Atheism." "Delightful news," he remarked: "since the days of Isaiah and Micah have the whole Jewish nation been so gliding? If the Cardinal so read History, it is a merit to Atheists" (106).

Robert Browning did not like Newman or logic but he apparently knew some of Newman's writings. He allowed his Bishop Blougram to mouth part of this disjunction:

> What are the laws of nature, not to bend
> If the Church bid them?—brother Newman asks.
> * * *
> Still, when you bid me purify the same,
> To such a process I discern no end.
> Clearing off one excrescence to see two.
> There's ever a next in size, now grown as big,
> That meets the knife: I cut and cut again!
> First cut the Liquefaction, what comes last
> But Fichte's clever cut at God himself (11.702-3, 737-44).

James Joyce, an admirer of Newman's prose, created in *A Portrait of the Artist as a Young Man* a young hero who has abandoned his Catholic faith. When asked if he intended to become a Protestant, he replied: "I said that I had lost the faith. . . but not that I had lost self-respect. What kind of liberation would that be to forsake an absurdity which is logical and coherent and to embrace one which is illogical and incoherent?" (Joyce, 515).

A theological rejection of Newman's disjunction came from George Tyrrell, who as a Jesuit priest greatly admired Newman's developmental concept of Christianity. In his *Autobiography* Tyrrell contrasts Newman's Catholicism as the outcome of his theism with his own movement from Catholicism *to* a higher theism and a re-evaluation of his Catholicism (112). And in *A Much-Abused Letter* he suggests that there are ways to remain Catholic without adhering to Newman's strict sense of Catholicism. The exact meaning of Catholic doctrines is not always really known, and, besides, it is the life of Christianity, not its doctrines, that is of highest value. Perhaps it can be said that this position has been taken up by a fair number of Catholics in the twentieth century. Perhaps also often accepted is Tyrrell's dislike of Newman's "all-or-nothing" principle; thus, he writes, "I would infinitely rather see a Catholic country protestantized than de-Christianized; I would rather see it de-Christianized than bereft of all religion" (99, n 11).

Nevertheless, in the immediate post-Modernist Church, much of Newman's uncompromising disjunction remained alive. Graham Greene, who knew and admired Newman's writings, reflects its life in the urgency felt by his characters for option of either Catholicism or unbelief/atheism. His characters seem obsessed with choosing one or the other; there is no compromise. Querry in *A Burnt-Out Case* is haunted by a sense of necessity that he must believe all or nothing. And the male lover in *The End of the Affair* reflects: "I have never understood why people who can swallow the enormous improbability of a personal God boggle at a personal Devil" (51).

Finally, Carl Jung has noted the phenomenon of the twentieth century that while Protestants tend to abandon the particular doctrines of their churches only to re-formulate some other form of sectarian or humanistic religion, Catholics who leave their church tend to develop a "secret or manifest inclination toward atheism.... The absolutism of the Catholic church seems to demand an equally absolute negation, while Protestant relativism permits variations" (Jung, 23). Since Newman appears to have partially foreseen in 1831 what Jung wrote in 1938, I will allow him to have the last word: "The Children of evangelical parents, if they see the world, will generally turn liberals; on the same principles as the sons of Rome turn infidels" (L, II, 308).

WORKS CITED

1. Ford K. Brown. *Fathers of the Victorians*. Cambridge, 1961.
2. Susan Chitty. *The Beast and the Monk: A Life of Charles Kingsley*. New York, 1975.
3. Samuel Taylor Coleridge. *Aids to Reflection*. London, 1904.
4. Graham Greene. *The End of the Affair*. London, 1962.
5. Gerard Manley Hopkins. *Poems and Prose of Gerard Manley Hopkins*. ed. by W.H. Gardner London, 1953.
6. Walter Jost. *Rhetorical Thought in John Henry Newman*. Columbia, South Carolina, 1989.
7. James Joyce. *The Portable James Joyce*, ed. by Harry Levin. New York, 1946.
8. Carl Jung. *Psychology and Religion*. New Haven, 1938.
9. Henry Edward Manning. "The Workings of the Holy Spirit in the Church of England," *England and Christendom*. London, 1867.
10. Francis W. Newman. *Contributions Chiefly to the Early History of the Late Cardinal Newman*. London, 1891.
11. John Henry Newman. *Apologia Pro Vita Sua*, ed. by Martin J. Svaglic. Oxford, 1967. Noted in text as *Apologia*.
12. Ibid., *Callista: A Sketch of the Third Century*. London, 1962.
13. Ibid., *An Essay in Aid of a Grammar of Assent*. London, 1891.
14. Ibid., *An Essay on the Development of Christian Doctrine*. London, 1891.
15. Ibid., *The Idea of a University*, ed. by I.T. Ker. Oxford, 1976.
16. Ibid., *The Letters and Diaries of John Henry Newman*, ed. by C. Stephen Dessain *et al.*, vols. I-VI Oxford, 1978-84; XI-XXII London, 1961-72; XXIII-XXXI. Oxford, 1973-7. Noted in text as L.
17. Ibid., *Loss and Gain: The Story of a Convert*. Oxford, 1986.
18. Ibid., *Sermons Preached before the University of Oxford*. London, 1872. Noted in text as OUS.
19. Ibid., *Tract 85*, "Holy Scripture in its Relation to the Catholic Creed, Discussions and Arguments*. London, 1918.
20. David Newsome. "The Evangelical Sources of Newman's Power," *The Rediscovery of Newman: An Oxford Symposium*, ed. by John Coulson and A.M. Allchin. London, 1967.
21. William Robbins. *The Newman Brothers*. Cambridge, Mass., 1966.
22. Jean Guy Saint-Arnaud. *Newman et L'Incroyance*. Paris, 1972.

23. George Tyrrell. *Autobiography and Life of George Tyrrell.* London, 1912.
24. *Ibid., A Much-Abused Letter.* London, 1906.
25. Maisie Ward. *Young Mr. Newman.* London, 1948.

GEORGE TYRRELL:
Devout Disciple of Newman

David G. Schultenover, S.J.

George Henry Tyrrell, the former Jesuit who was excommunicated for his public criticism of Pope Pius X's encyclical *Pascendi dominici gregis* (1907), claims to have received his theological method from John Henry Newman. While one could mount a credible case for that claim, the scope of this paper is more modest. It will attempt to describe the beginnings of Newman's influence on Tyrrell, both in regard to his predisposition to that influence and in its early expressions in published works and correspondence.

Tyrrell was not a systematician. He was an essayist in every sense of that word. He carried on theological conversations, and from time to time drew together the results into a volume or set of volumes. Too, he was shamelessly eclectic, appropriating and adopting from everyone he read, making others' ideas his own, and sometimes not giving credit where credit was due. This failure is particularly evident in his early appropriations of Newman, and it is puzzling, as he often cites figures to whom he owed far less. I do not mean to impute plagiarism. Tyrrell simply did not always keep track of where his ideas came from, so he could not always give credit even if he wanted to.

Tracing influences on Tyrrell's thought, therefore, is problematic. Unless one finds a direct reference or attestation on Tyrrell's part, imputation of influence becomes tenuous, a matter of opinion. Still, because I am so convinced that I see Newman's shadow across nearly everything Tyrrell wrote, I venture this I hope not unduly opinionated essay.

First Confession—Earliest Influences

On 20 May 1906 Tyrrell replied to an inquiry from Raoul Gout, a young French Protestant who was preparing a thesis on Tyrrell's theological development: "I am a little embarrassed by your questions, which presuppose in me a mastery of Newman and an expert's acquaintance with his works, for which candour forbids me to take credit. The truth is that I have never read him very much, and cannot at all pretend in this respect to stand on the same level as Mr. Ward, or Mr. Williams, or Père Bremond."[1] But there was more to it than that. Tyrrell, ever prone to exaggerate for effect, in this case understated his grasp. He went on: "I have read *most* of his writings at least once; except the 'Plain Sermons,' the volume of the 'Via Media,' that on 'Athanasius' and that on 'Justification.' I have never read 'Tract 90.' But I have read the 'Grammar of Assent' three times, and the 'Essay on Development' about as often."[2] But there was still more. Apparently he had forgotten that in 1893, when he was about to review Wilfrid Ward's books on his father, he had told Ward that he was beginning his *fourth* re-reading of the *Grammar of Assent*;[3] that in 1901 he had told Maude Petre he had "gone back to the *Apologia* for the seventh time";[4] and that in 1901 he had told Ward that he had *very* carefully studied the last of the *University Sermons* in preparation for a critique of Newman's concept of the deposit of faith.[5]

The fact is, from one fateful day in 1885 when, as a callow seminarian, Tyrrell opened *A Grammar of Assent*, he became and ever remained, as he described it, "a devout disciple of Newman."[6] At first Tyrrell absorbed Newman indiscriminately. In time he came to see certain limitations which led him to depart on the issue of the nature of dogma. But in the end he returned to Newman's basic position, although with a significant twist. However one reads Tyrrell's relationship to Newman on particular issues, there is no question but that Tyrrell's way of thinking theologically, his psychology of religion, was forever etched with the image of John Henry Newman.

Newman became foundational for Tyrrell for several reasons: (1) Over against the dry rationalism and naive realism of approved neoscholasticism of the late nineteenth century, Newman was simply the most compelling theologian within Tyrrell's purview; (2) although Newman did not accept the philosophical presuppositions of British empiricism, he had to communicate within that horizon of discourse, and so he spoke a non-scholastic language with which Tyrrell was instantly sympathetic; and (3) a rather subjective and not well known reason, Newman fed Tyrrell at a moment when he was starving for meaningful responses to gnawing doubts and criticisms about the state of his own soul and was casting about for a salutary alternative to neoscholasticism.

The *Grammar of Assent*, Tyrrell confessed to Gout, effected "a profound revolution in my way of thinking, in the year 1885, just when I had begun to feel the limits of scholasticism rather painfully. I think it is quite psychologically conceivable that one who had read but little of the writings of a philosopher might be more deeply impregnated by his principles or his spirit than one who had read him more assiduously and completely."[7]

Predispositions to Newman

I take this confession as an invitation to suggest the psychological factors that account for Tyrrell's attraction to Newman, factors that Tyrrell failed to tell Gout. For instance, that his Tory father had died several months before Tyrrell was born; that for his first eighteen years he lived a vagabond existence, changing residences sometimes two and three times in a single year; that in the absence of a stabilizing, paternal influence, his elder brother Willie—brilliant but agnostic and usually boarding at school—became his oracle; that his mother, devoted and loving, was his father's opposite and instilled in Tyrrell a democratic spirit and loathing for play-acting and sham. Whatever continuity and consistency Tyrrell enjoyed in his most formative years were supplied by his mother's devotion and the care of Dr. Charles Benson, the kindly and evangelical headmaster of Rathmines School, Dublin. Tyrrell's childhood presents a picture of opposites. On the one hand, he forged strong emotional ties both within and outside the family; on the other hand, the context for those ties was destabilization and confusion, which paradoxically accounts for some of the strength of those ties.

As to distinctively religious upbringing, Tyrrell recalls that at the age of ten he graduated from the status of nonbeliever to unbeliever, and that until age fourteen he was essentially godless and amoral. Then a breakthrough occurred. At Willie's taunting, George, now aged fourteen, labored through Bishop Joseph Butler's *Analogy* with a measure of appreciation that astounded Willie, who forthwith tried to reassert his influence by annihilating Butler's arguments. Willie's *tour de force* impressed George, but it failed to touch the seed of faith and nonrational apologetics sown in his heart by this first, adolescent reading of Butler.

Years later, when Tyrrell read Newman's *Apologia*, he learned that Butler had also affected Newman; that he had in fact supplied for Newman "two main intellectual truths" that run "through very much that I have written," namely (1) the sacramentality of life that undergirds not only the sacraments but also the doctrine of the communion of saints; and (2) the principle of probability as the guide of life rather than certitude.[8]

Those two principles became Tyrrell's lifeblood, as Henri Bremond testified in his eulogy over Tyrrell's grave. No one knew Tyrrell interiorly better than Bremond, who was also a Newman scholar. On 21 July 1909, standing in the Anglican churchyard at Storrington, Sussex, in easy view of the Premonstratensian Priory where Tyrrell sometimes stayed between his dismissal from the Jesuits and his excommunication, Bremond observed to the mourners:

> No greater mistake could have been committed about him than the mistake of those well-meaning opponents who looked upon him as the modern apologist of private judgment and of individualism in religion. He wanted a Church, both from the sense of the necessity of a social organization of the Christian idea, and still more, perhaps, from his profound belief in, and his intense love for, the sacramental side of religion. No dogma was dearer to his heart than the dogma of the communion of Saints, of which I confidently repeated to his dying ears the sweet, short and simple formula: *Credo in communionem sanctorum*. Of his sacramental aspirations we have a touching proof in the paper dated January 1st, 1909, in which he states his wishes about his own funeral. There he says that he wished nothing to be written on his grave, except his name and the fact that he was a Catholic priest, to which was to be added the emblem of the Chalice and the Host—of which we have his own rough sketch.[9]

From conversion to death George Tyrrell was soul-companion to Newman, fed by the same worship and the same favorite doctrine.

Newman's Story *a rebour*

But as an impressionable fourteen-year-old, even if Tyrrell's head was rather fixated by Willie's rationalist onslaught, his heart had reasons of its own. Fascinated by the paradoxical and mysterious complexities of Butler's apologetic, Tyrrell began experimenting with the fringes and trappings of Butler's High Churchism. The Romish sacerdotal, sacramental, and liturgical elements of orthodox Anglicanism fascinated him. At first he tried St. Bartholomew's Church, regarded in Dublin as mildly High Church and a nest of Jesuitry. Then, encouraged by a ritualist companion, he graduated to Grangegorman, a church feverish with an advanced case of popery and sacramentalism. Tyrrell was on a straight trajectory to Rome.

It was less a matter of intellectual conviction than a matter of music. As Tyrrell reflected in his *Autobiography*, "there was something pretty about the name Grangegorman," and his friend's suggestion that he try it "stuck in my ear as a mote might have stuck in my eye."[10] It is difficult here not to see in Tyrrell a conscious comparison between Newman's conversion experience and his own. In his *Apologia* Newman used similar language to explain how Keble's work, *The Christian Year*, had affected him:

> Keble struck an original note and woke up in the hearts of thousands a new music, the music of a school, long unknown in England. Nor can I pretend to analyze, in my own instance, the effect of religious teaching so deep, so pure, so beautiful. I have never till now tried to do so; yet I think I am not wrong in saying, that the two main intellectual truths which it brought home to me, were the same two, which I had learned from Butler, though recast in the creative mind of my new master.[11]

Although Newman's *Apologia* informed and enlightened Tyrrell's religious experience, Tyrrell was also aware that his experience was quite different from Newman's:

> In that pure soul the presence of God in the voice of conscience was from the first . . . as self-evident as the fact of his own existence; although the outward evidence of the world's condition seemed to him to make for atheism, and to stand as a cumulative difficulty against this luminous interior intuition.[12] I often wonder whether it was at the suggestion of some early instructor, or by some spontaneous spiritual instinct, that he was brought thus to look for God within, as the mystics do, instead of without, as is the way with savages and children, whose theology is symbolic and materialistic. To me this conception [God in conscience] came at the end, and not at the beginning. Not merely was my earliest reason in revolt against the external, fetishistic God of the popular imagination, but when I came to hear of sacramental and supernatural indwelling I conceived it in the literal terms in which it was expressed, as the ingress of the external Deity into the soul—a notion, if possible, more unreal and more make-believe than the other—but of the natural union of the soul with God, as with the very ground of her being, I had no notion. I was too inquisitive, too eager for clearness, to accept the popular materialism; and of the spiritual truth I had learned nothing beyond words: *Foris Te quaerebam et intus eras*[13].

Obviously Tyrrell was also comparing his experience with Augustine's. He assiduously read and often quoted Augustine, perhaps because Newman had credited Augustine's dictum "securus judicat orbis terrarum" ("the whole world judges with assuredness") with pulverizing his *via media* and sending him definitively to Rome. It was the insight of this saying that undergirds the doctrine of the communion of saints and Newman's "mind of the church" which later became Tyrrell's.[14] Newman came to see in the Catholic Church the world's most universal representation, and so for him it was the Catholic Church that judged with assuredness. For Tyrrell, the saints, those who had "put on Christ," formed a communion at the heart of the Church. They were the Church's primary teachers because they were closest to the mind of God. And Tyrrell, dreading his own insecure footing, wanted desperately to belong to that community of assuredness. But his approach to Catholicism was very different from Newman's.

Newman came to Catholicism, Tyrrell explained, out of his practical and speculative theism; Tyrrell, vice versa:

> I, in my dark and crooked ways, almost began with Catholicism, and was forced back, in spite of myself, to theism, practical and speculative, in the effort to find a basis for a system that hung mid-air save for the scaffolding of mixed motives which made me cling to it blindly, in spite of a deep-down sense of instability.[15]

"Dark and crooked ways" seems to refer to Tyrrell's heartheld conviction that exploration into Roman Catholicism was the certain path for him, though his motives were at least opaque and quite possibly false.

In speaking thus in the first half of 1901 when he was writing his autobiography, Tyrrell likely had in mind two of his recently published essays: "Abuse of External Means of Light," first delivered in 1899 as a Lenten conference to Oxford students and subsequently published in *External Religion*; and "Rationalism in Religion," published three months earlier, in which he referred to Newman's three essays of the same generic title. In his conference, Tyrrell spoke of mysteries as "truths fringed with darkness," an image that parallels Newman's characterization of revelation as a mystery of light and darkness, or as doctrine viewed now on its illuminated side, now on its unilluminated side.[16]

Tyrrell's point was that he had entered into a process blindly by faith, by listening to a voice that he did not yet recognize (that is, by the light of intellect). So he clung desperately to the "scaffolding" of Catholicism until he was able to work his way down (via Newman's *Grammar*, as we shall see) to a reasonable foundation for what otherwise was a blind leap. Intellect would always leave the flight of faith unilluminated, but it could and must illuminate the launching pad. "The end of the process," Tyrrell continued,

> is that my dominant interest and strongest conviction is Theism; and dependently on this Christianity; and thirdly Catholicism, just in so far as Newman may be right; just in so far as it is the necessary implication of conscience....
>
> In the measure that I was keen for Catholicism I became equally keen for every thing that favoured theism,

> immortality, and the fundamentals of religion in general; wishing that so fair a flower might have an imperishable root. Not that I was sincere enough now to admit my really uncured doubts in these matters; for in the fact of praying and reforming myself I blindly and wilfully assumed the truth of what I wanted to be true. But the ghost was there and would rise at times; and so I clutched at all that would lay it—all that would make me internally honest and at peace.[17]

But that internal honesty and peace were still some ten years in coming.

Shortly after the onset of Grangegormanism, Tyrrell fell under the sway of Robert Dolling—the later Father Dolling—a young social activist, who, though a convinced sacramentalist, was liberal in his use and adaptation of ritual. He emblazoned on Tyrrell's soul that evangelical qualifier of all laws: "The Sabbath for man, not man for the Sabbath." He consequently disabused Tyrrell of Grangegormanism with its "Jansenistic narrowness" and "Tory High Churchism" and unwittingly left him with no alternative but to avail himself of the only other dispenser of sacramental consolations: the Roman Catholic Church. So Tyrrell began to steal into Roman churches for mass and benediction and even confession, a practice he had taken up at Grangegorman.[18]

Another crucial event that moved Tyrrell toward Rome was the sudden death of his brother Willie. That bitter disappointment provided another one of those nonrational motives that energized Tyrrell's journey: "I confess my brother's death so deepened my contempt of ordinary life that I became more anxious than ever to be really convinced that the fair dreams of Catholicism might prove true."[19] This disclosure compares strikingly to the famous passage from the *Apologia* where Newman laments the evil of the world and concludes "that either there is no Creator, or this living society . . . is in a true sense discarded from His presence." But Newman could not doubt the existence of God. That was a conviction beyond reason, beyond the evidence of the senses. So he argued about the world: "*if* there be a God, *since* there is a God, the human race is implicated in some terrible aboriginal calamity. It is out of joint with the purposes of its Creator."[20]

To bolster his flagging spirits and desperate hope that Catholicism might prove true, Tyrrell did not look to intellectual arguments——Willie had dashed that approach——but he turned to the book of life, to the experience of the communion of the saints. He began to read Montalembert's *Monks of the West*. "This concrete presentment of the reality and force of religion in action made me first wish to be, not merely respectably moral, but like these men, who were enthusiasts and wholly God-possessed." This vicarious experience fueled Tyrrell's need to hope in the God he could not touch with his mind. For the most part his natural skepticism lay dormant, but from time to time it would arise like a storm that on passing would leave him with a "sense of isolation and heartsickness."[21]

The Fateful Word

It was in the midst of one of these episodes that Tyrrell experienced what he regarded as a kind of *locutio divina*, not unlike Augustine's *tolle et lege* and Newman's *securus judicat orbis terrarum*. His head was still full of Montalembert's portrait of St. Benedict, when, on 21 March 1877——he remembered few dates so precisely——feeling particularly hopeless about his moral state, he paused in his reading of compline and "straight in the teeth of [his] Protestant conscience" prayed to St. Benedict for help. When he resumed reading, what leaped out at him were the words: "*Quoniam in me speravit, liberabo eum; protegam eum quoniam cognovit nomen meum; clamabit ad me et ego exaudiam eum; in tribulatione, eripiam eum et glorificabo eum.*"[22]

It was as some kind of answer to this prayer, Tyrrell believed, that he first met Frank Maturin, the son of Grangegorman's pastor, and then Dolling. Under Dolling's guidance Tyrrell smartened up his halfhearted and desultory academic efforts enough to matriculate at Trinity College in October 1878. He then accepted Dolling's invitation to go to London and assist him with a postal workers' guild at St. Alban's (Holborn). Dolling had hoped to show Tyrrell sane Anglo-Catholicism in action and thereby prevent his terminal step to Rome, for he knew not only that Tyrrell's heart was still enraptured by the "fair flower" of Catholicism but also that his mind would not let his heart rest until he had reached down to the flower's root. Throughout his life, it was always a case of his mind following his heart, reflection following action, a principle he found validated in the *Grammar of Assent* and later in Blondel's *L'Action*.[23]

It is important to appreciate the instability of Tyrrell's life and the tenuousness with which he was working his way to a theological explanation of his spiritual journey if one is to grasp Newman's radical importance to Tyrrell. Picture this: at the age of eighteen, having grown up without a father, with a mother who loved him but needed to change residences frequently, with an older agnostic brother whom he worshipped but whom death snatched from him, he decides to uproot himself from his only ties of affection and continue his spiritual odyssey in a totally foreign context. In what could only have been a confusing and confused state, Tyrrell departed Dublin on 31 March 1879 and arrived in London, as he put it, on the Feast of All Fools to begin a new era of his life.

In the first few days of his stay at Dolling's guild house, he was less than impressed with the casual familiarity of the residents, visitors, and clergymen, all of whom seemed no more to each other than mere acquaintances. He was even less impressed with the ritualistic propensities and preoccupations of certain "unwholesome young lads" who reminded him of the sort described in Newman's *Loss and Gain*. Just one week later, on Palm Sunday, while at the blessing of palms at St. Alban's, he was overcome with the "sense of levity and unreality about the whole proceeding" and left the church feeling sick, angry, and disappointed.

While waiting for Dolling, he wandered into Ely Place and the crypt of St. Etheldreda's Catholic Church. There, midst the smell of a dirty Irish crowd and a perfunctory and graceless ceremony, he found his heart's desire.

> Of course it was mere emotion and sentiment, and I set no store by it either then or now, but oh! the sense of reality! Here was the old business, being carried on by the old firm, in the old ways; here was continuity that took one back to the catacombs; here was no need of, and therefore no suspicion of, pose or theatrical parade; its aesthetic blemishes were its very beauties for me in that mood.[24]

The reasons of the head were there but lying unobserved behind the reasons of the heart. Years later Tyrrell let the cognitive content of that experience come to awareness:

> I should say now that what I missed [at St. Alban's] was that appeal to our historical sense which precisely the same

ceremony would have made in a Catholic church, where it would have been the utterance of the great communion of the faithful, past and present, of all ages and nations, and not merely of agents acting in defiance of the community to which they belonged. This it is, I fancy, and not any intuition of the Sacramental Presence, that makes so many say that they never *feel* at a ritualist function, however reverent and correct, as they *feel* at a Catholic function, be it never so careless and irreverent.[25]

Tyrrell underscored "feel" in this paragraph because he wanted to insist that the contact and continuity with the communion of saints was primarily a matter of *sense* rather than of reason or intellectual argument and conviction. While he discounted the emotional element of the experience, he was not discounting the feel or sense of it. What occurred in the crypt of St. Etheldreda's was a clear example of what Newman described variously as faith, swayed by antecedent considerations or prepossessions, coming finally to acquiesce in evidence otherwise defective.[26] In Tyrrell it was a case of assent triggered by intuition and attention to the voice of conscience.

Tyrrell never returned to the Anglo-Catholic experiment. He turned his mind to Thomas' *Summa*, but also continued to study the lives of the saints. Quite by chance he came across Paul Feval's *The Jesuits*, a "perfervid eulogium" of the Society of Jesus which, quite devoid of intellectual content, conjured up in his imagination a picture of a zealous and courageous company of men who worked singlemindedly *per fas et nefas* for the Catholic cause. It was certainly not rational powers that convinced Tyrrell in those first few days after leaving home and arriving in London, that he should seek admission not only into the Roman Catholic Church but into the Society of Jesus as well. It was rather his imagination and feelings.

Within two weeks of setting foot on English sod, Tyrrell was knocking at the door of the Jesuit Farm Street Church and was instantly admitted to instructions. A wholly specious syllogism from James Mumford's anti-Protestant apologetic, *The Catholic Scripturist* (1662), fell upon Tyrrell's mind like another *locutio divina* and swept away any lingering doubts: "Given that there must be a Church on earth claiming infallibility, no body that disclaims it can be that Church; and if only one body claims it, that must be the Church. But only the Roman Catholic body claims it, *ergo*. . . ."[27]

Learning Catholicism and Jesuitism

On 18 May 1879 George Tyrrell was received into the Roman Catholic Church and would the same day have been received into the Jesuits as well, except that canon law required converts to wait at least one year. So, next best thing, Tyrrell was sent to Cyprus to work at a fledgling Jesuit college, staffed by a motley band of Jesuits working to convert the spiritual descendents of Photius. This experience was supposed to introduce the young convert to Catholic and Jesuit ways——no thought having been given to the massive instability of Tyrrell's recent and distant past, psychological factors being at that time of no account.

Tyrrell was in Cyprus less than three months when the government closed the college because Father Riotta, a Sicilian Jesuit, could not resist instructing his students on the dire consequences of remaining in heresy. So Tyrrell was sent to finish out his apprenticeship in another college in Malta, where he found the Jesuits to be no less motley. From his telling, they would speak to him of their troubles but not to one another. Disturbed but undaunted by this experience, Tyrrell went from there straightaway into the Jesuit novitiate outside London.

Here Tyrrell's master, himself a convert, self-assured and authoritarian, regarded questions as aggressions of the evil spirit. Almost immediately Tyrrell was in trouble, for, although his wish to believe dominated his need to know, he did need to know, especially after his recent experience of Jesuit life. So after several confrontations not only with his master, who threatened him with expulsion, but also with his provincial, he stifled his inquisitive impulses and bent his will to conform to that degree of docility required for permission to pronounce vows. In the end, Tyrrell did pronounce vows with his classmates, but his superiors decided that, as an antidote to his "ignorant questionings and dissatisfactions," he should by-pass the usual two years of classical studies and leap immediately into three years of neoscholastic philosophy.[28] Little did they realize they were sending Tyrrell directly on the road to Newmanism.

Finding Newman

At the philosophate at Stonyhurst nonrational influences again held sway——in the persons of two professors, Fathers Thomas Rigby and Joseph Rickaby. Rigby, a devotee of strict Thomism, immediately swept Tyrrell into his train more by the power of personality than by intellect, while Rickaby, the local Newman expert, stepped in to help Tyrrell rebuild his spiritual mansion so laboriously yet tenuously constructed under the direction of his master of novices but now collapsed by the first wind of systematic doubt. It was most likely Rickaby who placed Newman's *Grammar of Assent* into Tyrrell's hands in 1885 and thus occasioned that "profound revolution in my way of thinking . . . just when I had begun to feel the limits of scholasticism rather painfully."[29] Newman fell upon the scene like a buoy tossed to a shipwrecked man. But the buoy turned out to be much more than merely the closest thing to hand that floated. It was practically the only thing. And it arrived at a time when the young Tyrrell, having passed through the troubled waters of conversion and into negative, reactionary, and rationalistic Catholic apologetics, was desperately seeking a rational grounding of his largely nonrational life-experiences. Newman instructed Tyrrell on the grammar of his assent. He provided the only rational explanation for nonrational religious experience that made sense. And it was in the distinctively non-scholastic language of Newman's intellectual horizon, British empiricism, a language that Tyrrell's scholastic censors were later and regularly to score without further ado as *"piis auribus offensiva."*[30]

Newman and the Modernist Quest

If one is to accept Tyrrell's own valuation of his indebtedness to Newman, one can date his first contact with modernism to his first reading of Newman in 1885. Not that this judgment makes Newman a modernist. But it was Tyrrell's judgment that Newman was at least the *father* of modernism, because, innocent of scholasticism and formed against the backdrop of empiricism, he naturally theologized in the living thought-forms of his culture.[31] Thomas Aquinas, Tyrrell pointed out, had done the same with Aristotelianism. With his "essentially liberal-minded" spirit and "elastic sympathy with contemporary culture" Thomas had successfully translated the "deposit of faith" into a marvelous dogmatic system based on the popular thought-forms of his day. But scholasticism, instead of imitating Thomas' method——as Newman had done——simply impounded his system and thus failed to keep pace with the inquiring mind of the Enlightenment that now required to know not only what we believe, but what we are doing when we believe.[32]

Twenty years after his first reading of Newman, Tyrrell was for a brief period convinced that the modern world had so by-passed the church and revolutionized thought that not even Newman would be able to answer its needs. On 19 February 1905 he wrote to his friend Baron Friedrich von Hugel: "I feel Newman cannot help us any more. It is not the articles of the Creed, but the word 'Credo' that needs adjustment."[33] But Tyrrell soon repented and returned to his original assessment that Newmanism *as a method* was enduring. It was Newman, Tyrrell had told Ward in 1893, who would "unbarbarise us and enable us to pour Catholic truth from the scholastic into the modern mould without losing a drop in the transfer," and thus Tyrrell would set out "to prosecute [his] analysis of the *Grammar of Assent*."[34]

Fourteen years later, in the aftermath of Pius X's condemnation of modernism, Tyrrell wrote to Albert Houtin:

> It is important in England to insist that Newman, and the more moderate 'Modernism' has been condemned. Personally I believe Newman was an incurable ecclesiast, fighting for ecclesiasticism with modern weapons and that these weapons (i.e. his Grammar of Assent etc.) were of use to Modernists in their war against Scholasticism. As Luther would have burned Harnack, so Newman would have burned Loisy. But so far as 'Newmanism' means, not his scope and motive, but his method, Newman is the father of Modernists; and that method condemned in the Encyclical is undoubtedly his.[35]

One could argue that Tyrrell had ulterior motives for linking Newman with modernism. After all, Tyrrell had recently been excommunicated for his public criticism of *Pascendi* in the London *Times*, where he first made the connection between Newman and modernism, and to claim such a prominent patron might possibly give the anti-modernists pause. But Tyrrell's claim, seemingly opportunistic in the current crisis, is no different from his position of 1885. From the first he recognized the substantial difference between Newman's method and the aprioristic and ahistorical method of scholasticism, and he began immediately to expropriate Newman. I would go so far as to say that Tyrrell penned his last essay, as well as his first, from a Newmanian perspective, and that his entire literary output can be seen as a conversation——and sometimes argument——with Newman.

Newman's Shadow on Tyrrell's Apologetic

We cannot present all the evidence for this judgment, as it is too pervasive. We shall focus only on some of Tyrrell's earlier writings. In an article of 1899, "A Point of Apologetic," Tyrrell explicitly distinguished *A Grammar of Assent* from scholasticism. The context for that distinction was his effort to validate new tracts for new times——for example, Chateaubriand's apologetic (and by implication Newman's)——aimed at the will and affections because scholasticism's apologetic, which was aimed at the intellect, had fallen into disrepute. There was need, Tyrrell argued tongue-in-cheek, to accommodate the remedy to the disease,

> to frame an argument that would appeal to the perverse and erratic mind of the day, rather than to an abstract and perfectly normal mind, which, if it existed, would "need no repentance." That a given medicine is the best avails nothing if it be not also one which the patient is willing to take. If a man has closed his teeth against everything that savours of scholasticism, we must either abandon him or else see if there be any among the methods he will submit to, which may in any wise serve our purpose.[36]

Tyrrell's entire apologetic was coined in its basic and enduring thrust in the image of J. H. Newman. In its essence that apologetic aimed to establish the dogmatic principle, that is, the act of obedience before the will of God manifest in revelation and its authentic interpreters, as the heart of religion over against latitudinarianism or liberalism that made reason the touchstone of religious truth. And, therefore, by *Pascendi*'s definition, Tyrrell was no modernist.

In his first strictly apologetic effort, Tyrrell used his review of Arthur James Balfour's *Foundations of Belief* to make a point against the empiricists. With Newman he argued that if scientists were honest enough to question their own presuppositions and to supply reasons *why* phenomena behave as they do——instead of merely telling us *what* they do——if they were forced to see that the only principle they allow, namely, causality, can only imprison them within a system of rationally explicable phenomena, they will have to admit that they hold their premises on the basis of some external authority, that being in most cases what is fashionable to believe. Newman's position was that "man is *not* [first and foremost] a reasoning animal; he is a seeing, feeling, contemplating, acting animal," that even the strictest scientific proof requires the prior *belief* that the Q.E.D. is reachable, and that the mind acting according to its laws will arrive at truth.[37] Tyrrell argued that empiricism's attempts to account for ethical behavior and our search for and instinctive appreciation of beauty and truth are futile. These attractions can be explained only by positing the existence of an interior standard of the Good, True, and Beautiful, which one knows instinctively, if inadequately, by intuition. The reason why some people see an either/or choice between faith and reason or religion and science is that their psychological motives have beclouded their reasoning, and they are not very transparent to themselves. Tyrrell did not elaborate on this point here, but saved it for his 1902 publication, *Religion as a Factor of Life*, where he pointed to love (meaning will-union with those of like mind and heart) as the grounding of all action whether mental or moral.

I cannot help but see Newman's twelfth University Sermon as well as his entire *Grammar of Assent* behind Tyrrell's argument. The burden of that sermon and actually of Newman's entire apologetic is to establish that, however integral to human living reason is, it is not the safeguard of faith, but that faith's safeguard is "a right state of heart."

> This it is that gives it [faith] birth; it also disciplines it. This is what protects it from bigotry, credulity, and fanaticism. It is holiness . . . or the spiritual mind . . . which is the quickening and illuminating principle of true faith, giving it eyes, hands, and feet. It is Love which forms it out of the rude chaos into an image of Christ; or, in scholastic language, justifying Faith, whether in Pagan, Jew, or Christian, is *fides formata caritate*. . . . It was lack of love [or sympathetic feeling] towards Christ that the Jews discerned not in Him the Shepherd of their souls. "Ye believe not, because ye are not of My sheep. My sheep hear my voice, and follow me." It was the regenerate nature sent down from the Father of

Lights which drew up the disciples heavenward,—which made their affections go forth to meet the Bridegroom, and fixed those affections on Him, till they were as cords of love staying the heart upon the Eternal.

Newman added a note on this passage that would have thrilled Kant. He pointed out that reason cannot be the safeguard of faith because "the mind cannot master its own reasons and anticipates in its conclusions a logical exposition of them," so that as it turns out, a right heart safeguards reason as well as faith.[38]

Thus Tyrrell saw that one transcends the self, whether in science or in religion, only by trusting one's senses to reveal the being that caused the sensations. "Faith in the Kantian sense—that is, a reasonable submission to quasi-instinctive beliefs and sentiments, philosophically unjustified—is as necessary for science as for ethics or theology."[39] In religion, this trust takes the form of believing what is revealed on the authority of those we trust—first our parents, then our teachers. As we mature and learn to think and judge for ourselves, we find supporting reasons for beliefs, but these reasons are merely supportive and do not constitute proofs.

Tyrrell was here saying no more than Thomas had said in his *Summa contra gentiles*, namely, that natural theology is inadequate as a defence of belief, however valuable it might be as an after-test or negative criterion.[40] But now he had the whole weight of Newman's *Grammar of Assent* behind his anti-rationalist stance. For Newman, true religion is essentially *revealed* religion, *revealed* knowledge, not knowledge arrived at through argument. His paraphrase of Jesus' injunction, "He who has ears to hear, let him hear," was, "if any man will do His will, he shall know of the doctrine."[41] Newman's conviction was that true religion requires submission of reason to mysteries, not mysteries to reason, for to reiterate, "man is *not* a reasoning animal; he is a seeing, feeling, contemplating, acting animal."[42]

The Faith of the Millions: A Rationale for Newmanian Apologetics

Less than a year after Tyrrell reviewed Balfour, he published his first rationale for Newmanian apologetics. He titled it "A Change of Tactics" and made it the lead article of his 1901 two-volume collection, *The Faith of the Millions*, but gave it the new title, "A More

Excellent Way." Tyrrell's acknowledgement of Newman was, however, only implicit. He explicitly acknowledged and paralleled Wilfrid Ward's essay, "The Rigidity of Rome," which, for its part, is explicitly Newmanian throughout. Tyrrell argued that, when dealing with the Protestant-Catholic controversy, it might make *logical* sense to face the authority issue first. But such a tactic only leads to arguments in which Catholics so exaggerate the principle of authority and Protestants the principle of freedom, that neither side is willing to consider a *via media* even long enough to realize that "such medial positions one after another have been tried and have given way, and have thereby demonstrated the necessity of a living, infallible guide, if unity of faith is to be preserved among Christians."[43] Behind this passage almost certainly lies Newman's argument in his *Apologia* that the *via media* was pulverized by the argument from infallible authority: *securus judicat orbis terrarum*; as well as his argument in the *Apologia* and *Essay on the Development of Doctrine* that an infallible teaching authority is implied in the giving of a revelation as a protection against the inevitable distortion of revelation left to the anarchy of unaided, fallen reason.[44]

Thus, with Newman, Tyrrell could not advocate a liberal approach to apologetics that would in any way compromise the dogmatic and infallible principles of Roman Catholicism. The tactic he was now advocating was akin to Chateaubriand's, namely, to sidestep the logically first issue (authority) and instead focus on an entirely different level. The Church must win hearts first, minds second. She must woo rather than whip. "Were one to judge her methods solely in the light of the Protestant controversy," Tyrrell argued,

> one might easily infer that her office in regard to the Truth was simply aggressive and defensive—bellicose in every sense. Nothing could be more unlike the conduct of her Divine Master, whose work she continues. He came to state, to proclaim, to reveal; not to argue, controvert, or defend: and such is her mode of procedure so far as the world at large is concerned. She reveals herself in her intellectual and ethical beauty, as God's good gift to man. She invites men to come to her but does not desire to force herself on their acceptance.[45]

The church must "speak to the heart of this people." She must trade polemics for apologetics that manifest "the Catholic religion in its ethical and intellectual beauty" as the "desire of the nations." What was needed, Tyrrell continued, were apologists who knew and sympathized with both sides, but who also "have at once a comprehensive grasp of the 'idea' of Catholicism and are possessed with its spirit, and who are no less in touch with the spirit of their own country and age."[46]

Parallels between these passages and certain passages in Newman's *Apologia*, *Grammar of Assent*, and *Essay on Development* are striking. In the *Apologia* Newman confesses how forcefully he was struck by Ambrose's dictum, "Non in dialectica complacuit Deo salvum facere populum suum":

> I had a great dislike of paper logic. For myself, it was not logic that carried me on; as well might one say that the quicksilver in the barometer changes the weather. . . . All the logic in the world would not have made me move faster towards Rome than I did.[47]

In the *Grammar* Newman argues that the intellect ultimately is slain not by propositions, but by "the intellectual and moral character of the person maintaining them, and the ultimate silent effect of his arguments or conclusions upon our minds."[48] In another place, he confesses, "I say plainly I do not want to be converted by a smart syllogism; if I am asked to convert others by it, I say plainly I do not care to overcome their reason without touching their hearts."[49] For Newman was convinced

> that faith, though an intellectual action, is ethical in its origin. . . ; that we must begin with believing; that as for the reasons of believing, they are for the most part implicit, and need be but slightly recognized by the mind that is under their influence; that they consist moreover rather of presumptions and ventures after the truth than of accurate and complete proofs; that intellectual coherence of what we believe comes as a reward of faith not as its condition.[50]

Nova et Vetera: Doctrine for Living

In the next few years Tyrrell gave concrete expression to his announced "change of tactics." There are too many instances to note them all. I will notice just a few of the works that tend to get bypassed either because they never caught the attention of church authorities—as the works were primarily devotional—or because students of Tyrrell have not figured out how they fit into the development of his "modernist mind."

Tyrrell's aim was to speak first to the heart and therefore to present Catholicism first in its beauty and attractiveness. Accordingly in the preface to his first book, *Nova et Vetera*, he announced his desire to dress old truths in language, not necessarily gorgeous or elegant, but attractive enough to "make us stop and listen." He would purposely avoid the elegant turn and sophisticated argument, because the wisdom of the Gospel "is hid from the wise and prudent and revealed to little ones," and that wisdom is real and "does not leave them as it finds them in their ignorance and littleness, but gives them understanding and a quick-minded intuition as unerring as instinct." The book is a series of meditations, which, seemingly disordered, were bound together, Tyrrell suggested, "with a unity of spirit or ethos . . . the spirit of devotion to the Sacred Heart, the idea of the *Benignitas et Humanitas Dei Salvatoris nostri*."[51] Significantly, Tyrrell's first meditation is on the hymn, "Jesu dulcis memoria, dans vera cordis gaudia": "Love or charity is that joy which the heart derives from the contemplation of what is lovely or fair. . . . This joy is to see God as He is . . . ; a contemplation of God under the aspect of His goodness, beauty and truth . . . 'that Beauty whose Vision is joy'."[52]

Newman's influence permeates the work, not only in its portrayal of the beauty of Christianity in all its mysteries (note the great frequency of the word "beauty") but also in the consistent effort to convey to unknowing readers——and hence to console them about——the truth of the indwelling God:

> Is not the authority of Truth and of God identical? As in the dictate of conscience, so in that of reason, we should recognize the voice of a *person* who is subsistent Rightness and Truth. This is the secret, perhaps, of Augustine's colloquial method of reasoning. What reason says to him, God says to him; and he answers to his own reasonings as to the voice of God. Through the defect of the instrument or

medium, the message is often garbled and perverted, nor can it at all times be accepted as Divine. Yet whatever truth there is in it is God's own Word, conveyed to the soul. Thus as God is always serving us and labouring for us in Nature, and we do not recognize it, so He is continually speaking to our inmost heart, and we take the words as from nowhence or as from ourselves.[53]

For Tyrrell, as for Newman, the indwelling God speaking through and to conscience is our teacher, and reason would be a perfect reflection of that interior voice were the instrument not impaired by sin. "Natural reason and conscience convey to us the will of God. . . . When enlightened by Catholic faith, the voice of conscience is none other than the voice of Christ."[54] In the absence of right reason and in praise of intuition, Tyrrell made the following reflection on the text, "Thou has revealed [the mysteries of the Kingdom of Heaven] to little ones":

Our clearest moments of insight are often those when, through weakness and weariness, our mind is least under control, when concentration and voluntary attention is least possible; when reason slumbers, but intellectual vision is still awake and alert. It looks as though intellect were a clear pond which when least ruffled reflects heaven more deeply and truly; receiving passively in a moment what reason, with its bustling activity, misses after hours or years of searching. . . . It is generally observed that the moment of passage from sleep to waking, or from waking to sleep, is one of brighter intuition; that children and simple folk divine many truths which sophisticated minds muddle over vainly; and that truth, like happiness, is coy, and flies from those who seek her directly or too anxiously.[55]

It was *Nova et Vetera* that brought Tyrrell and von Hugel together. Given the ghost of Newman behind nearly every page, and given the fact that von Hugel had read all the major works of Newman and corresponded with him, it is not surprising that *Nova et Vetera* should have occasioned an invitation to Tyrrell that led to a lifelong friendship and collaboration. Three years after their first meeting, the baron baptized Tyrrell in Newman's name. He was ecstatic over Tyrrell's incisive critique of the English Catholic bishops' pastoral letter condemning liberalism, and wrote to Tyrrell from Rome: "Not since Newman have we English-speaking Catholics had anything like as sweet and deep an 'organ-voice,' as adequate an expression of the truest, most constitutive forces within ourselves, as is that which God has now given us in you."[56]

Seminal Essay: "The Relation of Theology to Devotion"

It would not be too wide of the mark to suggest that Tyrrell's criticism of the joint pastoral jarred the baron's memory of Newman's essays in the *Rambler*, particularly of his final essay, "On Consulting the Faithful in Matters of Doctrine," which explicated decisively Newman's long-held theology of the laity as foundational for any theology of the Church. There is no unequivocal evidence that Tyrrell read this essay, but it is hard to imagine that he could have passed over the one article above all others that caused trouble for Newman both at home and in Rome. But above all, it is hard to imagine that Tyrrell did not have this essay in mind—or at least Newman's great work on the Arians whose third edition appended a revision of this essay—when he wrote "The Mind of the Church," his various responses to the joint pastoral, and most especially his seminal essay, "The Relation of Theology to Devotion."[57] In these works Tyrrell virtually quotes Newman's words:

> The body of the faithful is one of the witnesses to the fact of the tradition of revealed doctrine, and because their *consensus* through Christendom is the voice of the Infallible Church . . . its *consensus* is to be regarded: 1. as a testimony to the fact of the apostolic dogma; 2. as a sort of instinct, or deep in the bosom of the mystical body of Christ; 3. as a direction of the Holy Ghost; 4. as an answer to its prayer; 5. as a jealousy of error, which it at once feels as a scandal . . . . [And] while devotion in the shape of dogma issues from the high places of the Church, in the shape of devotion . . . it starts from below.[58]

Even if Tyrrell had not seen these ideas so pointedly expressed in Newman's essay, he was quite capable of pulling them out of the *Grammar of Assent*, where the heart of Newman's teaching occurs in his discussion of *phronesis* or the illative sense, that power in the individual to make a "real" as opposed to a "notional" assent in judgments of faith and conscience. *Phronema*, for Newman, is obviously the counterpart in the mystical body of Christ to *phronesis* in the individual and is that instinct deep within the *"orbis terrarum"* that holds fast to the entire deposit of faith. The workings of *phronema* are suggested in this passage from the *Grammar of Assent*:

> It was fitting that those mixed unlettered multitudes, who for three centuries had suffered and triumphed by virtue of the inward Vision of their Divine Lord, should be selected, as we know they were, in the fourth, to be the special champions of His Divinity and the victorious foes of its impugners, at a time when the civil power, which had found them too strong for its arms, attempted, by means of a portentous *heresy in the high places of the Church*, to rob them of that Truth which had all along been the principle of their strength.[59]

Numerous passages in Tyrrell's writings reflect the focus of this passage, but none more forcefully than these from "The Relation of Theology to Devotion":

> God has revealed Himself not to the wise and prudent, not to the theologian or the philosopher, but to babes, to fishermen, to peasants, to the *profanum vulgus*, and therefore He has spoken their language, leaving it to the others to translate it (at their own risk) into forms more acceptable to their taste. . . . Devotion and religion existed before theology, in the way that art existed before art-criticism; reasoning, before logic; speech, before grammar.[60]

Or this one from the Introduction to *The Faith of the Millions*, which begins with Ambrose's dictum quoted by Newman in his *Apologia*:

> God has not willed to save His elect by logic;[61] . . . the Gospel is preached to the poor and simple, and hidden from the wise and prudent. Nor can it well be denied that Christ's attitude towards those who sat in the chair of Moses—towards the theologians and casuists of the Jewish religion, was one of almost uncompromising hostility; that this very antagonism of spirit and principle was the proximate cause of His murder at their hands. His denunciations of

their formalism, their unreality, their trivial pedantry and hair-splitting, their lack of all sympathy with the quickening spirit of pure religion, their slavish letter-worship, their lust of domination, were persistent and almost fierce. He beheld with compassion the multitudes wandering and harassed, as sheep having no shepherd, because their leaders were blind leaders, keeping the key of the kingdom of knowledge; not entering themselves, nor suffering others to enter.[62]

It would be a simple task to marshal texts to show Tyrrell up as an anti-intellectualist, a voluntarist, or a quietist. But in quoting selectively, one distorts Tyrrell's thought. He must be taken whole. He was not anti-intellectual. In coming down on the side of devotion, he was expressing a conviction supported generously by Newman, that devotion is more basic to religion than after-reflection on religious experience. But he was also attempting to redress a rationalist imbalance that he found in the prevailing theology of the church.

Tyrrell's quarrel was not with reason but with rationalism, not with theology but with theologism. He took his cue from Newman. When Newman aimed to establish conscience as the primary principle of religious living, he meant conscience as considered within the framework of a human community; so when Tyrrell emphasized devotion he aimed to establish it in its proper dialogical relationship to dogmatic and ecclesiastical structures, and this in order to reset the balance, not to create a new dogmatism.

With Newman to the End

So much more needs to be said about Tyrrell's debt to Newman that must be left for a later study. We have not, for instance, even touched on Tyrrell's wrestle with Newman's understanding of the "deposit of faith" and development of doctrine, an issue that preoccupied Tyrrell throughout his last five years. But we may conclude the present study by giving the bare outlines of Tyrrell's thoughts thereon.

His penultimate word on the issue of revelation and doctrine is given in *Through Scylla and Charybdis* (1907), a gathering of twelve essays showing the progression of his thought in relation to Newman's from 1900 to 1907. Tyrrell's final word was given in the posthumously published *Christianity at the Cross-Roads*. There he sided with

Newman's view that the "idea" of Christianity (the content of revelation) remains identical throughout history, but its embodiment in formulae and institutions continually develops. He went beyond Newman, however, in admitting an occasional revolution as sometimes a natural part of development. Newman did not, and perhaps could not, see the problems raised for apologetics by historical criticism, particularly in reference to scripture. Thus, as Tyrrell understood him, Newman was able to assume identity between the "idea" of Christ and Christianity and the "idea" of Roman Catholicism, so he set out merely to establish identity between the "ideas" of early and late Roman Catholicism. The modernists, however, saw that historical criticism required Newman's assumption itself to be criticized, because historical critics charged that the "idea" of Roman Catholicism deviated early on from the "idea" of the historical Jesus and earliest Christianity. Thus modernists believed that they had to try to prove by the methods of the critics what Newman could assume. They had to try to establish by historical criticism identity not only between the "ideas" of early and late Roman Catholicism but also and foremost identity between the "idea" of the historical Jesus and earliest Christianity and the "idea" of Roman Catholicism whether early or late. They did so by using Newman's method, but they adapted it to the data of historical criticism——not the biased criticism of Protestant liberalism, but (in Tyrrell's view) the more strictly scientific criticism of Loisy, Weiss, and Schweitzer.

By 1909, therefore, the year of his death, Tyrrell had returned to a position that recognized the validity of Newman's theory but also its need to be modified. This Tyrrell attempted in *Christianity at the Cross-Roads* by showing that the categories of eschatology and apocalyptic, as preserved in Roman Catholicism throughout history, were the vehicles of identity between the "idea" of Christ and Christianity and the "idea" embodied in Roman Catholicism but lost both in liberalism and in scholasticism.

LIST OF ABBREVIATIONS

AL   Petre, Maude Dominica. *Autobiography and Life of George Tyrrell*. 2 Vols. London: Edward Arnold, 1912.
ERGT   *External Religion: Its Use and Abuse*. London: Sands & Co., 1899, 1906^4.
FMGT   *The Faith of the Millions: A Selection of Past Essays*. 2 vols. London: Longmans, Green & Co., 1901.
GT   George Henry Tyrrell
LOGT   *Lex Orandi: Or, Prayer and Creed*. London: Longmans, Green & Co., 1903.
NVGT   *Nova et Vetera: Informal Meditations for Times of Spiritual Dryness*. London: Longmans, Green & Co., 1897, 1902.

Works of John Henry Newman (Longmans editions)

Apo   *Apologia pro vita sua*, 1865, 1908
DA   *Discussions and Arguments*, 1836, 1911.
Dev   *An Essay on the Development of Christian Doctrine*, 1845, 1909.
Diff   *Certain Difficulties Felt by Anglicans in Catholic Teaching*, vol. 1, 1850, 1908; vol. 2, 1865, 1910.
Ess   *Essays Critical and Historical*, vol. 1, 1828, 1910; vol. 2, 1840, 1910.
GA   *An Essay in Aid of a Grammar of Assent*, 1870, 1909.
US   *Sermons Preached before the University of Oxford*, 1843, 1909.
VV   *Verses on Various Occasions*, 1867, 1909.

NOTES

1.   AL 2:209. Wilfrid P. Ward, with whom Tyrrell carried on an extensive correspondence and often disagreed, was preparing a two-volume biography of Newman. William J. "Willy" Williams was the author of *Newman, Pascal, Loisy and the Catholic Church* (London: Francis Griffiths, 1906) and numerous articles of a liberal slant in the Catholic press.

	Père Henri Bremond was a former Jesuit and longtime friend and correspondent of Tyrrell.
2.	AL 2:209.
3.	GT to Ward, 12 December 1893; in Mary Jo Weaver, *Letters from a Modernist: The Letters of George Tyrrell to Wilfrid Ward* (Shepherdstown, WV: Patmos Press and London: Sheed & Ward, 1981), p. 3.
4.	GT to Petre, 15 February 1901; AL 2:208.
5.	GT to Ward, 4 January 1904; Weaver, p. 92. Tyrrell's emphasis.
6.	GT to Ward, 22 September 1898; Weaver, p. 5.
7.	AL 2:209. Tyrrell was here taking a swipe at Wilfrid Ward who was hard at work on the Newman biography and who had recently slashed the biography by Tyrrell's friend Henri Bremond. In other words, Tyrrell was claiming for himself and for Bremond a better understanding of Newman than Ward had, who had read Newman perhaps "more assiduously and completely" than they had.
8.	Apo 19. See also GT, "Rationalism in Religion," *Month* 93 (January 1899) 1-16, reprinted in FM 1:85-114, an article inspired throughout by Newman.
9.	AL 2:443-44.
10.	AL 1:94.
11.	Apo 18-19.
12.	Apo 19: "Were it not for this voice, speaking so clearly in my conscience and my heart, I should be an atheist, or a pantheist, or a polytheist when I looked into the world. I am speaking for myself only; and I am far from denying the real force of the arguments in proof of a God . . . but these do not warm me or enlighten me; they do not take away the winter of my desolation, or make the buds unfold and the leaves grow within me, and my moral being rejoice. The sight of the world is nothing else than the prophet's scroll, full of 'lamentations, and mourning, and woe'."
13.	AL 1:111-12.
14.	Apo 116-17; Ess 2:35, 40-43, notes; Diff 2:303, 372. See GT, "The Mind of the Church," *Month* 96 (August, September 1900) 125-42, 233-40, repr. FM, 1:158-204; Lord Halifax [GT], "The Recent Anglo-Roman Pastoral," *Nineteenth Century* 49 (May 1901) 736-54; David G. Schultenover, S.J., *George Tyrrell: In Search of Catholicism* (Shepherdstown, WV:

The Patmos Press and London: Sheed & Ward, 1981), pp. 127-65.
15. AL 1:112.
16. ER 119; "Rationalism in Religion," pp. 93-94. Cf. Newman, Ess 1:30-101, esp. 41-45.
17. AL 1:112-13.
18. AL 1:131.
19. AL 1:119.
20. Apo 242-43.
21. AL 1:119.
22. AL 1:122. Ps 91:14-15.
23. See Schultenover, *Tyrrell*, pp. 72-77, 188-245.
24. AL 1:153.
25. AL 1:152-53. Cf. Newman, Apo 56, 197-98, 203-5; Diff 1:364-73, 393; 2:24.
26. See, e.g., Newman's description of the role of conscience in contrast to faith and reason as habits of mind, US 181-90. See also Dev 327-30, GA 159ff and especially 409-27 on revealed religion.
27. AL 1:158.
28. AL 1:249.
29. AL 2:209.
30. See, among other places, GT to Bremond, 18 January 1900, in Schultenover, *Tyrrell*, p. 101.
31. It was probably Newman's language, as much as his thought, that led Rome to regard him with suspicion. See Wilfrid Ward, *The Life of John Henry Cardinal Newman*, 2 vols. (London: Longmans, Green, and Co., 1912), 2:151-83. As Tyrrell quipped to von Hugel about Roman censors: "They are so very dense, so long as one avoids the 'male *sonans*' that one can say anything 'male *significans*'." GT to von Hugel, 4 December 1902, in Schultenover, *Tyrrell*, p. 239.
32. GT to von Hugel, 6 December 1897, in AL 2:45; GT, "Cardinal Mazzella," *Weekly Register* 101 (30 March 1900) 393. For confirmation of this analysis I am indebted to Nicholas Sagovsky's essay, "'Frustration, Disillusion and Enduring, Filial Respect': George Tyrrell's Debt to John Henry Newman," a paper delivered at a Newman symposium held in Birmingham, England, June 1983.
33. AL 2:220.
34. GT to Ward, 12 December 1893, in Weaver, *ibid.*, pp. 3-4.

35. GT to Houtin, 4 December 1907, Houtin Papers, Bibliotheque Nationale, Paris, Nouvelles acquisitions francaises, Fonds Houtin 15743-48, fl. 48. Tyrrell was not alone in his judgment that the encyclical condemned, if not Newman, at least Newmanism. It was also the conviction of Wilfrid Ward who was the foremost authority on Newman and who was himself decidedly not a modernist. On 2 November 1907, Ward wrote to John Norris, superior of the Birmingham Oratory: "Gasquet had ridiculed the idea that the Encyclical hit J. H. N., but as I told Norfolk three weeks ago it not only hits him but the analysis of modernism includes all on which his heart was set for 40 years and brands it as false and absurd.... We cannot defend him successfully without going in the teeth of the Encyclical, which brands also positions essential to his views.... I think the situation simply tragic." Quoted in Edward E. Kelly, "Newman, Wilfrid Ward, and the Modernist Crisis," *Thought* (Winter 1973), p. 515. See also GT, "Prospects of Modernism," *Hibbert Journal* 6 (January 1908): 241-55, esp. p. 243 where GT makes Newman's historical method the foundation of modernism.
36. *Month* 94 (August, September 1899) 113-24, 249-60; reprinted as "Adaptability as a Proof of Religion," in FM 2:296-347; passage quoted on p. 279.
37. DA 294; Ess, 2:353. See also Newman's whole discussion of assent and the illative sense in GA, esp. chap. 9.
38. US 234-35. In this connection see the passage from NV, 262-63, quoted below, p. 24.
39. "Mr. Balfour and *The Foundations of Belief*," *Month* 84 (May 1895) 27.
40. Thomas Aquinas, *Summa contra gentiles*, 1. cc. 4, 5.
41. GA 415.
42. DA 294; Ess, 2:353; cf. also Apo 243-61; GA 189-93, 288, 316-21.
43. FM 1:3. Cf. GT, "Rationalism in Religion," FM 1:110-12.
44. Apo 114-17, 243-45; Dev 79-92.
45. FM 1:6-7. Cf. Newman's admonition, "Brothers, spare reasoning, the apostles argued not but preached." VV 167. See also Diff 2:81-82.
46. FM 1:9.
47. Apo 169-70.

48. GA 302. Newman's observation on the force of personality over the force of intellect echoes through GT's works. See, e.g., AL 1, *passim*, on figures who influenced him (e.g. Henry Kerr, pp. 172-79; John Morris, p. 218; "Father 'M.'" [Thomas Rigby], p. 242); NV, pp.356-57.
49. GA 424-25.
50. Dev 327.
51. NV, 4th ed., iii-vii.
52. NV 1.
53. NV 356-57.
54. NV 405; cf. Apo 242 ff.
55. NV 262-63.
56. Von Hugel to GT, 28 May 1901, Petre Papers, British Library, Additional Manuscripts 44927.162. See GT, "The Recent Anglo-Roman Pastoral," *Nineteenth Century* 49 (May 1901) 736-54. This article, published under Lord Halifax's signature, was by GT, except for the introduction and conclusion. On the joint pastoral affair, see Schultenover, *Tyrrell*, pp. 143-65.
57. *Month* 94 (November 1899) 461-73, reprinted in FM and again in *Through Scylla and Charybdis* (London: Longmans, Green, & Co., 1907).
58. Newman, *On Consulting the Faithful in Matters of Doctrine* (New York: Sheed & Ward, 1961), pp. 63, 73. 105.
59. GA 486, italics mine.
60. FM 1:239, 252.
61. Ambrose's dictum quoted in Apo 169. See also GT, LO 211.
62. FM 1:xv-xvi.

GROWTH THE ONLY EVIDENCE OF LIFE:
Development of Doctrine and
The Idea of a University

Philip C. Rule, S.J.

I

"The rubric 'development of doctrine' has been in use since John Henry Newman, *An Essay on the Development of Christian Doctrine*," observes George A. Lindbeck (13n). Fellow theologian Jaroslov Pelikan observes that Newman's essay is "the almost inevitable starting point for the investigation of the development of doctrine" (3). Thus Newman and the idea of development in religious doctrine are almost synonymous. This raises a most fascinating question. Why Newman? Why at this particular time in the middle of the 19th century? Surely the idea itself was not new. Under the various terms of growth, change, process, progress, evolution, and development the concept was current in the late eighteenth and early nineteenth centuries. It has in fact been around since the beginning of western civilization as John Nisbet has shown exhaustively in his two general studies of the idea. Karl Weintraub has demonstrated that around 1800 "our modern sense of history and of individuality grew from the fusing of an emergent genetic sense and a growing concern for singularity" (332). So, if the idea was in the air, why was Newman the first one to thus exploit it in theology?

A similar question arose some twenty years ago for Erik Erikson in his reflections on "Autobiographical Notes on the Identity Crisis" in a seminar dedicated to the questions of "how major transforming concepts or theories developed, and what [is] the climate propitious to such developments" (v). His essay attempts to "lay out some of the possible reasons for my having been the person who, at a given time in his life and in the history of psychoanalysis, came to observe and to name something by now so self-evident as the identity crisis and to explain, in fact, why it now seems so self-evident" (730). Apart from clinical and anthropological observation Erikson finds the concept rooted concretely and autobiographically in his identity as an adopted son of his stepfather and his subsequent "adoption" by Anna and Siegmund Freud. To the best of my knowledge, no biographer or scholar of Newman has asked that question in any detail about Newman. The question could, of course, also be asked of Darwin. As Richard Altick has pointed out, with the admitted exception of some "crucial additions," *Origin of Species* "was largely a brilliant synthesis of many scientific ideas already current. What was new was Darwin's explanation of organic mutability" (226). Walter Ong, for example, in discussing the intellectual milieu of the *Essay* rightly points out that it is imminent in his early works and anticipatory of subsequent writing thus giving "a unified significance" to the history of his writings, but like others before and after Ong does not ask about the autobiographical origins of so pivotal an idea; he simply assumes Newman borrowed it from the current discourse ("Newman's Essay," 3).

This neglect of the autobiographical origins of the idea of development is no more dramatically exemplified than in Ian Ker's recent and otherwise authoritative biography which devotes only fifty-three of its 750 pages to the first thirty-two years of Newman's life and in those fifty-three pages he nowhere deals explicitly with the formation of the key insight of his personal and intellectual life. Even Henry Bremond's life, which purported to study Newman's "intellectual, emotional, and inner life" (p. 37), says nothing about the idea of development. Wilfred Ward's biography, which devotes 118 pages to the *Essay*, spends only 53 pages on the first forty-four years of his life. And yet he calls it "a record of the genesis of his thought" (I, 3). Maisie Ward tried to redress such obvious neglect in *Young Mister Newman* where she says, quoting Newman himself, "we rarely know much of men in their most interesting years—the years when they were forming—'from eighteen to twenty-eight or thirty'" (vii). One need not be much of a psycho-biographer to find this designation of the "formative years" rather naive especially when dealing with someone as emotionally and intellectually precocious as Newman.

Much had happened in Newman's intellectual development before he reached the ripe age of twenty. Meriol Trevor, of all biographers up to her time, comes closest to suggesting what I am addressing here. Newman, she writes, "had transferred the idea of growth from the individual to the group on the highest personal level, before it was discovered on the lowest and basic level of biology." She then suggests a line of pursuit, saying that "it is possible to trace the course of this growth because of his exceptional self-awareness, which some have considered self-preoccupation" (4). Unfortunately, having put her finger on one of the key sources, she fails to follow through in her otherwise excellent narrative biography.

It is my intention here, therefore, to trace the origins and conceptualization of Newman's fundamental, almost self-defining, insight in the first twenty-five years of his life before suggesting how both the *Essay on Development* and later the *Idea of a University* grew out of the gradually shaping insight and are both rooted in it, exemplifying that both in the unfolding of revelation and the cultivation of the intellect, development is the central guiding insight. I am suggesting in what follows that certain traits of character and temperament, certain practices, and certain experiences all converged to make Newman the right person with the right idea at the right time in the study of the history of Christian doctrine, and somewhat incidentally in terms of magnitude, in the contemporary ongoing dialogue about what university education should be. My procedure will be to pursue him through what I see to be the formative years, from birth to the age of twenty five, by following him through volume one of the *Letters and Diaries*, like a gleaner looking for what previous biographers and scholars have, I am convinced, overlooked.

II

We might begin with a seemingly trivial entry into a boyhood pocketbook. In 1810, at the age of nine, he pencilled in his first entry, a biblical truism which upon reflection might well be seen as emblematic of his life to come: "Train up a child in the way he should go, and when he is old, he will not depart from it" (LD,I,5). In the *Autobiographical Writings* there is a small passage of some twenty-one lines written over a period of seventy-two years. The initial entry written in 1812 at the age of eleven suggests how precociously self-conscious he had become at so early an age: "John Newman wrote this just before he was going up to Greek on Tuesday, June 10, 1812, when it wanted only three days to his going home, thinking of the time (at home) when looking at this he shall recollect when he did it" (5). This projecting of the future moment occurs in later years when, for example, he writes his mother from Oxford: "I have no doubt I shall look back with regret to the time I was at Oxford and my birthday of 18" (LD,I,62).

In the notebooks and diaries and letters written throughout his life there is a definite pattern of looking back to the past and forward to the future. In 1807 he left his home at Ham near Richmond for good, going off to school at Ealing. Almost sixty years later he wrote "it has ever been in my dreams" (LD,I,4). In 1886 he said it was a place "Which I dreamed about when a schoolboy as if it was Paradise" (LD,I,4). In 1816 after his father's financial failure, Newman wrote to his aunt Elizabeth about leaving Norwood, saying "he must have been conscious to himself that he would never see it (as his home) again" (LD,I,26). To his brother Frank he wrote in 1820 from Oxford: "For the calm happiness I now enjoy I cannot feel thankful as I ought. How in my future life, if I do live, shall I look back with a sad smile at these days!" (LD,I,82). What one senses here is a vivid consciousness of his being on the move—of moving from one place to another, of reaching back from a present point to a past one in a sort of Augustinian consciousness of the self stretched across time. It is as if he was ever in the presence of himself growing, a phenomenon poignantly borne out by a 1874 memo scribbled on a Latin oration delivered at Oriel in 1823: "I read this now for the first time these fifty-one years with sad tenderness, as if I loved and pitied the poor boy so ignorant of the future, who then wrote and delivered it before the Provost and Fellows, now almost all dead, but to whom I then looked up with great reverence and loving pride" (LD,I,157). In this "sad smile" and "sad tenderness" one hears echoes of the Virgilian time-bridging exhortation "Haec olim forsan et meminisse juvabit" (One day you will enjoy looking back even on what you now endure), or of the Wordsworthian vision "That in this moment there is food and life / For future years."

A second important aspect of Newman's early years is his dedication to the arduous task of composition. In an autobiographical memoir of 1874 he says, "though in no respect a precocious boy, he attempted original composition in prose and verse from the age of eleven, and in prose showed a great sensibility and took much pain in matters of style" (AW,29). While at Oxford "he wrote a critique of the plays of Aeschylus on the principles of Aristotle's Poetics, though original composition at that time had no place in school examinations" (AW,40). In an 1872 transcription of some early journal entries he writes that "the unpleasant style in which it is written arises from my habit from a boy to compose" (AS,149). The highly developed sense of introspection and self-consciousness revealed in the early acts of memory and imagining the future cited above can now be combined with an introspection or inwardness heightened and refined by sustained and rigorous efforts at original composition. As Walter Ong has pointed out, all writing—far short of the laborious kind we are witnessing here—has an interiorizing effect on a person. The cultural transition from orality to literacy literally restructures human consciousness. If as Ong says, "writing heightens consciousness," one can imagine the impact of such sustained and arduous exercise on an already self-conscious writer (Orality,82). It was, in fact, in the sustained experience of the writing process that Newman formally conceptualized the subjective insight of development—something growing from a seed into a full blown fruit. Two telling examples suggest this. In 1821 an essay he had submitted for an English Essay prize failed to win. Looking back thirty years later he writes: "This Essay gives evidence I had not yet attended to *composition*--i.e. taking an *idea* and developing it. I believe the same fault is to be found in my Essay on ancient Slavery. Perhaps I did not begin to attempt this difficult accomplishment (which even now, November 1851, is what tries and distresses me in writing) till I had been writing Sermons for some time" (Culler,23). This becomes even more explicit in his struggles with Latin composition. In an 1855 essay included later in *Idea* he records his own experiences through an imaginary obliging tutor, Mr. Black, who confesses "I had some idea of the style of Addison, Hume, and Johnson, in English; but I had no idea what was meant by good Latin style." Thus, he continues, "I was aiming to be an architect by learning to make bricks" (Idea,368). Newman's apparently lifelong struggle with genuine composition—unfolding an idea in his mind while committing it to writing—certainly sensitized him to the organic growth of ideas in any human mind which is itself growing and developing as it moves across a spectrum of time through heightened and expanding consciousness.

It is also clear that Newman at an early age began to see explicitly this developmental growth model at work both in the human thought processes and in the life pattern of an individual. Upon turning twenty-one he wrote his mother: "There is an illusion in the words 'being of age,' which is apt to convey the idea of some sudden and unknown change. That point, instead of being gained by the slow and silent progress of one and twenty years, seems to be divided by some strongly marked line, the past from the to-come" (LD,I,123).

Finally, another and more crucial event of his youth must be discussed—the conversion of 1816. Perhaps the best known and most often written about aspect of his early years, because of his own stressing of it in the *Apologia*, it nevertheless must be seen here as just one more element contributing to the subsequent fundamental insight about slow progressive change in general and doctrinal development in particular. Profoundly influenced by the writings of Thomas Scott, an evangelical clergyman, Newman says "for years I used almost as proverbs what I considered to be the scope and issue of his doctrine, 'Holiness rather than peace,' and 'Growth the only evidence of life'" (Apologia, 5). "Growth the only evidence of life." What single phrase could sum up more completely the entire tenor of Newman both intellectually and personally. His meticulous recording of the movements of his own life even at an early age, his deepening awareness of the developmental organic structure of human thought, and now a profound transition, a conversion, in his life as a Christian which he saw at the time and would see throughout his life as continuous rather than discontinuous, as organic movement rather than static stages, as development rather than corruption. In a lengthy letter of 1817 his former school master Walter Mayers described to the young convert what this kind of spiritual change is. "The change," he writes, "is what I would call conversion, or rather what I understand the Scripture would denominate conversion,—A change which is very rarely *sudden* or *instantaneous* but generally *slow* and *gradual*, arising often times from causes which appear at the times fortuitous, but which the mind when enlightened will discern to have been directed by God" (LD,I,32). This conversion is explored in autobiographical notes written in 1820-21 and later transcribed with editing in 1874. The following entry suggests how the stuff of life makes its way into his subsequent writings: "The reality of conversion—as cutting at the root of doubt, providing a chain between God and the soul (i.e. with every link complete) I know I am right. How do I know it. I know I know. How? I know I know I know &c &c (vide Grammar of Assent, p. 195-97, ed4)." (AW,150) In the *Apologia* he writes "a great change of thought took place in me" (4), but this change is elsewhere described as both quiet and continuous. The personal influence of Mayers and the writings of Scott while conducing to the feeling of election to eternal life, also grow out of his longstanding "mistrust of the reality of material phenomena" (4). Newman describes the particular circumstances of the conversion as quite serene. Finishing the school term at Ealing early, "thereby I was left at school by myself, my friends gone away—(that is, it was a time of reflection, and where the influences of Mr. Mayers would have room to act upon me. Also, I was terrified at the heavy hand of God which came down upon me" (AW,150). In June or July 1821, he writes "I speak of (the process of) conversion with great diffidence, being obliged to adopt the language of books. For my own feelings, as far as I remember, were so different from any account I had ever read, that I dare not go by what may be the individual case" (AW,166). Commenting on these very lines five years later, July 1826, he adds this reflection: "I am persuaded that very many of my most positive and dogmatic notions were taken *from books*. In the matter in question (conversion) my feelings were not violent, but a returning to, a renewing of, principles, under the power of the Holy Spirit, which I had *already* felt, and in a measure acted on, when young" (AW,172).

The converging pattern we have seen above—continuity of consciousness in recollecting the past and projecting the future, compositional activity, and conversion—come together in the combined concerns about his own spiritual growth and the unconscious shifting of his theological positions brought about by regular preaching. A diary entry for February 21, 1825, notes "dined in rooms and reviewed the past year" (LD,I,211). In a fuller entry for that date in *Autobiographical Writings* he writes that "the necessity of composing sermons has obliged me to systematize and complete my ideas on many subjects." He expresses regret that "this change of opinion" is occurring with "little opportunity for devotion or private study," that he lacks time for prayer and "stated self-examination" (204-5). On Sunday, July 17, of that same year he writes that "I may add to my above remarks on my change of sentiments as to Regeneration, that I have been principally or in great measure led to this change by the fact that in my parochial activities I found many, who in most important points were inconsistent, but whom yet I could not say were altogether without grace" (AW,206). In the autobiographical memoir of 1874 he points to this period, also as the beginning of "a great change in his religious opinions" (AW,73). Acknowledging "the force of logic and the influence of others," he credits personal pastoral experience for his growing conviction "that the religion which he had received from John Newton and Thomas Scott would not work in a parish; that it was unreal; that thus he had actually found as a fact, as Mr. Hawkins had told him beforehand, that Calvinism was not a key to the phenomena of human nature, as they occur in the world" (AW,79). This pattern of adult theological reflection would continue. In February 21, 1827 he reviews the previous year focusing on his religious growth (AW,210). By the time he was twenty four, the pattern of Newman's mind was clearly set. In *Loss and Gain*, Newman's thinly veiled conversion biographical novel, he writes of his hero that "it is impossible to stop the growth of the mind. Here was Charles with his thoughts turned away from religious controversy for two years, yet with his religious views progressing, unknown to himself the whole time" (202).

From this point in time we can date the twenty-year intellectual and spiritual Odyssey that would culminate in the *Essay*. In August, 1825, he was engaged in a long correspondence with his brother Charles who was undergoing a crisis of faith. At one point he counters Charles's qualms about the authenticity of certain texts in Scripture by pointing out that "the New Testament is not *Christianity*, but the *record* of Christianity" (LD,I,254), a statement that would no doubt have offended many conservative ears of the times. This position is clearly echoed in 1845 when he writes in the *Essay* that "it may be objected that the inspired document at once determines the limits of its mission without further trouble; but ideas are in the writer and the reader of revelation, not the inspired text itself" (56), a statement startling perhaps even for many today. Granted the earlier statement was directed to the genuineness of the gospels and the latter to the transmission of ideas and their subsequent growth in the minds of readers, the principle at stake is the same—the revelation of transcendent truth is caught up in the very complex and finite historical process of human understanding.

These twenty years preceding the Essay fall into three periods: 1826-1833, from the Oriel tutorship to the publication of *Arians of the Fourth Century*; 1833-1841, from the beginning of the Tractarian Movement to the publication of Tract 90; and from his rejection by the university and the bishops to his publication of the *Essay on the Development of Christian Doctrine*.

In May 1826, he wrote to his sister Harriet announcing "I am about to undertake a great work perhaps" (LD,I,284) referring her to a letter to his sister Jemima for a fuller explanation, a letter in which it is described as "a work which may take me—t!e!!-n!!!—years???

perhaps twenty—but that is a long time to look forward to—perhaps too long—for a reader and thinker must not look for a long life, and I reflect with a sigh that half my life is gone, and I have done nothing.—I hope I have laid the foundation of something" (LD,I,285). With Coleridgean bravado he lays out this immense task: "But what after all is the subject?—it is to trace the sources from which the corruptions of the Church, principally the Romish, have been derived—It would consequently involve a reading of all the Fathers—200 volumes at least—(you saw some good stout gentlemen in Oriel Library—Austin 12 folio volumes Chrysostom 13 do.—) all on the principal Platonists, Philo, Plotinus, Julian, etc—an inquiry into Gnosticism—Rabbinical literature—and I know not what else—perhaps much, much more—am not I bold?" (LD,I,285). This boldness prompted him to write his friend Samuel Rickards about an encyclopedic and systematic review of the Old English divines (LD,I,309-10), a task to which he would in fact address himself almost ten years later but first he had to produce what would be his initial, albeit implicit, application of the theory of development to doctrinal change. *The Arians of the Fourth Century,* a work which had been commissioned for an historical series, when finished evoked from William Rowe Lyall, one of the editors, the comment that "Mr. Newman's views seem to me more favourable to the Roman writers, than I should like to put forward in the Theological Library" (LD,III,105). If his initial study of the early church and the Fathers led him to a Catholic reading of doctrinal history, his subsequent reading of the Anglican Fathers backed him into it. Attempting to use these theologians systematically in presenting the Anglican "via media" in *Prophetical Office of the Church* (1837) and *Lectures on Justification* (1838) Newman discovered that they were not historians when they dealt with history. Actually, as early as 1831 writing to Samuel Rickard to whom he had initially proposed such use of these theologians he commented that "the standard Divines are magnificent fellows, but then they are Antiquarians or Doctrinists, not Ecclesiastical Historians—Bull, Waterland, Petavius, Baronius and the rest—of the historians I have met with I have a very low opinion—Mosheim, Gibbon, Middleton, Milner, etc—Cave and Tillement are highly respectable, but biographers" (LD,II,371).

Clearly Newman had found no adequate model for reading that past and its texts and was gradually articulating his own, a theory that would explain the facts, rather than twist the facts to fit a theory. It is indeed a felicitous coincidence that the year 1845 witnessed not only the publication of Newman's *Essay* but also of Poe's short story "The Purloined Letter," for both exemplify what may be fairly called a "Romantic" epistemology, one which considers the role of imaginative insight as equal to or superior to reason and logic. Poe's master sleuth, M. Dupin, tells his companion why the Prefect of Police failed to find the stolen letter: "'The measures, then, . . . were good in their kind and well executed; their defect lay in their being inapplicable to the case, and to the man. A certain set of highly ingenious resources are, with the Prefect, a sort of Procrustean bed, to which he forcibly adapts his designs'" (I,19). Later, Sherlock Holmes in a story clearly echoing and parodying Poe, "A Scandal in Bohemia," provides a similar answer to Dr. Watson as to why he has not yet solved his case: "I have no data yet. It is a capital mistake to theorize before one has data. Insensibly one begins to twist facts to suit theories, instead of theories to suit facts," (3). Newman's own experientially-based theory of development, ultimately based on his concept of the illative sense, would be the paradigm for this new reading and explanation of the facts of doctrinal history.

Thus, as Erik Erikson's insight into "identity" and "identity crisis" emerged from his "personal, clinical, and anthropological observations," (747) so Newman's insight into "development" grew out of his personal experience of the self as a developing entity, gathering and incorporating, so as to achieve a personal continuity of consciousness over space and time. As the individual, so the social phenomenon. Revelation is made to developing spiritual beings embedded in history—in space and time—and as he says with conviction in the *Essay*, "in a higher world it is otherwise, but here below to live is to change, and to be perfect is to have changed often" (63). This is only a maturer articulation of the insight achieved thirty years before: "Growth the only evidence of life."

III

In the *Essay* we find a convergence of the private and the public. Written as a personal synthesis of those arguments which brought him from the Anglican to the Roman Catholic Church, it is at once autobiography and theology. Karl Weintraub says that the proper form of autobiography is one "wherein a self-reflective person asks who am I? and how did I come to be what I am?" (1). What is here autobiographical in origin will become autobiography in form when in the narrative of the *Apologia* Newman traces from the inside, as it were, the forty four years leading up to the writing of the *Essay*. Yet the autobiographical note is struck here by the highly personal tone of the original 1845 Advertisement to the *Essay* where he apologizes for the frequent self-quotations "which are necessary in order to show how he stands at present in relation to various of his former publications" (x) and by the Dantesque echo at the end of the Introduction where he apologizes for the fact that his evidence is far from exhaustive. The bold enterprise once envisioned by the youth of twenty-five was daunting, but "much less can such an undertaking be imagined by one who, *in the middle of his days*, is beginning life again" (31 emphasis mine).

My interest here is focused exclusively on the first two chapters of the *Essay*. The rest of the chapters in Part I are simply the application of the theory to the antecedent probability of development and Part II is a detailed series of studies applying the notes of true development, seven notes which are in fact somewhat arbitrary and which Newman applies with decreasing degrees of thoroughness ranging from one hundred pages on the first to seven on the last. While it exceeds the limit of the present topic, it may be pointed out that even the choice and arrangement of doctrines treated serve autobiographical as well as objective theological needs. But the heart of the *Essay* is the discussion in Chapters I and II of the way the human mind works.

The opening words we read are that "it is the characteristic of our minds to be ever engaged in passing judgment on the things that come before us. No sooner do we apprehend than we judge; we allow nothing to stand by itself; we compare, contrast, abstract, generalize, connect, adjust, classify; and we view all our knowledge in the associations with which these processes have invested it" (33). It is tempting here to ask, is this the beginning of a treatise on doctrinal history, or on educational theory, or on assent to truth, or even a history of one's own religious opinions? It is clear that in all these cases the starting point for Newman is the nature of the human knower, the way the human mind works in the concrete.

His method in the first two chapters is to move from the nature of ideas growing in the individual mind to the nature of teaching and learning. Newman, first of all, who in the *Apologia* describes his youthful "mistrust of the reality of material phenomena" which made him "rest in the thought of two and two only absolute and luminously self-evident beings, myself and my Creator" (4), is not now thinking of a transcendent ahistorical self receiving divine truths in their completeness from a supremely transcendent being—God. However unquestioned the reality of the human spirit and the reality of a transcendent God, the human spirit is firmly embedded in history, in space and time, with all the limitations such a predicament implies. Thus an idea, "which represents an object or supposed object is commensurate with the sum total of its possible aspects, however they may vary in the separate consciousness of individuals" (34), "but there is no one aspect deep enough to exhaust the content of a real idea, no one term or proposition which will serve to define it" (35). "When an idea, whether real or not, is of a nature to arrest and possess the mind, it may be said to have life, that is, to live in the mind which is its recipient" (36). Once such an idea is possessed by the mind of many individuals its growth is slow and complex. This process Newman calls "its development, being the germination and maturation of some truth or apparent truth on a large mental field" (38). He explicitly rejects a logical or deterministic model of knowing when he says this "development of an idea is not like an investigation worked out on paper, in which each successive advance is a pure evolution from a foregoing, but it is carried on through and by means of communities of men and their leaders and guides; and it employs the minds as its instruments, and depends upon them while it uses them" (38). Then, foreshadowing both his argument for infallibility in Chapter II and his later awareness of the risks involved for a religious community in sponsoring the cultivation of the intellect, as he would recommend in *Idea*, he says that "this it is that imparts to the history of both states and of religions its specially turbulent and polemical character. Such is the explanation of wrangling, whether of scholars or of parliaments. It is the warfare of ideas under their various aspects striving for the mastery, each of them enterprising, engrossing, imperious, more or less incompatible with the rest, and rallying followers or rousing foes, according as it acts upon the faith, the prejudice, or the interests of parties or classes" (39). Ideas develop in minds, consciously or unconsciously, peacefully or contentiously, ordinarily over long periods of time, even at the end of which the complexity of a real idea is not fully exhausted or developed. Newman, like Coleridge before him, takes pleasure in pointing out that "with all our intimate knowledge of animal life and of the structure of particular animals, we have not arrived at a true definition of any one of them, but are forced to enumerate properties and accidents by way of description" (35).

The analogy with teaching and learning is drawn explicitly in the opening paragraph of Chapter II which, with typical rhetorical brilliance, summarizes the previous chapter. After describing how the historical fact of Christianity impresses a real idea on the mind and that idea then expands "into a multitude of ideas, and aspects of ideas, connected and harmonious with one another," he says this occurs because "it is a characteristic of our minds that they cannot take an object in which is submitted to them simply and integrally. We conceive by means of definition or description; whole objects do not create in the intellect whole ideas, but are, to use a mathematical phrase, thrown into series, into a number of statements, strengthening, interpreting, correcting each other, and with more or less exactness approximating, as they accumulate to a perfect image. There is no other way of learning or teaching. We cannot teach except by aspects or views which are not identical with the thing itself which we are teaching. Two persons may each convey the same truth to a third, yet by methods and representations altogether different. The same person will treat the same argument differently in an essay or speech, according to the accident of the day of writing, or of the audience, yet will be substantially the same" (55). Thus, Newman's "classroom" is one where uniquely individual minds struggle to communicate with other uniquely individual minds amid constantly changing times and circumstances. It is not the classroom of Dickens' Mr. McChoakumchild where one sees students sitting "like an inclined plane of little vessels then and there arranged in order, ready to have imperial gallons of facts poured into them until they were full to the brim" (*Hard Times*, 12). The method of teaching, of course, becomes the method of examining the historical process of unfolding revelation.

For anyone who might object that in the case of revelation, which is in fact a sort of teaching/learning situation, at least the textbook, speaks for itself, determines "the limits of its mission without further trouble," Newman counters, as we have seen, that "ideas are in the writer and reader of revelation, not in the inspired text itself" (56). For the problem is still the same: "the question is whether those ideas which the letter conveys from writer to reader, reach the reader at once in their completeness and accuracy on his first perception of them, or whether they open out in his intellect and grow to perfection in the course of time" (56). Newman is insistent on the analogue to human learning and understanding for he ends his point by reiterating that "unless some special ground of exception can be assigned, it is as evident that Christianity, as a doctrine and worship will develop in the minds of recipients, as that it conforms in other respects, in its external propagation or its political framework, to the general method by which the course of things is carried forward" (57).

The force of this argument within the context of the *Essay* leads to an argument for the antecedent probability of the development of doctrine throughout the history of the Church, which leads in turn to an argument for the antecedent probability of an infallible guide of that process (which is not deterministic as physical evolution would be) which need not concern us here except to point out that just as conscience for Newman is the "governor" or regulator of individual growth (George Eliot said "The strongest principle of growth lies in human choice"), so the multiplicity of opinions inevitably engendered over time by the conscious and unconscious exercise of the intellect must somehow be brought into unison if revealed truth is to be salvific and unifying. Describing the reality that results when "reason, as it is called, is the standard of truth and right," Newman concludes that individuals will tolerate no "common measure." The solution is again described in terms of teaching and learning; for it is precisely education, as he will stress in the *Idea* which causes the diversity. "There can," he says, "be no combination on the basis of truth without an organ of truth. As cultivation brings out the colours of flowers and domestication changes the character of animals, so does education of necessity develop differences of opinion; and while it is impossible to lay down first principles in which all will unite, it is utterly unreasonable to expect that this man should yield to that, or all to one" (90). And thus "the only general persuasive in matters of conduct is authority" (90). The rest of the *Essay* grows out of this insight into the processes of human understanding, communication, and interpretation. The revelation is divine and transcendent; the medium and recipients however are very finite and time bound. The process of development is very human, however divinely guided to its destined end. Development of doctrine, like teaching and learning, is a very subtle often frustrating but ultimately enriching process.

IV

By now it should be clear how much personal and subjective experience lies behind Newman's objective theological concept "development of doctrine." Let me now proceed to suggest how personal experience lies behind most of his thinking on education as expressed in *The Idea of a University* and pursue further the analogues between it and the *Essay*.

Dwight Culler has dealt magisterially with the subject and has shown how the writing of the *Idea* coincided with a move Newman's Oratorian community made from one part of Birmingham to another. Already planning to review his long years at Oxford—a trait we have seen before—as an acceptable model for University education, he now had the additional opportunity to sift through his incredible accumulation of writings and notes. He would not be reviewing in memory only but could cull from material ranging from his earliest exercises as a student to his published works. During the Oxford years Newman engaged in a confrontation with Edward Hawkins, Provost of Oriel, over the lecture vs. the tutorial method. The two elements Newman stressed in education, as Culler points out, were "the element of discipline or law and the element of influence. Influence is Mark Hopkins on one end of a log and a student on the other, and Newman considered this to be the heart of the educational process" (157). This role of personal influence runs deep in Newman's thought. In 1840, writing against the substitution of secular and scientific knowledge for religious truth, he said "deductions have no power of persuasion. The heart is commonly reached, not through the reason, but through the imagination, by means of direct impressions, by the testimony of facts and events, by history, by description. Persons influence us, voices melt us, looks subdue us, deeds inflame us" (DA,293). For Newman, although he would argue vigorously for the cultivation of the intellect as *an* end in itself, it is not *the* end of education. His parting comment to readers of the *Essay* is not a call for scholarly examination of this evidence and argument but a reminder that "time is short, eternity is long" (418).

Thus Newman advocated the tutorial method because teaching is a pastoral activity and teachers and students form a community of learners. "A University is," he says, "according to the usual designation, an Alma Mater, knowing her children one by one, not a foundry or mint, or a breadmill" (144-45). Newman was interestingly enough anticipated in this by the poet William Cowper whose poem "Tirocinium or a Review of Schools" advocated the tutorial method as better suited for dealing with "adolescents," which turns out to be the first use in the English language of that term as describing a developmental stage between childhood and adulthood (Cowper,353). What both decried was the regarding of students as impersonal receptacles to be filled or products to be manufactured. "Real teaching," Newman says, ". . . at least tends toward cultivation of the intellect; it at least recognizes that knowledge is something more than a sort of passive recognition of scraps and details; it is something and it does something which never will issue from the most strenuous efforts of a set of teachers, with no mutual sympathies and no intercommunion, of a set of examiners with no opinion which they dare profess, and with no common principles, who are teaching or questioning a set of youths who do not know them, and do not know each other, on a large number of subjects, different in kind and connected by no wide philosophy, three times a week, or three times a year, or once in three years, in chill lecture rooms or on a pompous anniversary" (147-48). In real teaching one finds a "multitude of ideas" which are "connected and harmonious" such as rise out of a community reflecting over time on the content of revelation as seen in the *Essay*. One finds truths which are not impersonally dictated but lovingly and not without difficulty communicated from person to person—not the communication of fragments and bits between total strangers.

Newman's stress on the developmental model is borne out both by his explicit ideas and his choice of words. He recommends Grammar as the first step in intellectual training "which is to impress upon a boy's mind the idea of science, method, order, principle and system; of rule and exception, of richness and harmony." The second is Mathematics which gives him "a conception of development and arrangement from and around a common centre" (xix). In describing the history of his own views on liberal education he speaks of "a fuller development and more exact delineation of the principles of which the University was representative" (p.2). His own views "have grown into my whole system of thought, and are, as it were, part of myself. Many changes has my mind gone through: here it has known no variation or vacillation of opinion, and though this by itself is no proof of the truth of my principles, it puts a seal upon conviction, and is a justification of earnestness and zeal" (4). Again the study of style, Cicero's for example, is important because "it is the expression of lofty sentiment in lofty sentences, the 'mens magna in corpore magno.' It is the development of the inner man" (281). Finally, the literature of a people is seen as a development of a nation or a culture: "The growth of a nation is like that of an individual; its tone of voice and subjects for speech vary with every age" (310).

Just as the Church runs the risk of contamination from its contact with the world, it runs an equal risk in isolating itself. So in true education one runs risks—either losing an intellect cultivated simply for its own sake or destroying or impairing it by training it only for some useful or specific task. In the *Essay* he asks "whether all authority does not necessarily lead to resistance" (50) and admits "education of necessity develops differences of opinion" (107). So in *Idea* he says "Knowledge viewed as Knowledge, exerts a subtle influence in throwing us back on ourselves, and making us our own centre, and our minds the measure of all things. This then is the tendency of that Liberal Education, of which a University is the school, vis., to view Revealed Religion from an aspect of its own,—to fuse and recast it,—to tune it, as it were, to a different key, and to reset its harmonies. . . . A sense of propriety, order, consistency, and completeness gives birth to a rebellious stirring against miracles and mystery, against the severe and the terrible" (217-18). This is the risk one takes if one conceives of the human mind as an organism and not a machine.

What Newman advocates is a philosophic habit of mind at once precise and capacious, one that can examine detail minutely and comprehend the whole systematically, one that does not look out to the world and the universe only from a limited disciplinary point of view, however adequate that may be in exploring its particular subject, but one which sees the whole as a whole. Thus he argues in Part I on University Teaching for the rightful and necessary place of theology in the university faculty and curriculum if the whole of truth is to be the subject of learning and in Part II on University Subjects he warns against the narrowing effects of Useful knowledge "which may resolve itself into an art, and terminate in a mechanical process, and a tangible fruit" (112).

V

I should like to conclude by briefly discussing another strong influence on Newman, one already suggested in passing. As late as 1872 Newman wrote that "Wordsworth's Ode is one of the most beautiful poems in our language" (LD,XXVI,56). In 1860, writing about the lives of the saints, he says that the real life is "a narration which impresses the reader with the idea of moral unity, identity, growth, continuity, personality" (HS,II,227), Finally, in 1845 speaking of the "conservative action of the past" in the *Essay* he writes that the "bodily structure of a man is not merely that of a magnified boy; he differs from what he was in make and proportions; still manhood is the perfection of boyhood, adding something of its own, yet keeping what it finds" (419-20). Clearly his own devout wish was that the movements both of his own life and that of the Church doctrinal life could be "Bound each to each by natural piety." Almost all of Newman's writings are, as I have been suggesting about the two works under consideration in particular, recollections of a past that has both a private and public dimension and significance.

As Wordsworth records in his poetry his movement from a period of youth when he saw the "splendour in the grass" and the "glory in the flower" to mature years which bring "the philosophic mind," so Newman in his essay on "Elementary Studies" in *Idea* begins with the undifferentiated vision of an infant and moves to that mature differentiated vision which "gradually converts a calidoscope into a picture," and concludes that "the first view was more splendid, the second the more real; the former more poetical, the latter more philosophical" (331). The Wordsworthian diction is obvious. Less obvious, perhaps, is that it opens the way to the *Grammar of Assent* with its illative sense that fuses imagination and reason. In *The Prelude* Wordsworth's life and reflections would lead him to the source of that philosophic mind—at times called the "Imagination—here the Power so called / Through sad incompetence of human speech" (VI, 592-93). At other times it is called "spiritual Love [which] acts not nor can exist

>Without Imagination, which, in truth
>Is but another name for absolute power
>And clearest insight, amplitude of mind,
>And Reason in her most exalted mood   (XIV,188-92)

Or, again, it is called "intellectual Love," for

>Imagination having been our theme,
>So also hath that intellectual Love,
>For they are each in each, and cannot stand
>Dividually.   (XIV,206-209)

Read in this light the writer of the *Essay* is not a disinterested historian but a concerned reasoner. Read in this light the writer of *Idea* is not an educational theorist but a loving and concerned teacher, concerned to bring out the full uniqueness of each individual committed to his care. What Wordsworth compressed into the word "imagination" Newman would finally call the "illative sense." In the *Grammar of Assent*, echoing both the *Essay* and *Idea* almost verbatim, he says "everyone who reasons, is his own centre; and no expedient for attaining a common measure of minds can reverse this truth" (345). Here all Newman ideas converge: doctrines tend toward their fulfillment, their perfection or individuality; education tends to bring out the uniqueness, the individuality of the human person; and now he tells us that the illative sense is the perfection of that human individuality on the cognitive level: "What is the peculiarity of our nature, in contrast with the inferior animals around us? It is that, though man cannot change what he is born with, he is a being of progress with relations to his perfection and characteristic good. Other beings are complete from their first existence, in that line of excellence which is allotted to them; but man begins with nothing realized (to use the word), and he has to make capital for himself by the exercise of those faculties which are his natural inheritance. Thus he gradually advances to the fullness of his original destiny. Nor is this progress mechanical, nor is it of necessity; it is committed to the personal efforts of each individual of the species; each of us has the prerogative of completing his inchoate and rudimentary nature, and of developing his own perfection out of the living elements with which his mind began to be. It is his gift to be the creator of his own sufficiency; and to be emphatically self-made. This is the law of his being, which he cannot escape; and whatever is involved in that law he is bound, or rather he is carried on, to fulfil" (348-49). Thus whether it be in matters of doctrine, education, or the psychology of knowing, "Growth [is] the only evidence of life."

WORKS CITED

1. Altick, Richard D. *Victorian People and Ideas*. New York: Norton, 1973.
2. Bremond, Henri. *The Mystery of Newman*. London: William and Norgate, 1907.
3. Chadwick, *From Bossuet to Newman: The Idea of Doctrinal Development*. Cambridge, Cambridge UP, 1957.
4. Coburn, Kathleen. *The Self-Conscious Imagination*. London: Oxford, 1974.
5. Cowper, William, *Verses and Letters*. Ed. Brian Spiller. Cambridge, Mass: Harvard, 1968.
6. Culler, A. Dwight. *The Imperial Intellect: A Study of Newman's Educational Ideal*. New Haven: Yale UP, 1955.
7. Dickens, Charles. *Hard Times*. New York: New American Library, 1961.
8. Doyle, Arthur Conan. *The Complete Adventures and Memoirs of Sherlock Holmes*. New York: Bramhall House, 1975.
9. Erikson, Erik. "Autobiographical Notes on the Identity Crisis." *Daedalus* 99 (1970): 730-759.
10. Ker, Ian. *John Henry Newman: A Biography*. Oxford, Clarendon Press, 1988.
11. Lindbeck, George. *The Nature of Doctrine: Religion and Theology in a Postliberal Age*. Philadelphia: Westminster P, 1984.
12. Newman, John Henry. *Apologia Pro Vita Sua*. London: Longmans, 1895.
13. ——*John Henry Newman: Autobiographical Writings*. Ed. Henry Tristram. London: Sheed and Ward, 1956.
14. ——*Discussions and Arguments on Various Occasions*. London: Longmans, 1891.
15. ——*An Essay in Aid of a Grammar of Assent*. London: Longmans, 1891.
16. ——*An Essay on the Development of Christian Doctrine*. London: Longmans, 1894.
17. ——*Historical Sketches*. 3 Vols. London: Longmans, 1896.
18. ——*The Idea of a University Defined and Illustrated*. London: Longmans, 1896.
19. ——*The Letters and Diaries of John Henry Newman*. 31 Vols. I-X:Oxford: Clarendon Press, 1978--; XI-XXXIII: London: Thomas Nelson, 1961-1977.

20. Nisbet, Robert. *History of the Idea of Progress*. New York: Basic Books, 1980.
21. —. *Social Change and History: Aspects of the Western Theory of Development*. London: Oxford UP, 1969.
22. Novak, Michael. "Newman at Nicea." *Theological Studies* 21 (1960) 44-53.
23. Ong, Walter J. "Newman's Essay On Development in its Intellectual Milieu." *Theological Studies* 13 (1946): 3-45.
24. —. *Orality and Literacy: The Technologizing of the Word*. London: Methuen, 1982.
25. Pelikan, Jaroslov. *Development of Christian Doctrine: Some Historical Prolegomena*. New Haven: Yale UP, 1969.
26. Poe, Edgar Allan. *The Works of Edgar Allan Poe*. 5 Vols. New York: Collier, 1903.
27. Rule, Philip C. "Newman and the English Theologians." *Faith and Reason* 15 (1989): 65-90.
28. Siskin, Clifford. *The Historicity of Romantic Discourse*. New York: Oxford UP, 1988.
29. Trevor, Meriol. *The Pillar of the Cloud*. New York: Doubleday, 1962.
30. Ward, Maisie. *Young Mister Newman*. New York: Sheed and Ward, 1948.
31. Ward, Wilfred. *The Life of John Henry Cardinal Newman*. 2 Vols. London: Longmans, 1912.
32. Weintraub, Karl Joachim. *The Value of the Individual: Self and Circumstance in Autobiography*. Chicago: U of Chicago P, 1978.

Comments

In parenthetic citations the following standard abbreviations for Newman's writings are used: Apo: *Apologia pro Vita Sua*; AW: *Autobiographical Writings*; DA: *Discussions and Arguments*: GA: *Grammar of Assent*; Dev.: *Essay on Development*; HS: *Historical Sketches*; Idea: *The Idea of a University*; LD: *Letters and Diaries*. In the text of my essay, for brevity's sake, *The Idea of a University* and the *Essay on Development* are referred to as *Idea* and *Essay* respectively.

Virgil, *The Aeneid*. Trans. W.F. Jackson Knight (Harmondsworth: Penguin Books, 1956), p. 33. "Tintern Abbey,"ll., 64-5.

In "Newman at Nicea," Michael Novak points out how Newman discovered in the warring theological factions represented by Antioch and Alexandria the wrong and the right way of reflecting on revelation. It was the latter party which showed him that "it is of the nature of the human mind to see things only partially; to move gradually from vantage point to vantage point; to court first one extreme and then the opposite, back and forth, in climbing the ascent of wisdom. And the irreverence of mere logicism of the Arian mind is always a threat to us enroute." p. 452.

In my "Newman and the English Theologians" I show how Newman's sustained and systematic reading of the Reformation and Caroline divines led to disillusionment with them because of their static view of history.

In *Bossuet to Newman* Owen Chadwick shows how the traditional Christian belief in a fixed "deposit of faith" began to yield to the pressure of a growing sense of historicism. While thoroughly conversant with this history of theorizing about change and the indefectibility of revealed truth, Newman was influenced largely if not exclusively in these matters by Bishop Joseph Butler's *Analogy of Religion* (1736) which he first read in the summer of 1823.

Critics such as Clifford Siskin, would, of course, claim this developing conscious self is a product and ploy of a temporally defined and conditioned Romantic discourse, all the more delusively powerful because it is so "ahistorical." *The Historicity of Romantic Discourse*, p.12.

Kathleen Coburn says Coleridge "frequently noticed with something like triumph, the difficulties in defining the edges of the mineral, vegetable, and animal kingdoms, as if here he saw evidence of the process itself, growth, continuity with change, and change with continuity. In short, in looking at nature he saw the inside of the outside, and the outside of the inside—he felt, at his best, a small but functional part of all that lives, grows, changes, and creates." *The Self-Conscious Imagination* p. 63.

THE *SENSUS FIDELIUM* AND CATHOLICITY:
Newman's Legacy in the Age of Inculturation

Paul G. Crowley, S.J.

Los Angeles to Dublin, Nairobi to Taipei, Cairo to San Salvador: the faith of the Catholic church assumes such diverse cultural forms that it is difficult if not impossible to specify a normative sense of the one faith catholic.[1] Yet we persist in trying to specify the basis for the catholicity of the faith, understood not only as description of a worldwide faith, but as a source of unity even within the church itself.[2] Augustine understood catholicity to be the universal agreement by all sectors of the church about what constituted the truth of faith.[3] Vincent of Lerins held that it was that which was believed everywhere, at all times, and by everyone.[4] Things no longer seem so simple. Inculturation—the adaption of the faith to various cultures, and the appropriation by diverse cultures of specific traditions and theologies—has meant that the catholicity of the faith is now strained by a pluriformity of faith expressions, even after the magisterium has spoken.[5] How do we approach this problematic of catholicity and inculturation of faith in tension with each other?

Both Augustine and Vincent pointed in a promising direction by saying that the catholicity of faith is tied to the universal consent of the faithful about the content of faith. By consent is meant a consensus about the faith received and transmitted. Such consent rests upon a sense of faith, the *sensus fidelium*, held by all baptized persons. While *sensus fidelium* literally means "sense of the faithful," another rendering would be the "collective faith consciousness" of all the faithful which leads to a consensus of faith.

This notion of a collective faith consciousness has become a prominent feature of theological reflection since the Second Vatican Council.[6] The Council speaks in *Lumen Gentium* of the People of God, "the whole body of the faithful who have an anointing that comes from the holy one [and who] cannot err in matters of belief." That which guarantees this fidelity to the truth of faith is "the supernatural appreciation of the faith (*sensus fidei*) of the whole people, when 'from the bishops to the last of the faithful' [Augustine, *De Praed. Sanct.*, PL 44, 980) they manifest a universal consent in matters of faith and morals."[7] The Council thus acknowledged a tenet long held within the tradition of the church, that the faith is received and transmitted not solely through the teaching magisterium, but fundamentally through all the faithful, by virtue of the *sensus fidelium*.

Since the Council, the re-emergence of bishops' conferences, the assertion of local and regional church identities, the development of "popular" churches under various rubrics (base communities, non-geographical parishes, house churches, specific groups for marginalized peoples in certain cultures), and the changing patterns of lay participation in the ministries of the church since the Second Vatican Council, have all contributed to renewed theological interest in the *sensus fidelium*. My claim here is that a critical recovery of the *sensus fidelium* as a foundation for the church's self-understanding could help resolve the larger problem of the tension between catholicity and inculturation by providing a theological linkage between the universal faith and its local expressions in different times and places.

Owing to his extensive treatment of the *sensus fidelium* as an instrument of doctrinal development, John Henry Newman remains an indispensable point of departure. I shall begin by examining Newman's treatment of the *sensus fidelium* in order to glean from it certain principles which can be transposed to the current situation of faith, a situation made more complex than it was in Newman's day by two factors.

First, as Karl Rahner has noted, the Church within which the tradition is transmitted and doctrines are developed is a world church of many cultures, not primarily a European church.[8] This means that the pluriformity of practices, pluralism of theologies, and not infrequent disharmony within the Roman communion are perhaps more evident today than in Newman's time, or in the fourth century, to which so much of Newman's research was devoted. The current situation of a world church makes the discussion of the *sensus fidelium* a more daunting task than Newman might have imagined. In the second part of this paper, I will relate the *sensus fidelium* to the context of a world church.

Further, there has been a philosophic change since Newman's day, from an epistemological question, how the church knows the truth of the faith tradition, to a hermeneutical question, how the church, in different times and places, comes to understand the faith tradition. Communication of the faith from the church in one time and place to another requires delicate instruments of interpretation if the catholicity of the faith is not to be lost.[9] In the third part of this paper, I will discuss how a philosophy of interpretation, as exemplified by the work of Hans-Georg Gadamer, can aid in grounding the *sensus fidelium*.

A critical transposition of Newman's insightful work on the *sensus fidelium* not only requires an appropriation of Rahner's contention that we are in the third great period of the church today, that of the world church, but also that the church lives within a world culture which is held together primarily by instruments of communication, calling for a new rendering of the hermeneutics of faith transmission. In several key ways, Newman seems to have anticipated many of our current questions. At the same time, aspects of his thought come to life in the context of current theological problems and philosophical developments.

A. Newman's Contribution: the *Sensus Fidelium*

Newman's most famous presentation of the *sensus fidelium* occurs in the controversial *Rambler* article of July 1859 entitled "On Consulting the Faithful in Matters of Doctrine."[10] However, he began to develop this notion in his earlier *Lectures on the Prophetical Office* (1837)[11], and in Oxford University Sermon XV on doctrinal developments (1843), where the mind of the Church is virtually identified with "the secret life of millions of faithful souls."[12] The position taken by Newman in the *Rambler* article moves a few steps beyond his earlier thinking, and he had occasion to make such an advance. Ultramontanist fever was in high pitch in 1859, and threatened to eclipse the legitimate role of the faithful in the transmission and articulation of the faith in centers far from Rome, as well as to extinguish the legitimate theological and episcopal voices of faith in parts of Europe where papal authority, tied as it was to the secular power of the Papal States, was received variously. Apart from France, no place reflected the stresses and strains within the church over papalism more than England, and few suffered through this period more than Newman and the Oxford converts.[13] Newman's work on the *sensus fidelium*, therefore, was not merely an academic exercise. Indeed, the occasion of its writing, a dispute with Bishop Ullathorne over the proper role of the laity in education, was historically quite specific. But it raised for Newman a deeper theological question about the relationship between the laity and the church, and finally, about the nature of the church itself.

In characteristically docile yet diplomatic prose, Newman would write:

> As to the present, certainly, if there ever was an age which might dispense with the testimony of the faithful, and leave the maintenance of the truth to the pastors of the Church, it is the age in which we live. Never was the Episcopate of Christendom so devoted to the Holy See, so religious, so earnest in the discharge of its special duties, so little disposed to innovate, so superior to the temptation of theological sophistry. And perhaps this is the reason why the "consensus fidelium" has, in the minds of many, fallen into the background. Yet each constituent portion of the Church has its proper functions and no portion can safely be neglected.[14]

Later, in the "Newman-Perrone Paper," Newman was to argue that the possession by individuals of revealed truth—here called the "Word of God"—could be applied to the church as a whole. The laity as well as the episcopacy witness to their own understanding of the faith tradition and thus contribute to the ongoing transmission of God's Word.[15]

The foundation for this approach lies in the *Essay on the Development of Christian Doctrine* (1845). In the *Essay*, development, like faith itself, is shared by a communion of minds, each of whom is "ever engaged in passing judgment on the things which come before it."[16] The *Essay* establishes that Christianity lives in the church much as an idea does within an individual person. In some parts of the *Essay*, Newman draws a parallel between the mind of an individual and that of a wider society.[17] On the basis of such analogies,

Newman holds that the corporate person of the church is thus fittingly called the "mind of the church." He concludes from these references that a single idea lives in or takes possession of many minds, and that this single idea is viewed differently by each person in whom it lives:

> The idea which represents an object or supposed object is commensurate with the sum total of its possible aspects, however they may vary in the separate consciousness of individuals; and in proportion to the variety of aspects under which it represents itself to various minds is its force and depth, and the argument for its reality.[18]

Newman describes the way an idea lives simultaneously in many minds, ultimately in the mind of the church. The idea is like a cut diamond, which, as it is turned in the light, reveals a spectrum of colors and whose beauty is enjoyed from a variety of perspectives. This idea reaches its plenitude when it becomes the "common property" of many minds.

> The multitude of opinions formed concerning it . . . will be collected, compared, sorted, sifted, selected, rejected, gradually attached to it, separated from it, in the minds of individuals and of the community. It will, in proportion to its native vigour and subtlety, introduce itself into the framework and details of social life, changing public opinion, and strengthening or undermining the foundations of established order.[19]

The nature of the idea itself, with its "native vigour and subtlety" insinuating itself into many minds and ultimately into "social life," is the basis for the transposition in Newman's argument from the mind of the individual, who beholds the idea from a limited vantage point, to the mind of the church, where it is beheld from a multitude of such perspectives.[20] The idea retains a transcendent, quasi-Platonic status, but always in its state of being possessed by many critical minds:

> Thus in time it will . . . after all be little more than the proper representative of one idea, being in substance what that idea meant from the first, its complete image as seen in a combination of diversified aspects, with the suggestions and corrections of many minds, the illustration of many experiences.[21]

The one idea is known only through the countless mediations of personal experiences of faith in particular times and places. The basis for arguing from the mind of the individual to the mind of the church is therefore not the transcendent objectivity of the "idea," but the personal nature of the church itself, which, as Vatican II taught, is the "People of God" who live in history. Faith lives in and is transmitted through the *sensus fidelium* which is shared by all the faithful who together constitute the church.

How does an individual person actually share in this *sensus fidelium*, which both shapes and reflects the historical faith of the church? Here we return to the *Rambler* article of 1859. Apart from the obvious theological basis for such a sharing found in baptism and the practices of faith, Newman's answer lies in the mutual inspiration by the Holy Spirit of teachers and learners in the church, the *conspiratio pastorum et fidelium*. This *conspiratio* is a delicately balanced relationship between the teaching function of the church and the role of the laity in arriving at an explicit knowledge of the content of faith.[22] In this *conspiratio*, the teachers become learners, and the learners become teachers. The entire church is inspired to transmit the faith, and this transmission includes the doctrinal formulation of faith.

Newman had established the theological background for the thesis of the *Rambler* article in his study of the Arian controversy. In his earlier studies of church history, Newman was troubled to find that the function of transmitting and formulating the faith had not always manifestly been carried out by the expected teaching authorities, bishops and theologians:

> I could not find certain portions of the defined doctrine of the Church in ecclesiastical writers. . . . Up to the date of the definition of certain articles of doctrine respectively, there was so very deficient evidence from existing documents that Bishops, doctors, theologians, held them.[23]

In the *Arians of the Fourth Century*, Newman reached the bold conclusion that the faithful, with their "instinct" for faith (the *sensus fidelium*), and not the institution of the magisterium vested in the bishops, had maintained the faith catholic in the aftermath of the Arian controversy:

> The episcopate, whose action was so prompt and concordant at Nicea on the rise of Arianism, did not, as a class or order of men, play a good part in the troubles consequent upon the Council; and the laity did. The Catholic people, in the length and breadth of Christendom, were the obstinate champions of Catholic truth, and the bishops were not. . . .[24]

Wishing to avoid a simplistic distinction between clerical teachers and the non-clerical learners, Newman extends the term "faithful" to the entire church:

> In speaking of the laity, I speak inclusively of their parish-priests (so to call them), at least in many places; but on the whole, taking a wide view of the history, we are obliged to say that the governing body of the Church came short, and the governed were pre-eminent in faith, zeal, courage, and constancy.[25]

In the *Rambler* article, Newman explains that the tradition of the apostles was committed to the entire church *per modum unius*, but in different times and places; the channels of tradition are many and diverse.[26] The magisterium of the church, which in the nineteenth century as in our own, was claimed as one of the sure notes of catholic unity, is situated here *within* the living instinct for faith possessed by all the faithful, and not apart from it or even formally prior to it. Nevertheless, each part of the church, teaching and learning, has a distinct role to play.

The church continues to receive and to know the truth of faith to the degree that the faithful, inbued with a sense of faith, assist in transmitting the faith in its authenticity. This activity of receiving and transmitting is the human foundation of the "mind" of the church. As this mind becomes more explicitly known and universally shared in the *conspiratio pastorum et fidelium*, a real basis emerges for organically relating the authoritative teaching of the truth of faith by the magisterium to the confession of faith in the various forms that doctrine assumes. The truth of revelation is the developing subject matter of the entire church's faith, a faith which the church receives and transmits in the particular histories which together constitute its collective history.

The *sensus fidelium* is, therefore, a theological principle supported by the evidences of the church's collective history. A transposition of this theological principle to the situation of today's church calls for attention to the new situation of a "world church," and to the hermeneutical turn that theology has taken in recent years.

B. The *sensus fidelium* in a World Church

The dawn of a world church has raised the kind of questions about cultural incarnations of faith that were thought to have been more or less settled during the era of the European-centered church. For example, the seventeenth-century Chinese rites controversy, which concerned matters that would fall under the umbrella of inculturation today, was summarily settled by the removal of Jesuits from China; for about two hundred years, the matter was considered closed. Missionary work, with notable exceptions, tended to disregard the validity of non-European cultures, and was even less open to the possibility of forms of faith authentically deriving from a local culture. This was very much the rule in Newman's day, when, despite a great flourishing of missionary activity, the church, especially in England, was largely preoccupied with internal affairs defined by the cultural and political landscape of Europe.

As we have noted, Newman chose the Arian controversy, over which he had labored for years before, to illustrate his principle that the *sensus fidelium* is the guardian of the catholic faith in times of uncertainty in the church. His treatment of the controversy was in many ways novel, not least because he treated it not only as a doctrinal or theological controversy, but as an ecclesial and religious controversy, pitting different senses of faith against one another in a struggle over the meaning and practice of faith.[27] The Arian controversy reflects the role played by the faithful in the transmission of the faith in a cultural situation different from that of the mainline churches of the empire. It could be understood as an early example of the tension between the catholic faith and its inculturated theological forms. This state of tension was experienced by the faithful themselves, who held fast to their understanding of the catholic faith, though with distinctive local flourishes, ranging from riots to *anachoresis*. In Newman's treatment, the Arian controversy does not belong only to a world of ideas abstracted from history. While the creed became the battleground of the bishops in their struggles over authority, the underlying issue did not concern the bishops alone. It also concerned all the people of the church in Egypt and beyond, precisely because it involved the vagaries of local expressions of religious faith, as Newman's evidences so well attest.[28]

Robert Gregg and Dennis Groh have addressed this "local" dimension of the controversy in their ground-breaking book, *Early Arianism—A View of Salvation*.[29] There they argue that the religious issue was a conflict over the practices of faith linked to competing theologies of salvation: the moral heroics of the Arians, who found in Christ a moral exemplar, were pitted against the grace transmitted by Christ the consubstantial Son, a view advocated by Athanasius. Various sectors of the Egyptian church would have been favorable to Arianism. According to Gregg and Groh, the Arian view would have been given a warm reception among the desert monks, but an icy reception among the so-called "orthodox" hierarchy. Other local factors also contributed to the rise of Arianism in Egypt: the relations between Egyptian desert Christianity and the more formalized faith of the declining urban centers; the spiritualities of salvation espoused by the desert monks, and those espoused by the episcopal leadership; the spiritual authority enjoyed by monks and bishops; the popular perceptions of the rule of faith, its interpretation, and especially the use of scripture; and the precarious position of Egypt within the Roman empire in the early fourth century. The Arian controversy can then be seen less as an abstract doctrinal debate, and more as an example of the inculturation of the Christian faith in a setting quite different from the episcopal religious culture of Constantinople.

Viewed in this light, Newman's appeal to the *sensus fidelium* as the mainstay of the Catholic faith during the Arian controversy is a profound theological principle, and still useful in a world church. As new theologies continue to arise, not only in the Third World, but also in the "old" worlds of Europe and North America, the actual relation between these theologies and the Catholic faith tradition raises troublesome questions: What is the relationship between a local theology as the expression of an inculturated faith, and the apostolic tradition of the Catholic church? Is a given local theology an authentic expression of the apostolic tradition of faith, even in an inculturated form? Can a particular local theology address the faith of the larger church? Such questions cannot always be answered by the application of abstract principles or dicta. As in the Arian controversy, which extended far beyond Nicea, they may have to be answered in the main by the long-range test of the church's life of faith itself, which is reflected in the *sensus fidelium*.

We can conclude that the *sensus fidelium* in a world church is that faith consciousness of the entire church reached through the countless local experiences of faith that together constitute the collective history of the church's faith. It is therefore, an historical reality, and not an idealistic abstraction from the church's life of faith. The coordinates of this historical reality are the ways local churches receive and transmit from churches of other places and times the same Catholic faith, through worship, devotion, theology, teaching and works. The catholicity of the faith is thus maintained to the degree that the people of local churches communicate with other local churches, and share in a *sensus fidelium*. Such communication requires ongoing interpretation and judgment of what is received and transmitted from the churches of different times and places. The world church is a church of communication, and this fact calls for a hermeneutics of the transmission of faith.

C. The *sensus fidelium* in a hermeneutical universe

To say that Newman used the *sensus fidelium* as a hermeneutical principle, a principle by which the entire church interprets and judges forms of faith, seems far from Newman's intention. If anything, Newman's treatment of the *sensus fidelium* was epistemological: the idea of Christianity was borne by the *mind* of the church. The life of the church was, not only metaphorically, but in reality, a kind of knowing, and revelation was the subject-matter known. Though the language of hermeneutics would have been foreign to Newman's ears, its functional meaning would not: the *sensus fidelium* acts as the clearing-house wherein the content of the church's historical life of faith is gleaned from the shape of the faith in a given time and place.

What has changed since Newman's time are some fundamental assumptions about how the faith is transmitted from one situation to another, such that it remains the Catholic faith, even in a localized manifestation. The major philosophic development of our time, the shift from epistemology to hermeneutics, from the idea to language, must be taken into account if the *sensus fidelium* is to serve as an effective principle for relating the catholicity of faith to its inculturated forms. There is a foreshadowing of such a philosophic shift in Newman's own work.

As noted earlier, Newman holds in the *Essay on Development* that the process of development, like faith itself, is shared by a communion of minds, each of them "ever engaged in passing judgment on the things which come before it."[30] To judge is to move beyond a passive knowing of the content of revelation; it is to become critically engaged with it, sorting, sifting, selecting, rejecting, and gradually appropriating it. And this occurs within the church-context of a particular time and place. The content of revelation is thereby interpreted. Writing in a time before the hermeneutical turn had taken place in philosophy, Newman the historian in effect introduced a hermeneutical dimension into the discussion of development: The entire church receives and transmits the faith as it is interpreted or understood in particular historical and cultural situations.

The hermeneutical philosophy of Hans-Georg Gadamer is an apt vehicle for pursuing the direction indicated by Newman.[31] In Gadamer's principle of the "fusion of horizons," a wide tradition is understood, through the specificity of one of its monuments, within the coordinates of a particular vantage point. For example, the catholicity of the faith tradition, expressed in the "monument" of the Nicene Creed, could be interpreted somewhat differently from the perspectives of a fourth-century Eastern bishop and a twentieth-century Catholic from California. Each of these individuals could hold a radically different notion of the meaning of personhood. On the other hand, there is a certain continuity between the fourth-century understanding and the twentieth-century understanding, in the focus upon the unique relationship between the Father and the Son, which makes both understandings "catholic" as well as particularized.

In the example above, a current horizon of understanding is addressed by the horizon of an authoritative tradition. The horizons of the present and of the past encounter each other in and through a specific subject matter offered by the horizon of the past, and consequently enter into intimate contact. The act of understanding, even by the entire church of a particular time and place, is an effort by the "subject" (local church) to grasp something which seems either alien to or vanished from its horizon of understanding.[32] For example, a particular local church may be required, within its own horizon of understanding, to encounter and make its own, in a critical fashion, a particular Roman teaching on church practices, moral codes, or theological strictures.

What is involved here is an interpretation of past meanings within a current historically-conditioned consciousness. This is the "fusion of horizons."[33] In this fusion of horizons the subject's current horizon of understanding is broadened. The horizon of the tradition, in turn, becomes more sharply focused within the consciousness of the subject, in this case, within the faith consciousness of the local church. The result of this process is a new horizon of meaning which does not obliterate the former understandings, but rather transcends them. As Gadamer explains:

> Understanding is always the process of the fusion of horizons which were thought to be isolated by themselves. In the life of a tradition such a fusion of horizons is constantly to be found. . . . For there the old and new are always growing together toward something of living value, and generally without either being explicitly contrasted with the other.[34]

Thus, every such moment of understanding is provisional and incomplete, but involves a real "development" in the meaning of what the tradition says, and of the subject's understanding of what the tradition says.

Such a philosophic hermeneutics has some pertinence to the theme of catholicity, inculturation, and the role of the *sensus fidelium*. Inculturated forms of the faith, especially in local churches, constitute a horizon of understanding within which the faith tradition from the past is encountered and received. This reception, however, is a mutually critical one, in which the faith of the local church is shaped in part by the tradition from the past, and whereby the tradition from the past is reinvigorated and changed (or challenged) by the peculiarities of the local church culture.

The *sensus fidelium* comes into play here in that no such encounter can be rendered in abstraction from the ongoing "experience" of the faith in particular social, political, and cultural contexts of the local church. Most of the classical dogmas of faith have resulted from a long experience of faith in local cultures. When, in the aftermath of the Council of Nicea, it was asked why the doctrine of the Holy Spirit had not earlier been elaborated, Gregory of Nazianzus said that the experience of God in the history of revelation had not made it imperative to do so, until the age of the church had dawned.[35] The church was ready to dogmatize, to express what had remained latent in its collective heart, when the horizon of a particular faith consciousness (embodied in the fathers at Constantinople) was ready to meet the horizon of the faith tradition itself. But this could only have followed the winnowing process not only of many centuries of the experience of God, but also of the contest among several contradictory views, not least among them the Arian heresy.

The result of Constantinople was indeed a new dogmatic statement on the Trinity, but even this was not the *terminus ad quem* of the development of the doctrine of the Trinity, as the history of theology attests. More significantly, it was the classical statement of the church's faith which would authoritatively speak to future generations who themselves would come to understand it within the horizons of their own particular experience. Naturally, the magisterium came to play a significant role in mediating this experience and the church's dogmatizing about it. But even the most juridical form of the magisterium could not and never has obviated the *a priori* role of the *sensus fidelium* which has resulted from living the faith in particular historical circumstances.

Little that has been said here under the rubric of "philosophic hermeneutics" could not find abundant support in Newman's work on doctrinal development, although the philosophic turn toward hermeneutics helps us to read Newman in a new light. While Newman's notion of the "mind of the church" is at heart epistemological, the process of development itself is not thereby merely psychological or mental. While the idea of Christianity is held as an object of faith knowledge by the entire church, and by local churches in specific ways, the process of development is not purely conceptual or intellectualistic. It is firmly rooted in and shaped by the history of faith.[36] Newman's field of data excludes in principle no aspect of the life of faith (dogmatic, devotional, or practical). It is thus impossible to limit the discussion of doctrinal development to a matter of ahistorical knowledge. Even "Sermon XV," with its focus on reason and an aim narrower than that of the *Essay*, tells us that the "secondary and intelligible means by which we receive Divine Verities" include exposure to people "themselves in possession of the sacred ideas."[37] Development of the idea of Christianity may occur with the assistance of reason, but ultimately it is an event of a living faith, rooted in history, which, ever interpreted and understood anew, "extends into mystery."[38]

D. Newman's Enduring Legacy

Newman's work on the *sensus fidelium* pertained to receiving and transmitting the faith in its doctrinal forms. This included the origin of doctrines, the authority to teach them, and the critical reception of them. His most enduring contribution is not the organic pattern of development which he outlined, but the claim that the faith is transmitted and received by the faithful themselves—by the entire church of a particular time and place, in a dialectical relationship with the authority of the magisterium. The catholicity of the faith is thereby safeguarded.

This claim, regardless of its sound historical foundations, continues to astonish, and to challenge. It astonishes because the church cannot escape the ultimately healthy tension between a universal teaching function, and the implication that there are those in particular places who are taught. Yet in Newman's scheme of things, it is the people of particular places, the taught, who become the universal teachers. This claim continues to challenge us because it is so notoriously difficult to translate the theological value of the *sensus fidelium* into real social and historical terms. When we try to do this, through various applications of sociological analysis, the theological value seems squeezed out, or merely added as a gloss. The tension between catholicity and inculturation in our day leads us to look again at Newman's work, to draw out its implications in ways likely unimagined in the mid-nineteenth century, and to turn to advantage the astonishment and challenge provoked by Newman's accomplishment.

Perhaps no current ecclesial development more urgently invites us to do this than the theology of liberation. Here is a theological and a pastoral movement which arose within local churches, but which has been influenced by elements of the theological and pastoral traditions of the church in other locales, notably Europe. The theology of liberation is an instantiation of the pluriformity of the world church in a creative tension with the older tradition, and of the encounter between a particular set of local horizons of faith and the horizon of the mother church, itself historically-conditioned. The theology of liberation rests upon an assertion of a church model that begins with the *sensus fidelium*, not with hierarchical structures. It challenges other theological streams within the church, including those expressed by the hierarchical magisterium, to listen and to become engaged with the legitimate mediations of the faith tradition that have taken place within the local church contexts.

In view of the concrete opportunities for engagement presented by liberation theology, a contemporary theological, historical, and even sociological evaluation of the notion of the *sensus fidelium*, inspired by Newman, could serve as a helpful tool in treating the tension between the catholicity of faith and its inculturated manifestations.

NOTES

1. Most references to "faith" and the "church" here presume Roman Catholicism, and the problems peculiar to that communion. I recognize fully, however, that the questions raised here ultimately demand a more ecumenical theological treatment.
2. For a discussion of catholicity in both its geographic and qualitative senses, and of the relation between catholicity and inculturation, see Walter Principe, "Catholicity, Inculturation and Liberation Theology: Do They Mix?" in *Franciscan Studies* 47 (1987): 24-43.
3. *Securus judicat orbis terrarum* (the entire world judges with surety). See Newman's discussion of Augustine's maxim in *Apologia Pro Vita Sua*, ed. David J. DeLaura (New York: Norton, 1968), p. 98.
4. *Quod ubique, quod semper, quod ab omnibus creditum est* (what has been believed everywhere, always, and by everyone). See Vincent of Lerins, *Commonitorium*, Chapter 2, PL 5, 640.
5. For a thoroughgoing discussion of the issues involved in relating theologies arising from inculturation (local theologies) to the older traditions, see Robert Schreiter, *Constructing Local Theologies* (Maryknoll, N.Y.: Orbis Books, 1986). Schreiter notes, p. 37: "Local theology is certainly not anything new to Christianity. But a direct awareness and pursuit of it is relatively recent for most Christian churches. For Roman Catholics, the stress on universality has been such that it makes it difficult to think about how locality and universality are to be related."
6. For the distinctions between *sensus fidei*, *sensus fidelium*, and *consensus fidelium*, see Herbert Vorgrimler, "From *Sensus Fidei* to *Consensus Fidelium*," in *The Authority of the Believers*, Concilium series, ed. Johannes-Baptist Metz and Edward Schillebeeckx (Edinburgh, Scotland: T. & T. Clark Ltd, 1985), p. 3. Vorgrimler distinguishes between the *sensus fidei*, a knowledge of faith granted to those who possess faith; the *sensus fidelium*; and the *consensus fidelium*, the "agreement which arises among believers as a result of the sense of faith with regard to particular items of faith ..." Also see Francis A. Sullivan, S.J., *Magisterium: Teaching Authority in the Catholic Church* (Mahwah, N.J.: Paulist Press, 1983), p. 23: "The term *consensus fidelium* (agreement of the faithful) adds the element of univer-

sal agreement to the notion of *sensus fidelium*. It refers to the situation in which, on a particular issue of faith, the whole body of the faithful, 'from the bishops down to the last member of the laity', share the same belief." Newman is not always so precise, sometimes using *sensus fidelium* and *consensus fidelium* interchangeably.

7. See "Dogmatic Constitution on the Church [*Lumen Gentium*]," #12, *Vatican Council II: The Conciliar and Post Conciliar Documents*, ed. Austin Flannery, O.P., New Rev. Ed. (Northport, N.Y.: Costello Publishing Co., 1984), p. 363. Another key text is *Dei Verbum*, #8. For a thorough discussion of both these passages, see Sullivan, *Magisterium*, pp. 17-21.

8. See "Basic Theological Interpretation of the Second Vatican Council," in *Concern for the Church*, *Theological Investigations* XX, trans. Edward Quinn (New York: Crossroad, 1986), pp. 77-89. In this essay Rahner demarcates three epochs in the history of the church: the early church of Palestine; the church of the Hellenistic world, later becoming the church of European culture and civilization; and, in our own time, the church of the whole world, tied to no overarching culture or civilization.

9. The inspiration for this observation is given by Richard McKeon, who notes an historical progression of philosophic inquiry from metaphysics to epistemology to hermeneutics, as the subject matter changes from instances of being, to criteria for knowing, to modes of communication. If one accepts his categories, then one can conclude that we find ourselves in an age of communication, when the hermeneutical question is paramount. McKeon explains: "When concrete facts and existential data are examined to provide foundations for inquiry and discussion and reasons for what is presented as testable facts and certifiable truths, the problems of being and of thought do not disappear without detectable experiential traces or persisting existential remnants; types of being and modes of awareness are transmuted into problematic differences discovered in statements and actions. What is encountered in experience is not a world of constituted facts nor a set of definite data; facts and data are constituted and determined in what is said and done." See McKeon, "Ontology, Methodology, and Culture," in *Contemporary Philosophy/La Philosophie Contemporaine*, ed. Raymond Klibansky, Vol. III (Florence: La Nuova Italia Editrice, 1969), p. 101. It should be noted that the

hermeneutical here includes that which might fall under the contemporary theological rubric of "praxis"—what is said *and done.*

10. *On Consulting the Faithful in Matters of Doctrine,* ed. John Coulson (London: Geoffrey Chapman, 1961). [Hereafter cited as *Consulting*].

11. *Lectures on the Prophetical Office of the Church, Viewed Relatively to Romanism and Popular Protestantism* (London: J.G. & F. Rivington, 1837). At this early stage, Newman's thinking reflects his respect for the Vincentian Canon: "The highest evidence of Apostolical Tradition is where the testimony is not only everywhere and always, but where it has ever been recognized as tradition, and reflected upon and professedly delivered down as saving, by those who hold it" (p. 295). He distinguishes here between the "Episcopal Tradition," which is the authoritative teaching of doctrine, and the "Prophetical Tradition, existing primarily in the bosom of the Church itself. . . This is obviously of a very different kind from the Episcopal Tradition, yet in its origin it is equally Apostolical. . ." (pp. 298-299). Such a distinction allows him more ably to argue for the apostolic nature of the Church of England, which is a principal aim at this stage in his thinking about a *Via Media* between Romanism and Anglicanism.

12. "Sermon XV. The Theory of Developments in Religious Doctrine," *Fifteen Sermons Preached Before the University of Oxford* (New York: Scribner, Welford, & Co., 1872), p. 323.

13. See John Coulson's introduction to *Consulting,* pp. 1-20.

14. *Consulting,* pp. 103-04.

15. For further treatment of this theme, see Samuel D. Femiano, *Infallibility of the Laity: The Legacy of Newman* (New York: Herder and Herder, 1957), pp. 42-44 and 50.

16. *An Essay on the Development of Christian Doctrine,* 1878 revised edition, ed. C.F. Harrold (London: Longmans, Green and Co., 1949), p. 31.

17. For example, see *Essay,* sections II.1.1-2, pp. 51-53, where this is implied.

18. *Essay,* p. 32.

19. *Essay,* p. 35.

20. This transposition raises a question. It is one thing to say that the idea which motivates Christian faith realizes itself socially; it is another to say that this social realization takes place within a

The Sensus Fidelium and Catholicity 127

"mind," or "the mind of the Church." See Nicholas Lash, "Notions of 'Implicit' and 'Explicit' Reason in Newman's University Sermons: A Difficulty," *Heythrop Journal* 11/1 (January 1970), p. 49 about this point in Sermon XV: "The ambiguity in the fifteenth sermon . . . concerns the legitimacy of extrapolating the notion of an 'implicit *starting point*' from the descriptive psychology of the individual to a theory of doctrinal development." In my view, this problem is carried over into the *Essay* on development.

21. *Ibid.* For the quasi-Platonic status of the idea of Christianity, see Nicholas Lash, *Newman on Development: The Search for an Explanation in History* (Shepherdstown, W. Va.: Patmos Press, 1975), p. 51; J.-H. Walgrave, *Newman: Le développement du dogme* (Tournai: Casterman, 1956), pp. 171ff.

22. Yves Congar explains the specific meaning Newman assigned to this term *conspiratio*: "Non sans se référer a Möhler, et en liaison avec l'analyse de la connaissance que devait s'exprimer dans l'*illative sense* de la *Grammar of Assent*, Newman donne toute sa valeur au *sensus fidelium*, que les Pères grecs appelaient *phronema*. Cet instinct de la foi existe dans les fidèles en dépendance de l'*auditus fidei*, donc de la prédication hiérarchique, mais il ne se reduit pas à cette part de la hiérarchie: il lui ajoute un valuer propre, celle de la vie de l'*ecclesia* comme telle. L'Eglise enseignante n'est pas toujours l'instrument le plus actif de la grâce d'infaillibilité: on l'a vu, dit Newman, dans la crise arienne. L'Eglise n'est un organisme hiérarchiquement structuré, mais tout entier vivant. L'idéal est un *conspiratio pastorum et fidelium*." *La Tradition et les Traditions: Essai Historique* (Paris: Fayard, 1960), p. 261.

23. *Consulting*, pp. 63-64.

24. Appendix, Note V. "The Orthodoxy of the Body of the Faithful during the Supremacy of Arianism," in *The Arians of the Fourth Century*, Fifth Edition (London: Pickering and Co., 1883), p. 445. Newman reviews the entire Appendix in *Consulting*, pp. 77-101.

25. *Ibid.*

26. These channels of tradition function ". . . sometimes by the mouth of the episcopacy, sometimes by the doctors, sometimes by the people, sometimes by liturgies, rites, ceremonies and customs, by events, disputes, movements, and all those other phenomena which are comprised under the name of history . . . . It follows that none of these channels of tradition may be treated

with disrespect; granting at the same time fully, that the gift of discerning, discriminating, defining, promulgating, and enforcing any portion of that tradition resides solely in the *Ecclesia docens*." *Consulting*, p. 163.

27. See *Arians of the Fourth Century*, especially Appendix, Note V, pp. 445-468.
28. As Richard Vaggione has recently noted: "One of the most striking things about the Arian controversy is not merely its speed of propagation, but its popular nature and the polemical depths to which it almost immediately descended ... Taken together with the almost immediate spread of this controversy outside its home ground and its manifest appeal to non-intellectuals, we are faced with the implication that here indeed there was something at issue which transcended the formally expressed terms of the debate." "*Arius, Heresy and Tradition* by Rowan Williams," *Toronto Journal of Theology*, 5/1 (Spring 1989), pp. 66-67.
29. (Philadelphia: Fortress Press, 1981).
30. *Essay*, p. 31.
31. We rely here principally upon Gadamer's *magnum opus*, *Warheit und Methode: Grundzüge einer philosophischen Hermeneutik* (Tübingen: J.C.B. Mohr, 1975); ET: *Truth and Method* (New York: The Seabury Press, 1975). [Hereafter cited as WM and TM respectively].
32. "On the Scope and Function of Hermeneutical Reflection," *Philosophical Hermeneutics*, trans. and ed. David E. Linge (Berkeley: University of California Press, 1976), p. 21.
33. WM, pp. 289ff; TM, pp. 273ff.
34. WM, pp. 289-90; TM, p. 273.
35. Jaroslav Pelikan, *The Christian Tradition*, Vol. I, *The Emergence of the Catholic Tradition (100-600)* (Chicago: University of Chicago Press, 1971), p. 211.
36. One might take issue with Walgrave here, who claims that development in Newman is a characteristic of abstract knowledge, and that Newman's "idea" parallels Aquinas' *verbum mentis*. The similarities are superficial. Walgrave's reading is based upon the premise that the *Essay* is a search for the right means of arguing for development according to the principles of conscience, and then testing these means from the standpoint of reason. See Walgrave, p. 106, n. 8, and also pp. 33-34.
37. "Sermon XV," p. 333.

38. "Sermon XV," p. 318.

NEWMAN'S CONSCIENCE:
A Teleological Argument

Rev. Bernard J. Mahoney

John Henry Newman's argument from conscience to the existence of God is an example of a teleological argument because it argues from structure or design, in this case the structure of the operation of the human mind, to the existence of a superior being, God. The design of an object, in Newman's case—the human mind—incorporates its end or purpose, its final cause. Newman's argument, then, states that the human mind, in the operation of the conscience, "carries on our minds to a Being exterior to ourselves" (*Theism* 114). This argument proves that the very nature of the conscience, one of the acts of the human mind (Assent 80), as a sanction of right conduct (81), implies the recognition of an intelligent being (83), a Supreme Governor, a Judge, holy, just, powerful, all-seeing, retributive (84).

I

The structure of this presentation revolves around, first, the significance and importance of the argument from design, and second, the way in which Newman dealt with the intellectual challenge this argument presented. The argument from design was the intellectual mechanism that enabled the early modern British scientists to unite their old Christianity with their new discoveries. The close relationship between science and religion in the seventeenth century became an adversarial relationship in the nineteenth. The assumptions of the seventeenth century became controversies in the nineteenth.

Reflecting the Book of Genesis, seventeenth-century British scientists inherited the medieval view that creation is good; in fact, Nature is perfect. This perfection is reflected in the final causes contained in the works of creation. Thus, the scientists' "ultimate question was not 'why' but 'how.' How does this universal machine operate? How does this individual part contribute to the operation of the whole?" (Westfall 51). However, the seventeenth-century assumption that evidence of divine providence in nature was obvious was challenged by new nineteenth-century insights into the laws of nature. Alfred Lord Tennyson expressed this new insight in *In Memoriam* (#56, 13-16; Tennyson 261).

> Who trusted God was love indeed
> And love Creation's final law—
> Though Nature, red in tooth and claw
> With ravine shrieked against his creed—

Newman was a part of the discussion that attempted to resolve the conflict between the old assumption and the new hypotheses.

Francis Bacon made the clarion call in his *Advancement of Learning* (45) to abandon metaphysical speculation about final causality and search for the explanation of efficient causality. The operation of the efficient cause was seen as evidence of the existence of the final cause, who is, of course, God. Although the scientific discoveries of the seventeenth century by Galileo and Newton challenged the Ptolemaic assumptions about the universe and led to theological controversies in each century about the place of man in this new view of the universe, the teleological (Newton 369) assumptions of Newton remained intact. Without hesitation, he asserts, at the close of his *Principia*, that the system he so brilliantly proved "could only proceed from the counsel and dominion of an intelligent and powerful being" (Newton 369). Newton then asserts that although it is not possible to have "any idea of the substance of God. . . . We can know him by his most wise and excellent contrivance of things and final causes" (371). In addition, Newton also identifies all the attributes of the Christian God evident in this system. This Being is supreme, eternal, infinite, absolutely perfect, omniscient, omnipotent, "the Maker and Lord of all things" (370). Since "blind metaphysical necessity . . . could produce no variety of things," the "diversity of natural things . . . could arise from nothing but the ideas and will of a Being necessarily existing" (371). These wide-ranging conclusions could hardly be a direct result of his inductive observations and deductive reasoning, rather they are likely the result of the climate of opinion that accepted the assumptions of the Deists. Newman's conscience, on the other hand, pointed only toward a Supreme Judge; our knowledge of the divine attributes, for Newman, was the result of Revelation.

In the seventeenth century, English science was the most advanced and creative of any nation at that time. But this new science was influenced by both Protestant theology and by the mechanical view of nature. Influenced by Calvinism, the English scientists tried to see evidence of divine providence in a mechanical universe (Westfall 6). The analogy of the watch and watchmaker thus became common coin between both theologians and scientists. The investment in these intellectual efforts seemed to bear great fruit in the mutual support of science and religion. Christianity used divine providence to soften the harsher aspects of the mechanical view of nature, while natural science emphasized the "rational or demonstrable elements at the expense of suprarational mysteries" (11).

This same attitude is reflected in the article on "Theology" in the Third Edition of the *Encyclopedia Britannica* (1797). It states that the study of the principles of theology, which is also a science, requires much preparation; listening to a couple of lectures is not enough. The student "must study the works of God scientifically before he can perceive the full force of that testimony which they bear to the power, the wisdom, and the goodness of the author." Only by studying "the physical and mathematical sciences" before beginning to study theology will the student "obtain just and enlarged conceptions of the God of the universe." In an obscure nineteenth-century work, Thomas Turton clearly states the common opinion that the objects of Natural Philosophy are: "1. the discovery of the existence and attributes of a Creator, by investigating the evidences of design in the works of creation, material as well as spiritual; and 2. the discovery of his will and probable intentions with regard to his creatures, their conduct and their duty" (Turton 32). While it is clear that classical Greek philosophy considers teleology inherent in the cosmos, the teleological argument developed in England attempted to assert a far broader and larger understanding of purpose and function in the world of nature.

The Deistic metaphor of the clock and the clock-maker is evidence that the teleological argument is partially rooted in the Newtonian concept of motion. Since "motion is neither logically nor ontologically self-sufficient," Aristotle's position is that to be ignorant of motion is to be ignorant of nature ("Motion" 396). The early British scientists considered local motion, unlike Aristotle, as "the essential and exclusive constituent of change." Newton's mathematical formula explained the Law of Gravity and gave permanent credibility to the celestial observations and hypothetical conclusions of Copernicus, Kepler, and Galileo, to name just a few. It is just a short leap then to translate the intelligent Unmoved Mover of Aristotle into the Christian Creator who expresses his loving providence in all of His creation. Greek cosmology has thus been translated into a teleological proof for the existence of the Christian God. The philosophical tradition, handed down from the ancient Greeks, developed by medieval scholars, and enlarged by the seventeenth-century British scientists and theologians, attempts to demonstrate that the function and purpose in the physical world points to an intelligent organizer for the Greeks, and to an All-knowing Creator for the scholastics, and to a God of Providence for the seventeenth-century scientists and theologians. While the cosmological argument from motion was used both by Aristotle and by Aquinas to demonstrate the existence of an Unmoved Mover, the teleological argument of these scientists and theologians is primarily interested in establishing the existence of the First Cause. Classical Greek philosophy established Mind as the principal reality organizing physical structure, and those who developed various forms of the teleological argument were satisfied in establishing the connection between physical appearance and a first cause. The use of a series of efficient causes to establish and identify a Final Efficient Cause was the goal of most of the formulations of the teleological argument. Although Francis Bacon's system of Induction shifted the emphasis of scientific inquiry from final causality to efficient causality, Newtonians, for example, expressed great concern about the presence of final causality in the operation and function of nature. They saw "traces of one Creator" not only in the mathematical order of nature but also in the prophetic revelations (Jacob 80).

II

Newman's argument argues from a structure, in this case the structure of the human mind. Newman's argument is stated in a number of places from the University Sermons to the Grammar of

Assent. But in his unpublished monograph, titled *Proof of Theism*, he states his thesis:

> November 7, 1859. Ward thinks I hold that moral obligation is, because there is a God. But I hold just the reverse, viz. there is a God, because there is a moral obligation. I have a certain feeling on my mind, which I call conscience. When I analyze this, I feel it involves the idea of a Father and a Judge—of one who sees my heart, etc. (Theism 103).

The structure of the mind, for Newman, is stated in his *Grammar of Assent* in the typical terms of British Empiricism first formulated by John Locke (Assent 79). The operation of the mind begins with sense experience which produces an image, which then abstracts from the physical image a concept or an idea, whether simple or complex, to form the content of our knowledge. From the awareness of external phenomena through the senses in combination with a number of "instinctive perceptions," which are similar to Locke's notion of intuition (Locke 309), the mind generalizes to the notion of a Supreme Ruler and Judge. The conscience is the mental act which enables us to come to this judgement. The conscience, thus, enables us to give assent to the reality of our conclusion that the image produced by our mind is the image of a Supreme Judge, who is God (Assent 48). Hume had asserted that morality is not based in some form of intellectual activity, but in some form of real decision-making power or force, such "as conscience or a sense of morals" (Aiken 34). Newman, also, placed morality in the conscience which gives real assent to its concrete directives in contrast to the notional assent given to abstract intellectual propositions.

Newman lists the Conscience as one of the mental acts, along with reason, memory, and imagination. Newman asserts the fact that we have a conscience by nature as a first principle which, in good Aristotelian logic, does not need proof (Assent 80). He lists it alongside other mental acts, such as the memory, the reason, the imagination, and the sense of the beautiful. All these mental acts are part of the basic structure of the mind and perform the special functions by which we recognize our own consciousness, our own existence.

The argument from conscience to God is teleological for two reasons; first, the conscience contains within itself a final cause, i.e., the conscience itself implies a superior being, and second the conscience is empirically observed, i.e., the conscience, apparent to all by its dictates, is one of the mental acts that makes one aware of one's existence.

Newman establishes the first reason in his discussion of Natural Religion in his *Grammar of Assent* (295-310). He defines Religion as "the knowledge of God, of his Will, and of our duties towards Him" (295). He then asserts that there are three channels by which Nature gives us this knowledge; they are: one, our own minds; two, the voice of mankind; and three, the course of the world. He then goes on to assert that "the most authoritative of these three means of knowledge, as being specially our own, is our own mind" (296). Newman continues by saying that the "Conscience ... teaches us, not only that God is, but what He is; it provides the mind a real image of Him, as a medium of worship" (296). The "cardinal and distinguishing truth" the conscience teaches us is that he is not "a God of Wisdom, of Knowledge, of Power, of Benevolence," but that he is "a God of Judgement and Justice" (297).

Newman establishes the second reason by identifying the conscience as a "personal guide, and I use it because I must use myself" (296). The conscience is not only individual, but it is also universal. The conscience is not only "carried about by every individual in his own breast," but it is also "adapted for the use of all classes and conditions of men, for high and low, young and old, men and women, independently of books, of educated reasoning, of physical knowledge, or of philosophy" (296). In his *Proof of Theism*, Newman states that the conscience is as obvious as one's own existence. "If then our or my knowledge of our or my existence is brought home to me by my consciousness of thinking, and if thinking includes as one of its modes Conscience or the sense of an imperative coercive, and if such a sense, (when analyzed, i.e.) reflected on, involves an inchoate recognition of a Divine Being, it follows that I am, and is only not so clear an object of perception as is my own existence" (Theism 119).

The conscience has two functions, a critical and a judicial function. It is both "a moral sense and a sense of duty" (Assent 80). It presents approval or disapproval in the form of feelings. This moral sense is a part of the intellectual makeup of human beings rather than being a separate sense. It has the job of both "dictating and commanding" (82). The conscience is not only the "rule of right conduct," but is primarily the "sanction of right conduct" (81). The conscience activates our emotions of "reverence and awe" of hope and fear, especially fear" (82).

Newman's proof for the existence of God hinges on this sense of sanction essential to the conscience. Although he does allow some variation in the testimony that provides the definition of this God, he clearly asserts that this sense of sanction implies the existence of a Divine Sovereign and Judge. He does not assert that we see God as a creator, a maker, a doer out of nothingness, but we all see God as a Supreme Judge. Once again, Newman took the middle ground between the Deists who would assert only vague attributes to the Divine other than that of a creator, and between those seventeenth-century scientists who would assert the definite list of all the divine attributes of the traditional God of Christianity (77). His definition of God was a result of Revelation, but the conscience could only point to such an enlarged view. The conscience would give testimony that God is the Supreme Judge, while not clearly grasping the whole of Revelation.

In his *Proof of Theism*, Newman quotes first from his University Sermon. "Conscience implies a relation between the soul and something exterior, and that moreover, superior to itself; a relation to an excellence which it does not possess, and to a tribunal over which it has no power" (113). Then, quoting from his *Occasional Sermons*, Newman says "This is Conscience, and, from the nature of the case, its very existence carries our minds to a Being exterior to ourselves; for else whence did it come? and to a being superior to ourselves; else whence its strange, troublesome peremptoriness?" (114). Finally, quoting from his novel *Callista*, Newman says the conscience " . . . is the echo of a person speaking to me. . . . The echo implies a voice; a voice, a speaker. That speaker I love and fear" (116). Newman says that these "extracts" are representative of a position he has held for thirty years (121). These few quotations, then, establish his position that the conscience contains within itself a recognition of not only a superior being, but specifically a person; and that this recognition is universal.

The teleological argument Newman develops to prove the existence of God is quite different from the teleological argument in vogue in the nineteenth century. In his *The Idea of a University*, Newman calls the teleological argument based on natural theology a "most jejune study" (95). He was careful to distinguish natural theology, sometimes called physical theology, from "*Naturalis Theologia.*" The former he considered "really no science at all," while the latter was an integral part of his idea of a University. The former, physical theology, is "nothing more than a series of pious or polemical remarks upon the physical world viewed religiously," (95) while the later, natural theology in the proper sense, understands that there is an intelligent principle, "absolutely distinct from the world," (96) who has given all creatures "their work and mission and their length of days, more or less, in their appointed place" (97). What is more, on all rational creatures, this intelligent principle has "imprinted the moral law and given them the power to obey it" (97).

The teleological argument of Newton and Boyle identifies phenomena which imply the existence of the Christian God with all the divine attributes, while Newman's argument identifies a human activity that implies the existence of a person who can inspire love and fear. The teleological argument of Newton and Boyle concludes that the Christian God is the final efficient cause in a series of efficient causes, while Newman's argument concludes that the source of the feelings of love and fear is the existence of a final cause. The weakness of Newton's argument is that it makes this causal leap of faith that assumes a direct and immediate connection between the existence of the observed phenomena and the existence of the final efficient cause. Newman's argument also recognizes a set of phenomena, in this case, the phenomena of love and fear, and it makes a direct and immediate connection to a person who can cause this love and fear.

Newman says in his *Idea of a University* that "physical science is in a certain sense atheistic, for the very reason it is not theology" (228). He views theology on one end of the intellectual spectrum and science on the other. Theology explains and systematizes what God "has told us of Himself; of His nature, His attributes, His will, and His acts" (395). Then, as the theology gets closer to the physical end of the spectrum of knowledge, "it takes the counterpart of the questions which occupy the physical philosopher" (395). The physicist "contemplates facts before him; the theologian gives the reason of those facts. The physicist treats of efficient causes; the theologian of final. The physicist tells us of laws; the theologian of the Author, Maintainer, and Controller of them" (395). Since "truth cannot be contrary to truth," (405) Newman sees no essential conflict between these two approaches to knowledge.

Newman also distinguishes between the methods of theology and physics. First, the argumentative method of theology, akin to geometry, is deductive, while physics starts with the inductive method.

The phenomena of the physicist lie "in a confused litter, and needing arrangement and analysis," (400) while theology receives all its information in Revelation, and "retains the severe character of a science, advancing syllogistically from premises to conclusion" (401).

Newman goes on to describe and define his notion of theology. Theology "contemplates the world, not of matter, but of mind; the Supreme Intelligence; souls and their destiny; conscience and duty; the past, present, and future dealings of the Creator with the creature" (395). While maintaining his definition of theology, and his definition of natural theology as notional and scientific (Assent 43), he rejects the claims of the Argument from Design, which used the other definition of natural theology, also termed physical theology. Physical theology "is derived from informations," "the same evidences of design," (Idea 408) "which existed just as they are now, before man was created, and Adam fell" (411). These "informations" are only part of the truth; they tell us nothing of the "moral attributes of the Creator," which are vital to his argument from the conscience to God. Thus, while not rejecting the discoveries and new hypotheses of modern science since "truth cannot be contrary to truth," (409) Newman does reject the notion that modern science can add anything substantive to physical theology because it has to operate on the same observations it had always had.

Another reason why Newman rejects the claim of physical theology is that this "so-called science" tends to dispose the mind against Christianity (411). Physical theology can only speak of the laws of nature which physics makes clearer by its inductive logic. A vital part of Christianity for Newman was the existence of miracles, "which are of the essence of the idea of Revelation" (411). Since the science of physics should not be asked to explain miracles, which is a distraction from its purpose, (Idea 227) physical theology makes God into some kind of an idol since He would be identified "with His works" (411). In fact, this God "is not very different from the God of the pantheist" (412). Newman clearly shows an awareness of the arguments of Hume, and avoids arguing on the terms of the material world. For Newman, although physics could not contemplate the suspension of the physical laws, Revelation certainly could present such an eventuality to a theologian (Assent 232-3).

Although the new insights and new discoveries of modern science in astronomy questioned the place of man in the universe, Newman decided to quote the *De Argumentis* (#28) of Lord Bacon as his support. "Sacred Theology must be drawn from the words and oracles of God: not from the light of nature or the dictates of reason. It is written, that 'the Heavens declare the glory of God' (Ps. 19,1); but nowhere find it that the Heavens declare the will of God; which is pronounced a law and a testimony, that men should do according to it" (Idea 231). Newman argues that while Sacred Theology is based on Divine Revelation, conscience is also the part of the design of mind that enables a person to recognize the existence of a Supreme Intelligence, a person who is the Judge and arbiter of human behavior. The conscience is that part of the design of mind that enables a person to recognize the will of God.

Lord Bacon's comment that the will of God is not evident in the heavens is an example of the intellectual challenge that forced British philosophers and scientists to find a natural basis for morality in the internal structure of a human being. Raising morality solely on Revelation would mean that human benevolence would be based on criteria entirely dependent on some external force, albeit divine. If morality depended only on God's edicts, then human beings would/could not be blamed for not knowing what is good or bad without first knowing God's edicts ("Shaftsbury" 429). Along with the Earl of Shaftsbury, Newman rejected this position (Idea 409). The other alternative is to base morality on some part of human nature. Thomas Hobbes began the discussion by stating in his Second Natural Law, "found out by reason," that the sense of obligation comes only after the social contract is made with other human beings (Hobbes 87a). David Hume took a different position in his *Treatise of Human Nature*, one section of which was entitled, "Moral distinction not derived from Reason," and followed immediately by the section entitled "Moral Distinctions derived from a Moral Sense" (Aiken 31-48). Hume's position is that "the basis of moral judgements is not reason alone, but reason enlightening the moral sentiments of feeling" (Randall 822). "Morals excite passions and produce or prevent actions," which reason cannot do (Aiken 31). Newman also rejected this position.

Newman takes the middle ground between Hobbes and Hume. Newman's argument from the conscience of God is an examination of the epistemological process for ascertaining duty. The argument has three parts: one, it is epistemological because the argument requires that the conscience make a judgement (Theism 111); two, it is a process because the argument is based on the observation that the conscience is one of the mental acts that identifies consciousness (104); and three, it ascertains duty because the conscience not only intellectually discriminates between "acts as worthy of praise or blame," but also provides the sanction for human behavior in the emotions of fear and love (111).

III

It is fitting that Newman concluded his writing career with his letter to the Duke of Norfolk, published in 1875. In Section 5, Newman reaffirms his conclusions about the conscience. First, The Supreme Being "implanted this Law, which is Himself, in the intelligence of all His rational creatures, which is called the 'conscience'" (Ryan 127). Second, since the law of God is "the rule of our conduct by means of our conscience . . . it is never lawful to go against our conscience; as the fourth Lateran Council says, '*Quidquid fit contra conscientiam, aedificat at gehennam*'" (128). Third, the conscience is "a constituent element of the mind, . . . the voice of God in nature and in the heart of man . . . distinct from the voice of Revelation" (128). Fourth, the conscience is " . . . the universal sense of right and wrong, the consciousness of transgression, the pangs of guilt, and the dread of retribution" (132). The conscience is the echo of the voice of God that Newman fears and loves. For these reasons, it is clear, if asked to offer a toast, why Newman would offer the toast, "to the Conscience first, and to the Pope afterwards" (138).

CONCLUSION

One final issue needs to be confronted. Is this Proof from Theism convincing? For Newman, the answer is found in his distinction between notional and real assent. A logical argument produces notional assent; if the structure of the argument is correct, then one has to accept the conclusion. Thus, if the premises are true, then the conclusion is true. Since both Aristotle's *Metaphysics* and *Ethics* are teleological, the concept of causality is shared. The concept of motion requires a final cause, in this case, the Unmoved Mover. Newman's argument dovetails with these notions. If there is an action, in this case the action of praise and blame by the individual human mind, then there must be a Supreme Judge of these actions.

But Newman does not base his argument on notional assent alone, for "Life is not long enough for a religion of inferences" (Assent 72). Is this argument convincing enough to oblige me into giving real assent? The concrete images of praise and blame can move the concrete affections and passions to real assent, to action. This kind of assent is not only concerned about what is true, but also about "what is beautiful, useful, admirable, heroic," and ultimately about "what is individual and personal" (Assent 69), as Callista says, the voice "whom I love and fear."

The significance of Newman's conscience is that he attempted to deal with the act of Faith in the light of the psychology of his day. He was not afraid of take on any controversy and deal with the best scientific information available in the light of Revealed Truth. He was not worried that Revealed Truth would come off second best, but he did arrive at a view of human nature that could include both human freedom with its natural ability to search for and understand truth and Divine Revelation given to all human beings. Since it is obvious that not all people accept the same Divine Revelation, Newman developed a view of human nature that could resolve this apparent contradiction. How could one God speak in so many voices? It seems simple for some tyrant to demand allegiance, but it is another issue to realize that God demands intellectual honesty. A tyrant is quite pleased with the same drab intellectual uniform worn by his subjects, but God obviously encourages a unique and creative response from those who love him. A tyrant demands control of the media to ensure that all the subjects get only the "proper" point of view, while God demands that we search for the truth even if we discover only a part of truth, even if some of us grasp different points of view. One approach is to try to explain how some positions on truth are contradictory, whereas Newman's approach was to try to explain how human beings could see things differently. The concern, then, is not about Divine Revelation, which will stand firm no matter the strength of human intellectual assaults, but rather how human beings daily make moral choices here in this practical and complex world.

Newman firmly believed in truth and dedicated his life to justify why he took certain steps to search for truth, without regard to his "career" and without regard to the occasional painful confrontations. A recent book review of A.N. Wilson's *Eminent Victorians* makes this perceptive comment: " . . . Newman allowed his life to be guided by grand, persistent and compelling questions about morality and religion. 'John Henry Newman was no more able than anyone else to give us infallible answers to such questions . . . ' Nevertheless, 'for anyone who finds it impossible, quite, to put such questions out of their mind, Newman will always be a giant, and a hero'" (Simon 201).

WORKS CITED

1. Aiken, Henry D., *Hume's Moral and Political Philosophy* (Darien, Conn.: Hafner Publishing Co., 1970).
2. Bacon, Sir Francis, *The Advancement of Learning, Book II, VII, 7* (Chicago: Encyclopedia Britannica, Inc., 1952, Vol. 30 of *Great Books of the Western World*).
3. Boekraad, Adrian J., *The Argument from Conscience to the Existence of God* (Louvain: Editions Nauwelaerts, 1961).
4. Hobbes, Thomas, *Leviathan*, I, 14 (Chicago: Encyclopedia Britannica, Inc., 1952, Vol. 23 of *Great Books of the Western World*).
5. Hume, David, *An Enquiry Concerning Human Understanding* (Chicago: Encyclopedia Britannica, Inc., 1952, Vol. 35 of *Great Books of the Western World*).
6. Jacob, Margaret C., *The Newtonians and the English Revolution 1689-1720* (Ithaca, N.Y.: Cornell University Press, 1976).
7. Jammer, Max, "Motion", *Encyclopedia of Philosophy* (New York: Macmillan Publishing Co., Inc. & the Free Press, 1972).
8. Locke, John, *An Essay Concerning Human Understanding, II, ii* (Chicago: Encyclopedia Britannica, Inc., 1952, Vol. 35 of *Great Books of the Western World*).
9. Newman, John Henry, *An Essay in Aid of a Grammar of Assent* (New York: Longmans, Green and Co., 1947).
10. Newman, John Henry, *The Idea of a University* (Garden City, N.Y.: Image Books, 1959).
11. Newton, Sir Isaac, *Mathematical Principles of Natural Philosophy* (Chicago: Encyclopedia Britannica, Inc., 1952, Vol. 35 of *Great Books of the Western World*).
12. Randall, John Herman, *The Career of Philosophy, Vol. I From the Middle Ages to the Enlightenment* (New York: Columbia University Press, 1962).
13. Ryan, Alvan S., *Newman and Gladstone: The Vatican Decrees* (University of Notre Dame Press, 1962).
14. Sidwick, Henry, *Outlines of the History of Ethics* (London: Macmillan and Company Ltd., 1886; Boston: Beacon Press, 1960).
15. Simon, Linda, review of *Eminent Victorians* by A.N. Wilson, in *Smithsonian*, Oct. 1990, 200-02.

16. Sprague, Elmer, "Shaftsbury, Third Earl of (Anthony Ashley Cooper)", *The Encyclopedia of Philosophy*, (New York: Macmillan Publishing Co., and the Free Press, 1972).
17. Tennyson, Alfred Lord, *Poetical Works* (New York: The Macmillan Company, 1899).
18. "Theology", *Encyclopedia Britannica*, 3rd ed. (Edinburgh: A. Bell & C. Macfarquhar, 1797).
19. Thurton, D.D. Thomas, *Natural Theology* (Cambridge: at the University Press, 1836).
20. Westfall, Richard S., *Science and Religion in Seventeenth Century England* (The University of Michigan Press: Ann Arbor Paperbacks, 1973).

THE DEVELOPMENT OF DOCTRINE
IN JOHN CARDINAL NEWMAN AND ALFRED LOISY

Francesco Turvasi

Cardinal Newman was accused of being a modernist by modernists and scholastics alike because of his *Essay on the Development of Christian Doctrine*.[1] It is not my intention to defend Newman from the accusation of Modernism. My purpose is simply to make a comparison between the theory of the development of Christian doctrine as held by Newman and as held by Loisy.

Since development involves history and theology, it is appropriate, before making a comparison between Loisy's and Newman's conception of development, to define the method which is proper to historical research and to theology as it is conceived by Loisy and Newman. We will then analyze the terms of the development (*terminus a quo, terminus ad quem*, and the cause of the development), as they are understood by Loisy and Newman, and, on the basis of this parallel, we will define the meaning of the concept of development used by Loisy and by Newman. After this historical enquiry, we will consider the implications of the conceptions of development of these two scholars.

The works taken into consideration are mainly Loisy's *L'Evangile et l'Eglise* (1902) and *Autour d'un petit livre* (1903),[2] and Newman's *An Essay on the Development of Christian Doctrine* (1845) and *An Essay in Aid of a Grammar of Assent* (1870). Loisy's *L'Evangile et l'Eglise* has its counterpart in Newman's *Development of*

Christian Doctrine, and his *Autour d'un petit livre* has its counterpart in Newman's *Grammar of Assent*.

1

METHODOLOGY

One aspect of Newman's genius was his realization of the importance of the method to be used in the search for truth and certainty. He dealt with this point in every one of his works, especially in the *Oxford University Sermons* (the subject matter of which is the relationship between faith and reason), in *The Idea of a University*, and in the *Grammar of Assent*. Concerning the theological method, we must also add his sermon, "Contracted Views in Religion."[3]

In the *Grammar of Assent* the whole argument of methodology ultimately rests on the assumption that, in order to know by what kinds of mental operations we may trustfully advance to certainty, we have to investigate how the mind actually proceeds to conclusions which generate certainty in it, rather than to determine *a priori* how the mind has to proceed. After comparing the structure of the universe which "speaks to us of Him who made it" with the laws of the mind which are "the expression of His will," Newman adds that we should be bound by the laws of the mind, "to take them as they are, and use them as we find them," despite the difficulties which occur "in the interaction of our faculties." The following conclusion shows the intellectual and religious integrity of Newman on the subject:

> It is He who teaches us all knowledge; and the way by which we acquire it is His way. He varies that way according to the subject-matter; but whether He has set before us in our particular pursuit the way of observation or of experiment, of speculation or of research, of demonstration or of probability, whether we are inquiring into the system of the universe, or into the elements of matter and of life, or *into the history of human society and past times*, if we take the way proper to our subject-matter, we have His blessing upon us, and shall find, besides abundant matter for mere opinion, the material in due measure of proof and assent."[4]

It follows that, by not accepting the method which is proper to the subject matter of every science (and established by the Creator), we show a lack of faith.

1. THE HISTORICAL METHOD

We find in Newman's writings some hints which show that Newman could agree in principle with Loisy's conception of the historical method.

In his book *Autour d'un petit livre* (1903), Loisy defines the subject matter and method of historical inquiry as follows: "History apprehends only phenomena with their succession and their concatenation: it perceives the manifestation of ideas and their evolution; it does not attain the essence of things. If it concerns religious facts, it sees them in the limitation of their tangible form, not in their profound cause."[5] According to this definition, the historical method excludes both the knowledge of God and the divinity of Jesus Christ. He justifies this principle by appealing to the method of empirical science.

> God does not present himself at the end of the astronomer's telescope.... He is no more a personage of history than an element of the physical world. The divinity of Christ, though Jesus may have taught it, would not be a fact of evangelical history, but a religious and moral datum. This belief would pertain to the teaching of Jesus, and history would have to recognize it if the fourth Gospel were a direct echo of the Savior's preaching and if the word of the Synoptics on the Father who knows the Son and the Son who alone knows the Father were not a product of tradition.[6]

Concerning empirical science Newman uses a sentence which is literally identical to that which we find in Loisy: "The inquiry into physical [causes], passes over for the moment the existence of God. In other words, physical science is in a certain sense atheistic, for the very reason it is not theology."[7] Newman also states clearly that the knowledge of God is not the subject matter of a purely historical enquiry,[8] but of natural theology, either through the imperative of conscience or through the ontological argument.[9] Concerning the divinity of Jesus Christ Newman could not be more explicit in denying that it is the subject matter of the historical method: "Knowledge of these revealed truths is gained not by any research into [historical] facts."[10] If, in addition, we bear in mind the distinction between the different branches of knowledge, which Newman establishes in the *Idea of a University*, we can conclude that he could also agree with Loisy in affirming the autonomy of historical method.[11] In a letter to Richard H. Hurron, Newman wrote: "Why do you take for granted that I admit no historical errors in the Bible?[12] This is a question of fact—fact is fact, and can be proved." Then, after affirming his reverence for the sacred writer, he states plainly: "Certainly I will not shut my eyes to historical proof, nor am I inconsistent, as a Catholic, in saying so."[13] In another letter, addressed to Dr. Liddon, he wrote: "It is clear we shall have to discuss the question whether certain passages of the Old Testament are or are not mythical. It is one of the gravest of questions, and we cannot spend too much time in preparing for it."[14]

In Newman's time the historical method and biblical criticism were only beginning, but Newman perceived their importance and realized the impact they would have on traditional ideas about Sacred Scripture. We find in his writing several statements concerning biblical criticism of the Old and New Testament which show a singular affinity with Loisy's conclusion of historical method.[15] One statement concerning the New Testament is particularly interesting because it is an important factor in establishing the difference between Newman's and Loisy's conception of development. Newman deals, in some degree, with the problem which later on was qualified as the distinction between the Jesus of history and the Christ of faith. He analyzed the meaning of Peter's confession at Caesarea Philippi.

> "You are the Christ, the Son of the living God" (Mt. 16:16). St. Peter acknowledged Him as the Christ, the Son of God. So did the centurion who was present at his crucifixion. Did that centurion, when he said, "Truly, this was the Son of God," understand his own words? Surely not. Nor did St. Peter, though he spoke, not through flesh and blood, but by the revelation of the Father. Had he understood, could he so soon after, when our Lord spoke of His passion, which lay before Him, have presumed to "take Him, and begin to rebuke Him?" Certainly he did not understand that our Lord, as being the Son of God, was not the creature of God, but the Eternal Word, the only-begotten Son of the Father, one with Him in substance, distinct in Person. . . .

The Development of Doctrine

> Apparently, it was not till after His resurrection, and especially after His ascension, when the Holy Ghost descended, that the Apostles understood who had been with them. When all was over they knew it, not at the time.[16]

We must give credit to Loisy for having realized the distinction between the history and the faith of Christianity, and that the Gospels do not relate to us what Jesus Christ said *verbatim* and that they were informed by the faith of the first Christians. Newman, in the just quoted page concerning Peter's confession, shows that he, too, was, to some extent, aware of the distinction between history and faith. However, we should underscore an important difference between Loisy and Newman concerning the historical method. In his dispute with ecclesiastical authority, Loisy insistently protested that his two Books, *L'Evangile et l'Eglise* and *Autour d'un petit livre*, were historical in their subject matter and method. But in reality the books of Loisy dealt not only with history, but also with philosophy of religion. Loisy in *Choses passées* acknowledged that his book *l'Evangile et l'Eglise* contained an "apologetic part," and a "philosophical and historical element."[17] In *Quelques Lettres* he admits that in *L'Evangile et l'Eglise* and in *Autour d'un petit livre* "history occupied a very large place" but that they contained also a "theory of Christian development," i.e., philosophy or theology.[18] Baron von Hügel, a good friend of Loisy, called this point to Blondel's attention when he wrote: "What, for example, are the renowned pages 142-144 of M. Loisy's *L'Evangile et l'Eglise* if not philosophy?"[19]

This lack of distinction between the historical method and philosophy is the weak point of Loisy's system. While acknowledging that "history apprehends only phenomena with their succession and concatenation, and not in their profound cause," he does not hesitate to state that philosophy of transcendence made Jesus the Son of God. The reason that Loisy lost the insight of supernatural revelation and arrived at a rationalistic conception of revelation and dogma could be found in this lack of distinction between history and philosophy. Newman knew clearly the distinction between history and the philosophy of history.[20] He recognized that there is a personal element in historical research.[21] As he vigorously rejected the dishonest distortion of history for the sake of theory,[22] so he judged that, after establishing the facts, "all these successive processes of minute reasoning superintended and directed by an intellectual instrument [are] far too subtle and spiritual to be scientific."[23]

Given Newman's natural skepticism of the systematic philosophy of history, he could not agree when Loisy's philosophy "encroached" upon the historical method.

2. THE THEOLOGICAL METHOD

With theology, too, Newman insists that the method should follow the subject matter, and thereby he rejects any form of apriorism.

In order to understand how Newman establishes the proper method of theological science, and why he rejects the aprioristic method used by the theologians of his time, let us consider how certain dispositions of mind, such as patience, caution, humility, and obedience are necessary for discovering the method in scientific research, as is shown in the example of empirical science. The student of physics does not approach his subject matter with any pre-formed method. On the contrary, his study consists precisely in discovering the laws which govern physics and all his attention is directed toward this goal. His is the attitude of one who is learning, ready to discover something new. Knowledge of the subject matter will dictate the method he is to follow. He has to be very careful in obeying the subject matter. It would be simply foolish to pretend to impose on nature any aprioristic method. If he does not follow the laws of electricity or of atomic power, he runs the risk of being killed. The basic attitude of a true scholar is, therefore, humility and obedience, according to Francis Bacon's axiom: "Nature is dominated only by obedience to it." To get light, heat, or movement from electricity, we are compelled to study its properties without having the ridiculous pretense of changing them; and we apply them to our case, taking care to respect all of them. Otherwise, we won't achieve anything.[24] "Yet," Newman concludes, "though it seems to be so obvious a position when stated, that in forming any serious theory concerning nature we must begin with investigation, to the exclusion of fanciful speculation or deference to human authority, it was not generally recognized or received as such."[25] He adds that the imposition upon the science of "a language different from that which she really speaks" is as "unphilosophical as it is unchristian," because it does not take into account the laws which the Creator Himself put in nature.[26]

In theology, more than in the empirical sciences, the disposition of mind of "caution, modesty, patience and obedience," is extremely important. To find a method for theology we must first of all realize the nature of revelation and what God asks of man. For this reason, in his tenth Oxford Sermon, "Faith and Reason Contrasted as Habits of Mind," Newman appeals to several texts of Sacred Scripture to discover what attitude of mind is required in theology. Since Christianity is a supernatural fact of God's self-revelation which implies in man moral dispositions, it was unthinkable for Newman to approach Christianity from a preconceived and purely intellectual method. Newman wrote, "There is a vast distance between what it is in itself, and what it is to us. Light is a quality of matter, as truth is of Christianity; but light is not recognized by the blind, and there are those who do not recognize truth, from the fault, not of truth, but of themselves."[27] For this reason he energetically rejected the apologetics of his time, whose basis was miracles and whose instrument was the syllogism.[28] "If I am asked," he wrote, "to use Paley's argument for my own conversion, I say plainly I do not want to be converted by a smart syllogism; if I am asked to convert others by it, I say plainly I do not care to overcome their reason without touching their hearts. I wish to deal, not with controversialists, but with inquirers."[29] Newman sensed that the approach of apologetics "by syllogism" could give support to the rationalistic position. "Reason is subservient to faith," he wrote, "as handling, examining, explaining, recording, cataloguing, defending, the truths which faith, not reason, has gained for us, as providing an intellectual expression of supernatural facts, eliciting what is implicit, comparing, measuring, connecting each with each, and forming one and all into a theological system."[30]

In his sermon *Contracted Views in Religion* Newman makes a comparison between the attitude of the elder son in the parable of the "Prodigal Son" and the attitude of the theologians of his time. This gives him the opportunity to insist, in a explicit way, on the necessity of the use of the right method in theology.

> Men attach an undue importance to this or that point in receiving opinions or practices, and cannot understand how God's blessing can be given to modes of acting to which they themselves are unaccustomed. . . . They become not only overconfident of their knowledge of God's ways, but positive in their overconfidence. They do not like to be contradicted in their opinions, and are generally most attached to the very points which are most especially of their own devising. They

forget that all men are at best but learners in the school of Divine Truth, and that they themselves ought to be *ever* learning.[31]

It is no wonder that this kind of theology was hostile to Newman's *Development of Christian Doctrine*.[32] In France in 1905 F. Dubois wrote that "the prevailing tendency of recent studies in religious philosophy is to relegate the intellectual element of religion, belief and dogma to the background, and to regard religion principally as a feeling, an emotion or rather, according to the most popular formula, as a higher life, that is, an immanent activity in which spontaneity and the unconscious have a part to play equal at least to that of reflection." The author judged "this tendency to be a Protestant infiltration," and found its roots in the theology of Schleiermacher. The first on the list of Catholics who had "this tendency" was Cardinal Newman, followed by George Tyrrell, S. J. and A. Loisy.[33] Léonce de Grandmaison, S.J. and Jules Lebreton, S.J. did not hesitate to express their strong reservations concerning Newman's thought. Father de Grandmaison discerned "unequivocal traces of a state of mind bordering on that which sees in dogmatic statements only the authorized *symbols of unknowable truths*", and he mentioned the "bitter fruits" of Newman's anti-intellectualism.[34] Father Lebreton went further and blamed Newman for a certain nominalism.[35] E. Michaud declared that Newman strips dogma of divinity and leaves only "changing opinion," and that his theory of development and assent amounts in the end to a sort of sentimentalism.[36]

The aversion of scholastics to Newman's *Development of Christian Doctrine* finds its explanation in the fact that, in addition to being purely intellectualistic, scholastic theology had lost its contact with Sacred Scripture and Patristics. Newman's theory of development was deeply rooted in Scripture and Patristics, according to the theological method he had established. In Scripture, Newman, since his youth, had discovered the sense of divine Providence and of divine economy in the gradual revelation. This had provided him with the foundation of his theory of development.[37] In Patristics, as he states in the *Apologia*,[38] he had recognized the principle of doctrinal development.[39] Again, in his study of Patristics, he had realized the existence of the prophetical office working in the Church, which could be considered like the "atmosphere" of the development of Christian doctrine.

2

DEVELOPMENT OF DOCTRINE IN LOISY AND IN NEWMAN

In 1894 Baron von Hügel sent Newman's books to Loisy. Loisy confessed: "I studied them exhaustively. Newman's type of mind attracted me far more than did that of the Protestant theologians. I devoted myself assiduously to the study of his *Essay on the Development of Christian Doctrine*."[40]

In 1902 A. Loisy published *L'Evangile et l'Eglise*, which had the same goal as Newman's *Development of Christian Doctrine*. He commented that "If one may speak of the philosophical influence exerted on *L'Evangile et l'Eglise* and *Autour d'un petit livre*, one would have to take into consideration two very real and historically ascertained influences, those of Renan and Newman, although they were not systematic and, certainly, not exhaustive."[41]

In the introduction to *L'Evangile et l'Eglise* Loisy stated that "the aim of the work" was twofold. His first aim was "to catch the point of view of history." In this part from a purely historical point of view, Loisy dealt with the conception which Jesus Christ had of the Kingdom of God, and with the consciousness Jesus Christ had of his mission. His second aim was "to analyze and define the bonds that unite the two subjects [i.e., the Gospel, considered as a historical document, and the Catholic Church and its dogma concerning the divinity of Jesus Christ] in history."[42] Here Loisy shows step-by-step how the first Christians progressed from the notion of the Jesus of history, the simple Messiah, to that of his divinity. In this second part Loisy makes an explicit reference to the *Development of Christian Doctrine*, and to the application he had made of Newman's theory. Loisy says that "the paragraph concerning Newman resulted in a *widening* of his theory, in order to apply the idea of development not only to the history of Christianity, but also and first of all to the Biblical Revelation of the two Testaments, and these collections were themselves the fruit of historical development." Honestly he points out that "the attention of Newman was not drawn to this point."[43]

To realize the different conceptions of development which Newman and Loisy had, it is useful to point out three aspects: the *terminus a quo* of development, the *terminus ad quem* of development, the *cause* of development, and, in keeping with this analysis, to define the nature of the two conceptions of development.

1. TERMINUS A QUO

1. For Loisy the starting point of development is the historical data which we can draw from the Gospel through the historical method. These data are concerned with the conception which Jesus Christ had of the Kingdom of God, and with his messianic consciousness.

(1) Concerning the Kingdom of God Loisy states that "the message of Jesus is contained in the announcement of the approaching Kingdom, and the exhortation to penitence as a means of sharing therein. The object of Jesus' preaching was the reign of God, or the Kingdom of Heaven. The greater part of the parables bear either on the coming of this kingdom, or on the way of making ready for it. In the Lord's Prayer, Christ makes His disciples say, 'Thy Kingdom come!' All His teaching is given to prepare for the kingdom."[44] Against the thesis of Harnack, who stated in his book *Das Wesen des Christentums*, that the teaching of Jesus Christ was concerned with the revelation of God's fatherhood, Loisy shows that all the moral precepts of the Gospel are not an end in themselves, but a means for the Kingdom. Even the great precept of "love is not an end in itself; charity leads to the Kingdom, sacrificing the temporal to gain the eternal." What is the nature of the Kingdom of God? The Kingdom of God is purely eschatological. "There is no doubt," Loisy explains, that "all teaching of Jesus Christ is closely related to the eschatological conception of the Kingdom."[45]

(2) Concerning the historical image of Jesus Christ, the guiding principle of Loisy is the following: "Given a limited conception of the Kingdom of heaven, an equally limited conception of the mission of the Savior is sure to correspond."[46] After rejecting the historicity of the text of Matthew 11:25-30 and Luke 10:21-24, where we find a clear statement of Jesus' divine nature,[47] Loisy admits that Jesus "had the consciousness of being the Messiah."[48] As to its meaning, the title of Messiah (which has nothing to do with that of Son of God in the theological sense) relates to the meaning of the Kingdom of God. Thus, Loisy states, "As the Kingdom is essentially a thing of the future, the office of Messiah is essentially eschatological. Christ is the head of the society of the elects. The ministry of Jesus was only the preliminary to the Kingdom of Heaven and the fulfillment of the office of Messiah. In one sense Jesus was the Messiah, in another sense He was presently to become the Messiah."[49]

The Development of Doctrine

In *Les Evangiles Synoptiques*, on which he had been working since the end of 1899, Loisy summed up the image of the historical Jesus as follows: "A village craftsman, naive and enthusiastic, who believes the end of the world near at hand, believes in the establishment of a Kingdom of justice, in the advent of God on earth, and who, firmly set in this first illusion, assumes the principal role in the organization of the unrealizable city ... who recruits a small number of illiterate adherents, and provokes an unrest ... who could not escape a violent death, and who met it. His dream was frail and narrow as is our science."[50]

2. According to Newman the beginning of the process of development is the revealed truth committed to the Apostles. "To the Apostles the whole revelation was given, by the Church it is transmitted; no simply new truth has been given to us since St. John's death; the one office of the Church is to guard 'that noble deposit' of truth, as St. Paul speaks to Timothy, which the Apostles bequeathed to her, in its fullness and integrity."[51]

It is interesting to note that Newman points to a distinction in the understanding the Apostles had of Jesus, on the one hand, during His earthly life, and, on the other, after His death and resurrection. He finds that *historically* the Apostles' faith in the divinity of Jesus Christ (and consequently the full supernatural revelation) must be sought not during the life of Jesus but at Pentecost, with the descent of the Holy Spirit.[52]

Here we find the first basic difference between Newman and Loisy. While Newman explicitly stated that development begins with the revelation of the Holy Spirit, Loisy, consistent with his aim of showing the link between history and the faith of the Church, puts the beginning of the development in history, when the Apostles viewed Jesus simply as Messiah and not as the Son of God. While Newman admits a link between the understanding the Apostles had of Jesus during His life and the understanding they received from the Holy Spirit,[53] Loisy expressly denies any logical link between the Apostles' understanding of Jesus during his earthly life and their teaching after his death. "Custodians and preachers of a living religion," Loisy writes, "the first followers of the Gospel did not for a moment think themselves bound in their preaching either by the letter of the formulas Christ had used, nor by the material reality of past events; they did not consider themselves the guardians of a doctrinal essence which Jesus Christ never had the intention of preaching.... Jesus had been less the proponent of a doctrine than the initiator of a religious movement."[54]

2. TERMINUS AD QUEM

1. Starting from the historical data concerning the kingdom of God, preached by Jesus Christ, and the Messianic consciousness of Jesus, Loisy concludes to the following:

(1) Since the kingdom of God was essentially eschatological, and Jesus was conscious of being its agent, then Jesus could not at all have "systematized beforehand the constitution of the Church as that of a government established on earth and destined to endure for a long series of centuries." A conception "far more foreign still to His thoughts and to His authentic teaching" was "that of an invisible society formed for ever." "Jesus foretold the kingdom," Loisy states, "and it was the Church that came. She came enlarging the form of the Gospel, which was impossible to preserve as it was.... The view of kingdom has been enlarged and modified, the conception of its definite advent fills a small place."[55]

(2) The concept of Jesus as Messiah underwent a radical change. Loisy states, "Beginning at a very early date, the Greek interpretation of the Christian doctrine of the Messiah came into being... that Christ, Son of God and Son of man, predestined savior, became the Word made flesh, the Revealer of God to humanity.... The divinity of Christ, the incarnation of the Word was the only conceivable way of translating to Greek intelligence the idea of the Messiah."[56]

How did the Church arrive at the formulation of the divinity of Jesus Christ (whom history does not prove to be the Son of God) and at the subsequent Christological dogmatic statements? Loisy distinguishes two main changes.

"The first change, the most decisive, most important," and most radical was that which drew out of the *historical* conception of the Messiah a conception of a Jesus, Son of God, Revealer and Savior. This radical change, which Loisy terms *transformation*,[57] was accomplished by St. Paul and St. John.

> The Pauline theory of salvation was indispensable in its time, if Christianity were not to remain a Jewish sect without a future. The theory of the Incarnate Logos was also necessary when the Gospel was presented, not only to the proselytes of

The Development of Doctrine

Judaism in the Empire, but to the whole pagan world, and to everyone who had received a Hellenistic education.[58]

The second change has as its starting point the "theory" of St. Paul and St. John, and ends with the formulations of the hypostatic union of the Council of Constantinople and the Fourth Lateran Council.[59] The guiding principle which led to the final formulation of Christological dogma was formulated by Loisy in these terms:

> It is not astonishing that the result of so special a labor seems to lack logic and rational consistency. However, it is found that this defect, which would be fatal to a philosophic system, is, in theology, an element of endurance and solidity. . . . Orthodoxy seems to follow a kind of politic line, balanced and obstinately conciliatory, between the extreme conclusions that can be drawn from the data it preserves. When it can no longer perceive the logical agreement of the assertions it seems to set one against the other, it proclaims the mystery, and does not purchase unity of theory by the sacrifice of an important element of its tradition. . . . So it acted in the case of the Incarnation, when the dual nature was definitely affirmed in the one Person, and when it was necessary to take a stand simultaneously against Nestorianism and Monophysism.[60]

In *Autour d'un petit livre*, Loisy describes in detail the dialectic of this process of *transformation* until the Christological formula reaches its complete formulation.

(a) The first problem, faced by the early Church, was how to reconcile "the reality of evangelical history, and Paul's and John's theory, in order to make a coordinated system of them all."

> Are the Word and the Spirit, who come from God, divine personalities that are really distinct from the Father, the Creator? This problem was quite arduous; the Christian sense concluded by setting it in the affirmative.

But soon the question of the relationship between the Father and the other divine Persons, especially that of the Word-Christ, was posed.

The Word is of God, and personally distinct from the Father: yet is he absolutely God? And if he is the "first-born of creation," as St. Paul said, would he not be merely the first of creatures? Arius said yes. Athanasius and the Council of Nicaea answered no. The Word had to be consubstantial with the Father.

(b) There remained the task of defining the relationship between the divinity of Jesus Christ and his humanity.

Apollinaris thought he found the solution to the problem by admitting that, with regard to humanity and in the humanity of Jesus, the Word took the place of the spiritual soul. The Church condemned him: Jesus had been perfect man. Therefore, concluded Nestorius, He was a human person indissolubly united by a moral bond to the divine person of the Word. Nestorius is condemned: one must not divide Christ who is one.

(c) "If Christ is one, then human nature is incorporated with divinity, says Eutyches, and the unity of nature is implicated in the unity of person." In this case

Christ would not be man if human nature did not subsist in Him along with divine nature, according to the Council of Calcedon. The fifth ecumenical council adds that [human nature] is substantially united to the Word and subsisting in the Word.

(d) "Finally one asks himself if the unity of person does not entail the unity of will. The sixth council maintains two wills and two sources of action, to accede to two natures."

"The Christological dogma," Loisy concludes, "was henceforth fixed, as much at least as it could be, departing from the traditional data and ancient philosophy."[61]

2. According to Newman the *terminus ad quem* of development is substantially the same as its *terminus a quo*, since it is the explication of the supernatural revelation granted to the Apostles. Dealing with "the history of the doctrinal definitions of the Church," Newman states that

The Development of Doctrine

"the creed of the Church has been one and the same from the beginning. It has been so deeply lodged in her bosom as to be held by individuals more or less implicitly, instead of being delivered from the first in those special statements, or what are called definitions." These definitions are "but the expressions of portions of the one dogma which has ever been received by the Church."[62]

Newman explains that the principle which governs the explication of revelation can be called "*metaphysical* developments." He means that they are "a mere analysis of the idea contemplated, and terminate in its exact and complete delineation." In theology "the mind may be employed in developing the solemn ideas, which it has hitherto held implicitly and without subjecting them to its reflecting and reasoning power."[63] Since the development is "the carrying out of the idea into its consequences," Newman concludes that "creeds and dogmas live in the one idea which they are designated to express and which alone is substantive.[64]

3. CAUSE OF DEVELOPMENT

1. Loisy lists two conditions for the change in Christian thought.

The first condition was the very duration of Christianity. While Jesus Christ envisaged an eschatological kingdom, and the world continued to exist, the Church had to change Jesus' conception of the Kingdom: "If the end of the world had arrived in the years that followed the publication of the Apocalypse, the ecclesiastical development would not have taken place, and the Church even would hardly have existed. But the world did not perish: the Church retained a reason for existence and retains it still."[65]

The second condition was the impulse of propagandism. Once again, Loisy wrote, "The development of Christian dogma was brought about by the state of mind and culture of the earliest converts, who were Gentiles."[66]

The cause of both the origin and the successive transformations of Christian thought was the Greek philosophy of transcendence. This philosophy played the role of cause and effect, so that Jesus Christ was transformed from simply a Messiah to the Son of God. On the basis of this philosophy, the first radical *transformation* occurred when Greek philosophy made the historical Jesus a transcendent divine being. Loisy wrote, "Beginning at a very early date, the Greek interpretation of the Christian doctrine of the

Messiah came into being." Thus, "the Christ, Son of God and Son of man, predestined savior, became the Word made flesh, the Revealer of God to humanity."[67] The same philosophy is at the basis of the successive stages of Christological titles.[68] "It is evident," Loisy concludes, "that, with respect to this philosophy, the progressive definition of the dogma made complete sense.... Fundamentally, dogma defined only a metaphysical relation between Jesus and God, and it defined it especially according to the idea of the transcendent God."[69]

2. According to Newman the development of Christian doctrine is due to the very nature of revealed truth. "Time is necessary," he wrote," for the full comprehension and perfection of great ideas; and the highest and most wonderful truths, though communicated to the world *once for all by inspired teachers*, could not be comprehended all at once by the recipients."[70] In dealing with the cause of development he makes a remark which could appear to be a direct challenge to Loisy's conception. Newman says, "When developments in Christianity are spoken of, it is sometimes supposed that they are deductions and diversions made at random, according to accident or the caprice of individuals; whereas it is because they have been conducted all along on definite and continuous principles that the type of the Religion has remained from first to last unalterable."[71]

Newman states first that "for the convenience of arrangement [he] will consider the Incarnation the central truth of the Gospel, and the source whence we are to draw out its principles. This great doctrine is unequivocally announced in numerous passages of the New Testament, especially by St. John and St. Paul."[72] Then Newman points out two basic principles which govern development. The first one is an objective principle: "The principle of *dogma*, that is, supernatural truths irrevocably committed to human language, imperfect because it is human, but definitive and necessary because given from above."[73] The second principle is subjective: "The principle of *faith*, which is the correlative of dogma, being the absolute acceptance of the divine Word with an internal assent, in opposition to the informations if such, of sight and reason."[74]

At the beginning of his fifteenth Oxford sermon, where he deals with *The Theory of Developments in Religious Doctrines*, Newman gave a concise definition of the role played by faith in the development of Christian doctrine. He gives the example of Mary: "St. Mary is our pattern of Faith, both in the reception and in the

The Development of Doctrine

study of Divine Truth." He describes how Mary receives the divine truth: "She does not think it enough to accept, she dwells upon it; not enough to possess, she uses it; not enough to assent, she develops it; not enough to submit the Reason, she reasons upon it." Then Newman states the principle of faith which governs development by adding: "not indeed reasoning first, and believing afterwards, with Zacharias, yet first believing without reasoning, next from love and reverence, reasoning, after believing." In this way Mary "symbolizes to us, not only the faith of the unlearned, but of the doctors of the Church also, who have to investigate, and weigh, and define, as well as to profess the Gospel."[75]

4. THE NATURE OF DEVELOPMENT

Having explained the terms of development, as conceived by Loisy and by Newman, we must now evaluate the nature of the conceptions of development of the two scholars.

A. Loisy: Transformation

Loisy explains his conception of development in *L'Evangile et l'Eglise*, when he deals with Christian Dogma. After stating that the "Catholic Church does not even recognize the existence of this development [i.e., development from history to dogma], and condemned the very idea of it," he adds that the Church "never was conscious of it." The principle of Vincent de Lérins and Vatican Council I, "touching the development of dogma, applies in reality to the definitely intellectual and theological phase of its development," viz., Revelation. The principle does not apply "to the first budding and formation of beliefs, or at least includes in an abstract definition, much work for which this definition is no adequate expression." What Loisy adds is a clear reference to the historical data established by the historical method from which the development must take its beginning: "It is just the idea of development which is now needed to be developed [according to] a better knowledge of the past."[76]

Loisy formulates his thesis in these terms: "Christian thought at its commencement was Jewish, and could not be other than Jewish, although evangelical Christianity [i.e., Christianity according to the historical reconstruction of the Gospel] contained the *germ* of universal religion."[77] In *L'Evangile et l'Eglise* and in *Autour d' un petit livre*, where Loisy applies his theory of development, he uses again the terms "germ" and "seed" which are used also by Newman. After defining "the divinity of Christ as a dogma which grew in the Christian consciousness, but which was not expressly formulated in the Gospel," Loisy affirmed that this dogma "existed in germ only in the notion of the Messiah. . . . The essential elements of the notion of the Messiah were thus explained in a metaphysical doctrine."[78] But the term "germ," applied to the concept of Messiah, which is transformed into a metaphysical concept of divinity, is improper. The concept of Messiah not only does not contain the concept of a divine being, but is in conflict with it. A germ and a seed have immanent in themselves what they are destined to realize in their growth. A seed of corn can never produce a banana. The environment can favor or hinder its development, but not determine it in its nature.

We have already noted that Loisy terms the first radical change of the Jesus of history in the theory of St. Paul and St. John a *transformation*. This change could not be termed otherwise.[79] The Jesus of history, with his dream and illusion of the eschatological kingdom, has substantially nothing to do with the Jesus of faith of the Apostles and of the first Christians. Loisy admits that. In *Quelques lettres sur des questions actualles* Loisy could not be more explicit in this regard:

> If we take into account both Jesus' doctrine and the knowledge of his feelings, it is not only that we cannot establish as true, but also that we can establish as false, that Jesus Christ presented himself as the incarnation of a divine person, and that he was conscious of being God made man. The consciousness of Jesus manifests itself as a very pure human conscience, infinitely united to God, and sincerely persuaded of a providential mission, but humble before the Father, and, in his regard, having an attitude of prayer. Being said without paradox, no word, no impression, no act of the Christ of the Synoptics is fitting to a second person of the Holy Trinity.

"It is for this reason," Loisy concludes, "that the primitive tradition underwent such a great *deformation* in the fourth Gospel."[80]

The successive changes in the history of the Christological formulations are presented by Loisy as a real transformation of the initial datum. Dealing with Catholic worship, Loisy again conceives the change of Mosaic worship into Christian worship as a transformation. "While running the risk of corruption through the admixture of foreign elements," Loisy writes, "the Mosaic ritual realized successively the *transformation* (emphasis supplied) that its preservation and progress demanded."[81]

B: Newman: Vital Development

At the beginning of his *Essay on the Development of Christian Doctrine*, Newman defines the meaning of development as follows: "The word is commonly used, and is used here, in three senses indiscriminately, from defect of our language; on the one hand for the process of development, on the other for the result; and again either generally for a development, *true or not true*, (that is faithful or unfaithful to the idea from which it started,) or exclusively for a development deserving the name. A false or unfaithful development is more properly to be called a corruption."[82]

We have already noticed that Newman admits that the knowledge which the Apostles had of Jesus during his earthly life did not reach the point of recognizing him as Son of God. (Obviously Newman does not conceive, as did Loisy, a radical discontinuity between the knowledge the Apostles had of Jesus during his earthly life and the knowledge they received from the Holy Spirit after Jesus' death and resurrection.[83]). Therefore, Newman does not put the beginning of the development of doctrine in the Apostles' understanding of Jesus and his mission during Jesus' life. In this case we could not have a *true* and *real* development, but rather a transformation or corruption. "I call development," Newman writes, "being the germination and maturation of some truth or apparent truth on a large mental field. On the other hand this process will not be a development, unless the assemblage of aspects, which constitute its ultimate shape, really belongs to the idea from which they start. A republic, for instance, is not a development from a pure monarchy, though it may follow upon it."[84]

The starting point of an authentic development of Christian doctrine can be only the revelation of the Holy Spirit, because all successive dogmatic formulations are "implicitly" contained in this revelation.[85] Newman lists seven notes "to discriminate healthy development of an idea from its state of corruption and decay." They are the following: "There is no corruption if it retains one and the same type, the same principles, the same organization; if its beginnings anticipate its subsequent phases, and its later phenomena protect and subserve its earlier; if it has a power of assimilation and revival, and a vigorous action from the first to last."[86] He adds: "Such are seven out of various Notes, which may be assigned, of fidelity in the development of an idea. The point to be ascertained is the unity and identity of the idea with itself through all stages of its development from first to last."[87] The basic principle for recognizing the genuine development from corruption is the principle of "preservation of type." Using the analogy of physical growth, Newman states that "the adult animal has the same make as it had on its birth." Quoting Vincent of Lérins, he added: "Let the soul's religion imitate the law of the body, which, as years go on, develops indeed and opens out its due proportions, and yet remains identically what it was. Small are a baby's limbs, a youth's are larger, yet they are the same."[88]

C. Newman and Loisy Contrasted

It is astonishing that writers such as Wilfrid Ward could identify Loisy's conception of development with Newman's conception: "In a letter to von Hügel," Loisy wrote, "W. Ward praised *L'Évangile et l'Eglise* as showing a perfect knowledge of what Newman wanted and intended [with the Development of Doctrine]."[89] Although he recognizes Newman's influence, Loisy nevertheless explicitly affirms the different applications he made of the idea of development. Loisy "widened" [this is his expression] the idea of development by applying it not only to supernatural revelation, but also to history, while Newman limited himself to revelation.[90]

We find a first parallel between Loisy's and Newman's conception of development in an article published by Loisy in 1898 entitled "Christian Development according to Cardinal Newman."[91] Loisy shows clearly his personal conception of development. Loisy places continual emphasis on the "transformation" of dogma. Where Newman says: "Here below to live is to change, and to be perfect is to have changed often,"[92] Loisy writes, "Here below to live is to change, and that which has become perfect has done so only after many *transformations*."[93] Newman's term "change" has the meaning of a development of something which basically remains the same, while Loisy's term "transformation" implies a basic, essential mutation affecting the specific nature of the thing which is transformed.

Loisy remarks, "It is easy to understand that Christianity must have a development . . . because it was impossible, even for the most important points of belief, to adhere to the letter of Scripture without falling into a vain cult of formulas."[94] Newman's sentence is: "And, indeed, when we turn to the consideration of particular doctrines on which Scripture lays the greatest stress, we shall see that it is absolutely impossible for them to remain in the mere letter of Scripture, if they are to be more than mere words, and to convey a definite idea to the recipient."[95] Newman explains the meaning of his statement: "When it is declared that 'the Word became flesh,' three wide questions open upon us on the very announcement. What is meant by 'the Word', what by 'flesh', what by 'became'? The answers to these involve a process of investigation, and are developments."[96] Newman demands for his "development" only an explanation of what the words of Scripture mean. When he says that it is impossible to "remain in the *mere* [emphasis supplied] letter of Scripture", he implies that it is impossible to be satisfied merely with words alone without investigating the meaning they contain. Loisy, on the other hand, speaks of the impossibility of adhering "to the letter of Scripture." He omits Newman's qualification of "mere letter," and so he seems to imply that, even if we thoroughly understand the meaning contained in the "letter" of Scripture, it is still insufficient. The phrase which Loisy adds regarding a "vain cult of formulas" (which is not found in Newman's text) contains implicitly a rejection of dogmatic formulas.

With the publication of *L'Evangile et l'Eglise* and *Autour d'un petit livre* Loisy acknowledges the difference between Newman's theory of development and his own, and recognizes that he made a "broader application" of Newman's conception of development.[97] In Loisy's theory of development the cause of the radical and substantial change of the concept of Messiah, a simple human being, into a divine person is due to an exterior factor, viz., the Greek philosophy of transcendence. According to this principle, if Christianity, instead of going to Greece and Rome, had gone to India, the Kingdom of God and the person of Jesus Christ would have had a completely different change. Furthermore Loisy conceived the transformation through Greek philosophy as not even final because of the temporal nature of philosophy. Loisy supposes that transformation may undergo further transformation with the change of philosophy.

We can say that, since the starting point of the process of transformation is an image of Jesus which, as such, is completely foreign to and different from the image of Christ which was formulated by the Church, the extremes of development are completely heterogeneous, without any intrinsic and logical link. There is a true and substantial transformation. If we want to apply Newman's definition of development to Loisy's conception, we must say that Loisy's conception of development is *political* and must be termed a corruption rather then a development.

2. The starting point for Newman's theory of development is different from that of Loisy's. For Loisy the starting point is the rational knowledge of the Jesus of history; for Newman the starting point is supernatural revelation, granted to the Apostles, after Jesus' death. Newman explains this process of development by quoting his fifteenth Oxford University sermon:

> The mind which is habituated to the thought of God, of Christ, of the Holy Spirit, naturally turns with a devout curiosity to the contemplation of the object of its adoration, and begins to form statements concerning it, before it knows whither, or how far, it will be carried. One proposition necessarily leads to another, and a second to a third; then some limitation is required; and the combination of these opposites occasions some fresh evolutions from the original idea, which indeed can never be said to be entirely exhausted. This process is its development, and results in a series, or rather body, of dogmatic statements.[98]

For Loisy the principle of development is exterior to the essence of the object, while for Newman the principle belongs to the very essence and nature of the object. This principle is so vital and powerful that it can assimilate the culture. Newman calls it the "power of assimilation." In the physical world "whatever has life is characterized by growth, so that in no respect to grow is to cease to live." The growth consists in "taking into its own substance external material; and this absorption or assimilation is completed when the materials appropriated come to belong to it or enter into its unity." The same phenomenon occurs in Christian doctrine, according to Newman: "The stronger and more living is an idea, that is, the more powerful hold it exercises on the minds of men, the more able is it to dispense with safeguards, and trust to itself against the danger of corruption."[99]

While according to Loisy philosophy masters faith, according to Newman the reality of faith masters philosophy. In order to express its contents the faith changes the meaning of some philosophical terms (such as we see in the distinction between "person" and "individuated rational human nature," a distinction unknown in Greek philosophy, in order to define the union of the divine and human nature in the second person of the Holy Trinity). To express the revealed reality of divine love the faith creates new terms (for example, Agape).

For Newman faith is an internal principle, which expresses itself in an ever better and deeper way, rejecting by instinct whatever might destroy or diminish it. The reality which faith experiences is solely responsible for the theological formulation. "It is a rule of creation," Newman concludes, "that life passes on to its determination by a gradual, imperceptible course of change. . . . A true development, then, may be described as one which is conservative of the course of antecedent developments . . . it is an addition which illustrates, not obscures, corroborates, not corrects, the body of thought from which it proceeds; and this is its characteristic as contrasted with corruption."[100]

3

PHILOSOPHICAL AND THEOLOGICAL IMPLICATIONS OF DEVELOPMENT

After having explained Loisy and Newman's conceptions of development, we can now examine the philosophical and theological implications of the two conceptions of development, i.e., the meaning of Revelation and dogma, and the relationship between Revelation and dogmatic formulations.

1. REVELATION

A. Loisy: Human Intuition And Religious Experience

Loisy stripped revelation of its supernatural content when he claimed that the starting point of development was the historical Jesus (who is not God and who possessed characteristics incompatible with the possibility of his being divine) and that the transformation of his human personality into a divine being was a product of the Greek philosophy of transcendence. Everything is explained by a rational process. "According to the logic of reason," Loisy wrote, "if the idea of the Kingdom is not consistent with fact, then the Gospel as a divine revelation falls down to the ground, and Jesus is no more than a pious man who died as a victim of error rather than the servant of the truth that was in him."[101]

Consequently Loisy rejects as senseless the distinction between natural knowledge, or knowledge through reason, and supernatural knowledge, or knowledge through revelation.[102] He explains that "the beginning of revelation has been the perception, although rudimentary, which must exist between man, conscious of himself, and God who is present behind the phenomenological world." Loisy gives this definition of revelation: "Christian revelation, in its principle and in its starting point [is] the perception in Jesus' soul of the rapport which united Christ himself to God, and the perception of the rapport which binds all men to their heavenly Father. The perception of these rapports had a form of human knowledge, and it is only in this form that it could be communicated to mankind." In its "intellectual definition and verbal expression, revelation consists in ideas which were born in humanity. . . . In its native form it is a supernatural intuition and a religious experience."[103]

To the question of how we know God and the divinity of Jesus Christ Loisy rejects any intellectual proof of God's existence and appeals to the moral sense. "God is demonstrated neither by facts alone nor by reasoning alone," he writes, "but by the effort of the moral conscience, aided by knowledge and reasoning."[104] As to the divinity of Jesus (which has no objective significance) Loisy states: "The divinity of Christ is a religious and moral datum, whose certainty is obtained in the same way as that of God's existence."[105]

B. Newman: Supernatural Revelation

In the *Idea of a University*, Newman distinguishes between two orders of knowledge, natural and supernatural: "We may divide knowledge into natural and supernatural . . . two fields of knowledge in themselves . . . distinct from each other in idea." The source of natural knowledge is human reason, while the source of supernatural knowledge, whose object is the "Creator Himself in His fullness," is not "our natural faculties," but a "superadded and direct communication from Him." The very idea of Revelation "is that of a direct interference from above, for the introduction of truths otherwise unknown."[106] In the *Grammar of Assent*, after an analysis of natural religion, Newman gives this definition of revealed

The Development of Doctrine

religion: "'Revelatio revelata' is a definite message from God to man distinctly conveyed by His chosen instruments, and to be received as such a message; and therefore to be positively acknowledged, embraced, and maintained as true, on the ground of its being divine, not as true on intrinsic grounds, not as probably true, or partially true, but as absolutely certain knowledge, certain in a sense in which nothing else can be certain, because it comes from Him who neither can deceive nor be deceived."[107]

Newman sees the distinction between natural religion and revealed religion so clearly, and he judges it so necessary that he refuses any scientific proof of Christianity and formulates a principle, concerning conscience and Revelation, which will probably seem astonishing to many. For Newman conscience is the principle of natural religion, since it is the voice of the Lawgiver. Once God speaks to us directly through Revelation, His Word *replaces* the conscience. Here is the text of Newman:

> It must be borne in mind that, as the essence of all religion is authority and obedience, so the distinction between natural religion and revealed lies in this, that the one has a subjective authority, and the other an objective. Revelation consists in the manifestation of the Invisible Divine Power, or in the *substitution* of the voice of a Lawgiver for the voice of conscience. The supremacy of conscience is the essence of natural religion; the supremacy of Apostle, or Pope, or Church, or Bishop, is the essence of revealed.... Thus, what conscience is in the system of nature, such is the voice of Scripture, or of the Church, or of the Holy See, as we may determine it, in the system of Revelation.[108]

Consistent with his distinction between natural and revealed religion, Newman distinguishes between the way we know God and the way we know the divinity of Jesus Christ. Concerning the knowledge of God Newman is far from appealing to an irrational moral sense, as does Loisy. Newman argues from conscience whose imperative has an objective character of causality. Man realizes clearly that the imperative of conscience does not have its origin in him, but rather presupposes a Lawgiver.[109] Concerning the knowledge of Jesus' divinity, as presented by revelation, Newman, contrary to Loisy, denies that such knowledge can be obtained in the same way as the knowledge of God. Newman sees the source of the knowledge of

Jesus' divinity not in reason, not in historical science, but only in revelation received in faith. In this regard he makes a statement which could be directed to Loisy: "Knowledge of these revealed truths, is gained, *not by any research into facts*, but simply by appealing to the authoritative keepers of them."[110]

2. DOGMATIC FORMULATION

A: Loisy: Ideas Born In Humanity

Loisy had defined revelation as a natural religious intuition and as a religious experience which in its "intellectual definition consists in ideas which are born in humanity."[111] Consequently dogma is simply a relative expression of natural religious experience and does not have any intellectual value.

After having stated that the theology of St. Paul and that of St. John were "a great deformation" of the primitive tradition, Loisy adds: "One asks necessarily, after that, upon what does the dogma of the divinity of Jesus Christ rest and what is its meaning." His answer is: "The dogma of the divinity of Jesus Christ has ever been and is nothing else than a symbol, which is more or less perfect, destined to signify the rapport which unites the humanity personified in Jesus to God."[112]

In *L'Evangile et l'Eglise* Loisy writes: "The conceptions that the Church presents as revealed dogmas are not truths fallen from heaven, and preserved by religious tradition in the precise form in which they first appeared. The historian sees in them the interpretation of religious facts, acquired by a laborious effort of theological thought.... Traditional formulas are submitted to a constant work of interpretation wherein 'the letter that kills' is effectively controlled by 'the spirit that gives life.'"[113] In *Autour d'un petit livre*, after quoting the above-mentioned statement, Loisy asks: "Does this not deny that the dogma is true, that it is revealed, that it is immutable, that it is authorized by God in the teaching of the Church?"[114] In his answer he denies the supernatural objective meaning of dogma: "If one supposes that truth, in as much as it is accessible to human intelligence, is something absolute, that revelation has this character, and that dogma participates in it ... the assertions of the little book are more than rash, they are absurd and blasphemous. It is useless to tell you that they are in connection with another idea of truth, of revelation, of immutability, of authority; or rather they are in connection with the state of psychological and historical facts."[115]

B. Newman: Doctrines Contained In The Depositum of Revelation

To understand the meaning which Newman gives to Dogma we must appeal to the well-known distinction he makes between "real apprehension" and "notional apprehension."[116] To "real apprehension" corresponds "real assent" which is given to concrete reality; to "notional apprehension" corresponds "notional assent," which is given to an abstract concept. Of these two modes of apprehending propositions real assent is stronger, more vivid, than notional assent, because the experience of concrete facts is more effective than an abstract idea.[117] Applied to religion, Newman calls "real assent" the act of faith to the reality which is proposed by Sacred Scripture (Newman gives the example of the Holy Trinity, Father, Son and Holy Spirit). He calls "notional assent" the act of faith to the dogmatic propositions.[118]

In the fifteenth Oxford sermon Newman states the necessity of dogmas because of the condition of the human mind. "Creeds and dogmas live in the one idea which they are designated to express, and which alone is substantive; and are necessary only because the human mind cannot reflect upon that idea, except piecemeal, cannot use it in its oneness and entireness, nor without resolving it into a series of aspects and relations."[119] In the *Grammar of Assent* Newman shows the link which exists between Revelation and the authentic authoritative doctrines of the Church. The Catholic, who believes in the "*depositum* of Revelation," Newman writes, "believes in all the doctrines of the *depositum*. . . . It follows from this, that, granting that Canons of the Councils and the other ecclesiastical documents and confessions . . . are really involved in the *depositum* or revealed word, every Catholic, in accepting the *depositum*, does *implicite* accept those dogmatic decisions." Newman adds that "these various propositions are virtually contained in the revealed word," because of the authority of the Church: "To her is committed the care and the interpretation of the revelation. The word of the Church is the word of revelation."[120]

To show that dogma contains the *depositum* of faith, Newman adds another argument. The dogma is "the disavowal of error" and as such shows clearly its link to the *depositum*: "If a proposition is true, its contradictory is false. If then a man believes that Christ is God, he believes also, and that necessarily, that to say He is not God is false, and that those who so say are in error."[121]

3. VALUE AND RELATIVITY OF DOGMA

Concerning the relationship between Revelation and dogma we find in Loisy and in Newman divergent conceptions which are due to different conceptions of the value and relativity of dogma.

A. Loisy

Since for Loisy the dogmatic formula is a purely philosophical concept without any real link with the original concept about Jesus Christ, it follows that dogma lacks any objective intellectual value. "As doctrinal theory or dogmatic theology," Loisy writes, [the dogma is] an interpretation of faith by means of philosophy.... The ecclesiastical formula is not absolutely true, since it does not define the full reality of the object it represents: it is no less the *symbol of an absolute truth* [emphasis supplied]."[122] In the dogmatic formula Loisy sees only a moral value for religious education: "Dogmas are formulas of the traditional teaching, which have as their purpose to contribute to that work of religious and moral education which is the mission of the Church."[123]

Because "dogma defined only a metaphysical relation between Jesus and God, and it defined it according to the idea of the transcendent God,"[124] dogma will follow the fate of philosophy: "These formulas are not immutable; they are perfectible. No dogma is a pure product of the imagination. All have responded to a need of the Christian conscience, and consequently contain a moral sense which we must extract when the symbol itself has become outmoded [in French literally: *null and void*]."[125] Consequently Loisy envisages a further change or transformation of Christian dogma according to modern philosophy and modern science. In the light of this premise Loisy anticipates several transformations of dogma. Thus, he envisions

(1) The abandonment of the dogma of an intermediary between God and the world and between God and man. Loisy writes, "The evolution of modern philosophy tends more and more towards the idea of the immanent God, who has no need of an intermediary to act in the world and in man. Does the actual knowledge of the universe not suggest a criticism of the idea of creation? Does the

The Development of Doctrine

knowledge of the universe not suggest a criticism of the idea of creation? Does the knowledge of history not suggest a criticism of the idea of revelation? Does the knowledge of moral man not suggest a criticism of the idea of redemption?"[126]

(2) Furthermore, Loisy anticipates the abandonment of the idea of the divinity of Jesus Christ which was created by Greek philosophy. Loisy says, "Did the historical Christ bear witness that he was a person in the divine sense?.... Is it not true that the theological notion of the person is metaphysical and abstract, while in contemporary philosophy this notion has become real and psychological? Does that which was said according to the definition of ancient philosophy not need to be explained with respect to today's philosophy?"[127]

Loisy, consistent with his principle that philosophy is the cause of development, concludes with this statement: "If the problem presents itself now once again, it is much less because history is better understood than in consequence of the integral renewal which occurred and which continues in modern philosophy."[128]

B. Newman

In *Apologia pro Vita Sua*, Newman writes: "From the age of fifteen, dogma has been the fundamental principle of my religion: I know no other religion; I cannot enter into the idea of any other sort of religion. Religion as mere sentiment is to me a dream and mockery."[129] For this reason, during all his life he was an irreconcilable opponent of "liberalism," i.e., rationalism, "the anti-dogmatic principle and its developments."[130] Although "real apprehension has the precedence, as being the scope and the test of the notional," Newman states that in both cases the assent is unconditional and absolute, and that the notional has "its own excellence."[131] In the fifteenth Oxford sermon against the rationalistic prejudice that "there is no necessary or proper connection between inward religious belief and scientific exposition," Newman states clearly that "there is a general, natural and ordinary correspondence between the dogma and the inward idea."[132] In the *Grammar of Assent* Newman vindicates and exalts the exercise of the intellect upon the *credenda* of revelation.[133] Newman states that the dogmatic conclusions "are true, if rightly deduced, because they are deduced from what is true; and therefore in one sense they are a portion of the *depositum* of faith or *credenda*."[134]

In analyzing the distinction between "real assent" and "notional assent" and their respective values and functions, Newman deals with the two aspects of dogma which we have found in Loisy, viz. the value and the relativity of dogma. Newman says, "A dogma is a proposition; it stands for a notion or for a thing; and to believe it is to give the assent of the mind to it, as it stands for the one or for the other. To give a real assent to it is an act of religion; to give a notional, is a theological act. It is discerned, rested in, and appropriated as a reality, by the religious imagination; it is held as a truth, by the theological intellect."[135]

(1) Although Newman gives priority to real assent, he recognizes the necessity of notional assent to dogma. It is a "common mistake," Newman notices, "of supposing that there is a contrariety and antagonism between a dogmatic creed and vital religion. People resist the propositions that there is God, that there is a Trinity, but persist in believing in a God, in a Saviour, in a Sanctifier; and they object that such propositions are but a formal and human medium destroying all true reception of the Gospel, and making religion a matter of words or of logic, instead of its having its seat in the heart." To this objection Newman observes that "the propositions may and must be used, and can easily be used, as the expression of facts, not notions, and they are necessary to the mind in the same way that language is ever necessary for denoting facts, both for ourselves as individuals, and for our intercourse with others." Here Newman lists two reasons for the necessity of dogma in view of "real assent:"

(1) "[The propositions] are useful in their dogmatic aspect as ascertaining and making clear for us the truths on which the religious imagination has to rest. Knowledge must ever precede the exercise of the affections. We feel gratitude and love, we feel indignation and dislike, when we have the informations actually put before us which are to kindle those several emotions. We love our parents, as our parents, when we know them to be our parents; we must know concerning God, before we can feel love, fear, hope, or trust towards Him."

(2) "Devotion must have its objects; those objects, as being supernatural, when not represented to our senses by material symbols, must be set before the mind in propositions. The formula, which embodies a dogma for the theologian, readily suggests an object for the worshipper. It seems a truism to say, yet it is all that I have been saying, that in religion the imagination and affections should always be under control of reason. Theology may stand as a substantive

The Development of Doctrine

science, though it be without the life of religion; but religion cannot maintain its ground at all without theology. Sentiment, whether imaginative or emotional, falls back upon the intellect for its stay, when sense cannot be called into exercise; and it is in this way that devotion falls back upon dogma."[136]

(2) Newman is equally explicit in affirming a kind of relativity of dogma. Dogma is abstract and is partial.

As to dogma being abstract, Newman, after stating that dogmatic definitions are true because they are portions of the *depositum* of faith or *credenda*, adds: "They have, I readily grant, the characteristic disadvantage of being abstract and notional statements." Thus if we compare dogma with real religious assent, we see that "Devotion is excited doubtless by the plain, categorical truths of revelation, such as the articles of the Creed; on these it depends; with these it is satisfied. It accepts them one by one; it is careless about intellectual consistency; it draws from each of them the spiritual nourishment which it was intended to supply."[137]

As to dogma being a partial aspect of revealed truth Newman states in the fifteenth Oxford sermon, "Particular propositions which are used to express portions of the great idea vouchsafed to us, can never really be confused with the idea itself, which all such propositions taken together can but reach, and cannot exceed. As definitions are not intended to go beyond their subject, but to be adequate to it, so the dogmatic statements of the Divine Nature used in our confessions, however multiplied, cannot say more than is implied in the original idea, considered in its completeness, without the risk of heresy."[138]

NOTES

1. In the rank of modernists we find in England George Tyrrell, whom A. Houtin defines as a disciple of Newman and an "apologist of sentiment." Houtin writes, "Nobody has assimilated so deeply the doctrine or, it is better to say, the spirit of the doctrine of Newman" (A. Houtin, *Histoire du modernism catholique*, Paris, 1913, p. 53). George Tyrrell, after the issuing of the encyclical "Pascendi," did not hesitate to write that the pontifical document was directed against the *Development of Christian Doctrine* and the *Grammar of Assent*. The Italian E. Buonaiuti, by quoting Tyrrell's statement, adds that "England was the only country where modernism could count on a true and characteristic precursor [i.e., Newman] (E. Buonaiuti, *Le modernisme catholique* [Paris: Rieder, 1927], pp. 129-130). In France we find the Jesuit Henri Bremond, who wrote that "in putting conscience, Christian experience, and personal realization of the Divine at the base of the whole religious structure, [Newman] collaborates, without knowing it, in the work of Schleiermacher and his disciples." The French Jesuit thinks that "the *History of Arians* [of Newman] seems to be inspired by Schleiermacher" (H. Bremond, *The Mystery of Newman* [London: William and Norgate], 1907, pp. 332, 334 N.2). In an article, "Newmanism," E. Michaud wrote that Newman stripped dogma of its divine character and conceived it as "changing human opinion," and that "Newmanism" is nothing else than a "form of sentimentalism" (*Revue internationale de theologie*, 13 [1905], pp. 641, 646).

   Among the scholastics we can mention such authoritative names as Léonce de Grand-maison, S.J., and Jules Lebreton, S.J. The first stated that Newman saw in dogmatic statements "only symbols of unknowable truths" (*Etudes*, 1906, Vol. 109, pp. 721-750). The Jesuit probably did not realize that he used the same term (symbol of unknowable truths) which Loisy used to synthesize his religious agnosticism concerning dogma. Father Lebreton saw in Newman's work a certain form of nominalism (*Revue pratique d'apologetique*, 1907, p. 667).

The person who knew modernism and Newman's theory of development perfectly is the only one who would have expressed his reservations about the evaluation given to Newman's theory by modernists and scholastics: Alfred Loisy. He honestly acknowledged the different use he made of Newman's theory of development (see p.28).

2. Only the first book has been translated into English under the title *The Gospel and the Church* (New York: Scribners, 1904). Our quotations are taken from the original *L'Evangile et l'Eglise*, edition 1902.
3. *Parochial and Plain Sermons*, III, pp. 102-113 (Hereafter *PPS*).
4. *An Essay in Aid of a Grammar of Assent* (London: Longmans, 1913), pp. 351-352 (Hereafter *GA*).
5. A. Loisy, *Autour d'un petit livre* (Paris: Picard, 1903) pp. 9-10 (Hereafter *APL*).
6. *APL*, pp. 10, 130.
7. *The Idea of a University* (London: Longmans, 1931), p. 222 (Hereafter *IU*). In this regard Newman wrote on pp. 432-433: "Its [i.e., physics'] object is to resolve the complexity of phenomena into simple elements, principles; but when it has reached those first elements, principles and laws, its mission is at an end.... With matter it began, with matter it will end; it will never trespass into the province of mind.... The physicist, as such, will never ask himself by what influence, external to the universe, the universe is sustained; simply because he *is* a physicist.... If indeed he be a religious man, he will of course have a very definite view of the subject; but that view of his is private, not professional,—the view, not of a physicist, but of a religious man; and this not because physical science says any thing different, but simply because it says nothing at all on the subject, nor can it do so by the very undertaking with which it set out."
8. In a page of the *Apologia* (Hereafter *A*), which J. Walgrave (*Newman the Theologian* [New York: Sheed and Ward], 1960, p. 23) defines as "one of the finest pieces in the literature of the world," Newman writes: "Starting then with the being of a God ... I look out of myself into the world of men, and there I see a sight which fills me with

unspeakable distress. The world seems simply to give the lie to that great truth, of which my whole being is full. . . . Were it not for this voice speaking so clearly in my conscience and my heart, I should be an atheist, or a pantheist, or a polytheist when I looked into the world." After a description of human events Newman concludes: "What shall I say to this heart-piercing, reason-bewildering fact? I can only answer, that either there is no Creator, or this living society is in a true sense discarded from His presence." *Apologia*, p. 241-242.

9. *GA*, p. 104 f., and *Sermons Preached on Various Occasions*, p. 74.

10. *IU*, p. 446.

11. In a letter to George J. Milvart Newman reproaches theologians who intrude into questions of history: "Those who would not allow Galileo to reason 300 years ago, will not allow any one else now. The past is no lesson for them for the present and for the future: and their notion of stability in faith is ever to be repeating errors and then repeating retractions of them." Charles S. Dessain, *The Letters and Diaries of John Henry Newman* (London: Nelson), XXVIII, pp. 71-72 (Hereafter *LD*).

12. It must be recognized that Newman uses imperfect language when he speaks of "errors" contained in the Bible. Leo XIII in his encyclical "Providentissimus Deus" (November 18, 1893) rejected the opinion that the Bible contains "errors." Newman does not deny the divine inspiration of the Bible and consequently its inerrancy. His statement must be understood as meaning that in the Bible we find some historical facts which are not consistent with history (and this is not denying the divine authorship of the Bible, because the truth of Sacred Scripture is understood in another sense, as is clearly stated in the Constitution *Dei Verbum*, No. 11, of Vatican Council II).

13. *LD*, XXI, p. 482. In a memorandum Newman wrote about the necessity of conclusions generally received among Biblical and historical critics being fully and candidly discussed among Catholic theologians and men of science. Father Neville relates a statement of Newman in the highly improbable but not absolutely impossible event of becoming a Pope. "In a matter-of-fact manner, but with

grave seriousness," Newman stated that he would "appoint and organize commissions on various subjects," especially on "Biblical Criticism and the history of the Early Church;" and the commission would have to make a full and candid report to be dealt with by Newman's successor as he should think fit.

14. *LD*, XXVI, p. 66.
15. In 1883-1884 Newman wrote two essays about the inspiration of the Bible. The first was published in the *Nineteenth Century*, February, 1884; the second was written in reply to criticism of the first and was circulated privately by Newman. They are reprinted in *Stray Essays*. They do not show what Biblical criticism Newman had read, but they do show that, while he firmly adhered to the doctrine of the inspiration of Scripture, his adherence was combined with an acceptance of some critical conclusions. Thus he believed that Moses wrote the Pentateuch but used "foreign documents," that Daniel may not have written all the books attributed to him, that David may not have written all the Psalms, that there may have been two Isaiahs, and that there may be extraneous material in the received text of Mark and John. See *Stray Essays*, p. 23f.

After the publication of the *Origin of the Species* and *Essays and Reviews* Newman had no difficulty in accepting scientific and historical evidence against the apparent testimony of Sacred Scripture.

16. *PPS*, IV, pp. 254-256.
17. A. Loisy, *Choses passées* (Paris: Nourry, 1913), p. 248. (Hereafter CP).
18. A. Loisy, *Quelques lettres sur des questions actuelles* (Ceffonds: Auteur, 1908), p. 114.
19. R. Marlé, *Au coeur de la crise moderniste* (Paris: Aubier, 1960), p. 117.
20. Cf. *GA*, p. 364.
21. See *DCD*, p. 111 and *GA*, p. 364.
22. *Historical Sketches*, II, p. 342: "It is not honest to distort history for the sake of some gratuitous theory."
23. *GA*, p. 364.
24. The same consideration can be applied to the use of a computer.

25. *Fifteen Sermons Preached before the University of Oxford* (London: Longmans, 1909), pp. 7-8, (Hereafter *OUS*).
26. *OUS*, pp. 7-9.
27. *GA*, p. 410.
28. The theology dominant in Newman's time in the Anglican camp was that of William Paley (d. 1805). In his book, *The Evidence of Christianity*, Paley tried to demonstrate the truth of Faith by employing the method of syllogism. The basis of the syllogism was the miracles recorded in Sacred Scripture. The divine origin of the teaching of Jesus Christ and of the Church was proved by the miracles contained in the Gospel. The miracles were the proof that God authenticated the teaching of Jesus Christ and the foundation of the Church by Him.

    Not very different was the method of Catholic apologetics of that time. Based upon the same presupposition, Catholic theologians brought that method to the point of formulating a so-called "scientific faith." This kind of apologetics was first proposed by G. B. Franzelin, S.J., and sustained by Louis Billot, S.J., and Sebastian Tromp, S.J. Its formulation was as follows: Jesus performed miracles, which can be demonstrated historically. Miracles come from God and are signs on God's part that He sanctions the doctrine of Jesus Christ. Jesus declared Himself the divine legate and founded the Church. Therefore, it is proved historically that His doctrine and the Church, with its dogma and sacraments, have divine origin. See S. Tromp, *De revelatione christiana* (Rome: PUG, 1950), pp. 142-143.
29. *GA*, p. 425. Here we find the reason for Newman's motto in his Cardinalate Coat of Arms: "Cor ad Cor loquitur."
30. *DCD*, p. 336. It followed that this kind of theology denied the legitimacy and autonomy of science and particularly the historical method which dealt with Scripture. Father Giovanni Perrone, the most renowned theologian of Newman's time, did not think that Catholic exegetes had to trouble themselves much about the historical method, except insofar as it could defend dogma: "Nor do the hermeneutics and exegesis of Catholic Scripture scholars have any other purpose. The chief aim must be especially

to defend and maintain the interpretations of the Church against the impious novelties and attacks of heretics and unbelievers." (G. Perrone, *De locis theologicis* [Milan: 1857], p. 100). Hence theologians were accustomed to apply to science the moral qualification of "good" and "bad," insofar as science did or did not support their theological opinions. But, in reality the only qualification which is proper to every science is to be true or false.

31. *Parochial and Plain Sermons* (London: Longmans, 1891), pp. 108-109.
32. Writing to Bishop Wiseman from Rome on February 14, 1847, Newman indicated the suspicion he found among Roman theologians toward his thinking. "There is no disguising the fact that the only prominent theological professor here (Passaglia of the Coll[egio] Rom[ano]) is opposed to my book on Development. . . . Dr Grant has been speaking against my Essay, said it was my hobby, that I had set my mind upon it, and that though not at present dogmatically faulty, yet its principles would be condemned by the Church, if attention were turned to the subject." *LD*, XII, p. 42.

In Newman's journal we find this comment: "As to the great controversies of the day, about the divinity of Christianity &c, they think I am passé—at least this, (perhaps rather) that I have taken a wrong line in respect to them. At least I think the Jesuits do. They would think my line too free and sceptical, that I made too many admissions &c. On the contrary I *cannot* at all go along with them—and, since they have such enormous influence just now, and are so intolerant in their views, this is pretty much the same as saying that I have not taken, and do not take, what would popularly be called the Catholic line." Henry Tristan (Ed.), *John Henry Newman Autobiographical Writings* (New York: Sheed and Ward, 1957), p. 270.

33. *Revue du clergé français*, 41 (1905), p. 480.
34. *Études* (1906), Vol.109, 721-750; (1907), Vol.110, 39-69. At a later date in his book *Le dogme chretien* [Paris, 1928] Grandmaison omitted this judgment. H. Bremond ironically commented: "The hesitations, the fumblings, if I may be allowed the word, in the two admirable articles by

L. de Grandmaison have something pathetic about them. Like Balaam, he came to curse and yet he seems to murmur between the lines, 'How shall I curse him whom the Lord hath not cursed?'." *Revue pratique d'apologetique*, 3 (1907), p.666 note.
35. J. Lebreton, "Le primat de la conscience d'apres Newman", in *Revue pratique d'apologetique*, 3 (1907), p. 667.
36. "Newmanism" in *Revue internationale de théologie*, 13 (1905), pp. 641, 646.
37. In the Bible itself Newman found "a prophetic Revelation" in the form "of a process of development." In fact "the earlier prophecies are pregnant texts out of which the succeeding announcements grow; they are types. It is not that first one truth is told, then another; but the whole truth or large portions of it are told at once, yet only in their rudiments, or in miniature, and they are expanded and finished in their parts, as the course of revelation proceeds." The truth is that "the whole Bible, not its prophetical portions only, is written on the principle of development. As the Revelation proceeds, it is ever new, yet ever old." *DCD*, p. 64, 65.
38. *A*, pp. 197, 198.
39. See *GA*, p. 498; *Difficulties of Anglicans*, I, pp. 394-396. In his first book, *History of Arians*, Newman had been struck by the fact that in the first centuries of Christian history some Fathers and great ecclesiastical writers had spoken of the Son and His relation to the Father in a sense that comes near to subordinationism. It seemed clear, then, that the doctrine of Trinity as defined by the Councils of Nicea and Constantinople was not distinctly understood and professed in pre-Nicene times and that the most august truths of Christian faith had been shaped in the mind of the Church by a gradual process of development. See Jan Hendrick Walgrave, *Unfolding Revelation* (Westminster: Hutchinson, 1972), p. 198.
40. A. Loisy, *Choses passées* (Paris: Nourry, 1913), p. 164. There is an English translation with the title *My Duel with the Vatican* (New York: Greenwood, 1968).

In his *Mémoires* Loisy recorded that he read "Newman with enthusiasm," and he showed a great admiration for the man

and his doctrine: "He must be," Loisy wrote, "the most open theologian in the Holy Church since Origen." *Mémoires pour servir a l'histoire religieuse de notre temps*, I, pp. 421, 426. See also pp. 468-469, where Loisy gives a positive judgment of the theological genius of Newman.
41. *Mémoires*, II, pp. 560-561.
42. *EE*, p.vii.
43. *Mémoires*, I, p. 451.
44. *EE*, pp. 1, 36-37.
45. *EE*, p. 19.
46. *EE*, p. 39.
47. "Could it be said that the Father, who alone knows the Son, as the Son alone knows the Father, had also received a revelation from the Son of which he was to be interpreter, and was only the Father through his knowledge of the Son? Is there, then, a religion of the Son that the Father must teach, as the Son teaches that of the Father? Obviously the text indicates a transcendental relationship, whence springs the lofty dignity of Christ, and not a psychological reality, which in regard to God is clearly impossible. Father and Son are here simply religious terms, but have already become metaphysical theological expressions." *EE*, p. 44.
48. *EE*, p. 52.
49. *EE*, p. 102.
50. A. Loisy, *Les Évangiles synoptiques* (Ceffond: 1907), Vol. I, p. 252.
51. *Difficulties of Anglicans*, I, p.327.
52. "When our Lord was leaving His Apostles and they were sorrowful, He consoled them by the promise of another Guide and Teacher, on whom they might rely instead of Him. . . . The special way in which God the Holy Ghost gave glory to God the Son, seems to have been His revealing Him as the Only-begotten Son of the Father, who had appeared as the Son of man. . . . It was not till after His resurrection and especially after His ascension, when the Holy Ghost descended that the Apostles understood who had been with them." *PPS*, IV, pp. 251-256.
53. Cf. *PPS*, IV, p. 254 f.
54. A. Loisy, *Études evangeliques* (Paris: Picard, 1902), p. xiii.
55. *EE*, p. 111.

56. *EE*, pp. 139, 140.
57. See *EE*, p. 134: "The transformation was effected in spite of the traditional and conservative tendency inherent in every religion."
58. *EE*, pp. 136-137.
59. *EE*, p. 134.
60. *EE*, pp. 142-144.
61. *APL*, pp. 126-128.
62. *Difficulties of Anglicans*, I, p. 394.
63. *DCD*, p. 52.
64. *DCD*, p. 53.
65. *EE*, p. 117.
66. *EE*, p. 138.
67. *EE*, pp. 134, 139.
68. *APL*, p. 152.
69. *APL*, pp. 128, 152.
70. *DCD*, pp. 29-30.
71. *DCD*, pp. 323-324.
72. *DCD*, p. 324. Of St. John, Newman quotes this sentence: "The Word was made Flesh and dwelt among us, full of grace and truth." Of St. Paul, this one: "I live by the faith of the Son of God, who loved me and gave Himself for me."
73. *DCD*, p. 325.
74. *Ibid.*
75. *OUS*, p. 313.
76. *EE*, pp. 161-162.
77. *EE*, p. 134.
78. *APL*, p. 117, 147.
79. *EE*, p. 134.
80. A. Loisy, *Quelques lettres sur des questions actuelles* (Ceffonds: Autheur, 1908), pp. 148-149.
81. *EE*, p. 185.
82. *DCD*, p. 41.
83. See *PPS*, pp. 153-266.
84. *DCD*, p. 38.
85. See *DCD*, p. 52.
86. *DCD*, p. 171. In pp. 171-206 Newman explains in detail the seven Notes and in pp. 207-445 Newman makes the applications of the seven notes to the history of the first centuries of Christianity.

87. *DCD*, pp. 205-206.
88. *DCD*, pp. 171-172.
89. *Mémoires*, II, p. 173.
90. *Mémoires*, I, p. 451.
91. *Revue du clergé français*, 17 (1898), pp. 5-20.
92. *DCD*, p. 40.
93. *Art. Cit.*, p. 6.
94. *Ibid.*, p. 8.
95. *DCD*, p. 59.
96. *Ibid.*
97. "In [*L'Evangile et l'Eglise* and *Autour d'un petit livre*] history occupies a very large place. . . . As does the 'theory' of Christian development, of which I am not the inventor, although I made a *broader* application [emphasis supplied] of it than the Catholic authors who exploited it before." A. Loisy, *Quelques lettres* (Paris: Auteur, 1908), p. 144.
98. *DCD*, p. 52.
99. *DCD*, pp. 185, 188.
100. *DCD*, pp. 185, 188.
101. *APL*, p. 128.
102. See *APL*, p. 194.
103. *APL*, pp. 196, 198, 200.
104. *APL*, p. 215.
105. *APL*, p. 215.
106. *IU*, pp. 430, 445.
107. *GA*, p. 387.
108. *DCD*, p. 86.
109. See Adrian J. Boekraad, *The Argument from Conscience to the Existence of God* (Louvain: Nauwelaerts, 1961), p. 62 f.
110. *IU*, p. 446.
111. *APL*, p. 198.
112. A. Loisy, *Quelques lettres sur des questions actuelles* (Ceffonds: Auteur, 1908), p. 149.
113. *EE*, pp. 158-159.
114. *APL*, p. 189.
115. *APL*, p. 190.
116. Newman defines this distinction as follows: "There are propositions, in which one or both of the terms are common nouns, as standing for what is abstract, general, and non-existing, such as 'Man is an animal, some men are

learned . . .' These I shall call notional propositions, and the apprehension with which we infer or assent to them, notional. And there are other propositions, which are composed of singular nouns, and of which the terms stand for things external to us, unit and individual, as 'Philip was the father of Alexander,' 'the earth goes around the sun,' 'the Apostles first preached to the Jews;' and these I shall call real propositions, and their apprehension real." *GA*, pp. 9-10.

117. *GA*, p. 11.
118. Newman explains the relationship between "real assent" and "notional assent" with a fine image: "Break a ray of light into its constituent colours, each is beautiful, each may be enjoyed; attempt to unite them, and perhaps you produce only a dirty white. The pure and indivisible Light is seen only by the blessed inhabitants of heaven; here we have but such faint reflections of it as its diffraction supplies; but they are sufficient for faith and devotion. Attempt to combine them into one, and you gain nothing but mystery, which you can describe as a notion, but cannot depict as an imagination." *GA*, p. 132.
119. *OUS*, pp. 331-332.
120. *GA*, pp. 152-153.
121. *GA*, p. 148.
122. *APL*, pp. 200-201, 206.
123. A. Loisy, *Quelques lettres sur des questions actuelles et sur des evenements recents* (Ceffond: Auteur, 1908), p. 78. In *Choses passées*, after stating that he could not "accept literally a single article of the creed, unless it were that Jesus was 'crucified under Pontius Pilate'," Loisy describes the moral and social influence of the Catholic Church: "Yet religion appeared to me more and more in the light of a tremendous force that has dominated, and still was dominant in, the whole of human history. All its manifestations had had their limitations, their faults, and their abuses; still they represented practically the summed-up moral endeavor of the human race. The Christian religion, a continuation of that of Israel, was distinguished among all others by the loftiness of its ideal." (*Choses passées* [Paris: Nourry], 1913, p. 165.)
124. *APL*, p. 152.

125. A. Loisy, *Quelques lettres sur des questions actuelles et sur des evenements recents* (Ceffond: Autheur, 1908), p. 78.
126. *APL*, pp. 153-154.
127. *APL*, p. 152.
128. *APL*, pp. 128-129.
129. *A*, p. 49.
130. *A*, p. 48.
131. *GA*, p. 34.
132. *OUS*, pp. 319, 328.
133. *GA*, p. 147. This page is the best apology of Newman against the accusation of his anti-intellectualism brought by the scholastics. Newman explains the "natural, excellent, and necessary" exercise of the intellect as follows: "It is natural, because the intellect is one of our highest faculties; excellent, because it is our duty to use our faculties to the full; necessary because unless we apply our intellect to revealed truth rightly, others will exercise their minds upon it wrongly. Accordingly, the Catholic intellect makes a survey and a catalogue of the doctrines contained in the *depositum* of revelation, as committed to the Church's keeping; it locates, adjusts, defines them each, and brings them together into a whole. Moreover, it takes particular aspects or portions of them; it analyzes them, whether into first principles really such, or into hypotheses of an illustrative character. It forms generalizations, and gives names to them."
134. *Ibid.*
135. *GA*, p. 98.
136. *GA*, pp. 120-121.
137. *GA*, pp. 146-147.
138. *OUS*, p. 331.

ILLATIVE SENSE AND TACIT KNOWLEDGE:
A Comparison of the Epistemologies
of
John Henry Newman and Michael Polanyi

Martin X. Moleski, S.J.

The purpose of this essay is to show how two very different thinkers came to surprisingly similar conclusions about the nature of knowing. The claim made here is that Newman recognized the reality that Polanyi calls "tacit knowledge," while Polanyi recognized the reality that Newman calls "illative sense." Where Newman treated the tacit dimension as a matter of fact, Polanyi attempted to develop a theory to account for this fact.[1] What one man noted in passing, the other stopped to explore at length. Newman focused on the *capacity* of the mind to regulate itself by means of the illative sense; Polanyi concentrated on the *product* of this potency in the accumulation of tacit knowledge.

Illative Sense

Newman introduced the term, "illative sense," in the last three chapters of *An Essay in Aid of a Grammar of Assent*,[2] as a "grand word for a common thing."[3] This "grand word" refers to the theme of informal reasoning, to which Newman returned repeatedly over three decades of reflection.[4] In his 1840 sermon, "Implicit and Explicit Reason," Newman anticipated many of the points developed at greater length in the *Grammar*:

> The mind ranges to and fro, and spreads out, and advances forward with a quickness which has become a proverb, and a subtlety and versatility which baffle investigation. It passes on from point to point, gaining one by some indication; another on a probability; then availing itself of an association; then falling back on some received law; next seizing on testimony; then committing itself to some popular impression, or some inward instinct, or some obscure memory; and thus it makes progress not unlike a clamberer on a steep cliff, who, by quick eye, prompt hand, and firm foot, ascends how he knows not himself, by personal endowments and by practice, rather than by rule, leaving no track behind him, and unable to teach another. It is not too much to say that the stepping by which great geniuses scale the mountains of truth is as unsafe and precarious to men in general, as the ascent of a skillful mountaineer up a literal crag. It is a way which they alone can take; and its justification lies in their success. And such mainly is the way in which all men, gifted or not gifted, commonly reason,—not by rule, but by an inward faculty.[5]

The "inward faculty" which operates without rules and which is incapable of being fully formalized or articulated is, in the *Grammar*, called the "illative sense." It is the guardian of the mind's operations, determining "by personal endowments and by practice" when and how to bring the mind to make the act of assent that is the foundation of all human certitude:

> It is the mind that reasons, and that controls its own reasonings, not any technical apparatus of words and propositions. This power of judging and concluding, when in its perfection, I call the Illative Sense . . . [6]

The ninth chapter of the *Grammar* is entirely devoted to the illative sense. It is the keystone that completes Newman's epistemic investigations. In the tenth and concluding chapter, Newman uses the epistemology he has developed as a vehicle for theological reflection on natural and revealed religion.

Although the title of the *Grammar* may seem to promise that Newman will provide rules for the formation of correct assent, just as an English grammar provides rules for correct speech, the work itself is really written in opposition to efforts to formalize the conditions of belief. Where British empiricists were inclined to hold that 1) one must not believe what one does not understand and 2) one must not believe what cannot be proven, Newman took the opposite tack:

> ... Edward Caswall, a priest of the Birmingham Orator, wrote in his copy of the *Grammar*, after discussing it with Newman in 1877: "Object of the book twofold. In the first part shows that you can believe what you cannot understand. In the second part that you can believe what you cannot absolutely prove."[7]

It is the illative sense, operating informally, which licenses assent to what we cannot understand and to what we cannot prove. In the last analysis, Newman's *Grammar of Assent* declares that there are no rules adequate to determine the conditions of legitimate assent; it is only our own personal judgment that determines whom and what to trust.

It would be a rhetorical error—perhaps even a logical impossibility—to attempt a formal proof that the illative sense is the center of informal reasoning. Newman explores three certitudes that resist analysis: that Britain is an island, that the monks of the early Middle Ages did not compose the classics, and that we shall die.[8] Other examples and illustrations will be given in the discussion below. In place of formal proof, Newman offers an invitation to the reader to become personally aware of the peculiar inner guide that watches over all of our intellectual activity.

Tacit Knowledge

Newman died on August 11, 1890, in Edgbaston, England. Polanyi was born on March 11, 1891, in Budapest, Hungary, to a Jewish family that was "talented and intellectual."[9] After completing a degree in medicine, he found himself attracted to Christianity: "For a time particularly from 1915 to 1920 I was a completely converted Christian on the lines of Tolstoy's confession of faith."[10] Although he was apparently baptized as a Roman Catholic, he later claimed that "he had never been a communicant of a church."[11] Polanyi's interest in science led him away from medicine to the study of the adsorption of gases (how gases adhere to the surface of solids), X-ray crystallography, and reaction kinetics.[12] In 1948, Polanyi "retired from the professional pursuit of science to take up philosophy."[13]

Ten years later, he published his epistemic masterpiece, *Personal Knowledge: Towards a Post-Critical Philosophy*.[14]

The phrase "tacit knowledge" is used only rarely in *Personal Knowledge*,[15] but becomes more predominant in Polanyi's later writings as he developed the insight that "All knowledge is . . . either tacit or rooted in tacit knowing."[16] This is why knowledge is always *personal* knowledge; were it not for the tacit dimension of knowing, there would be no bar to the systematic depersonalization of knowledge. Because the root of knowledge always descends into silence, "we know more than we can tell."[17] Whatever articulate knowledge we possess is the focal point of tacit, subsidiary awareness:

> Viewing the content of these pages from the position reached in *Personal Knowledge* and *The Study of Man* eight years ago, I see that my reliance on the necessity of commitment has been reduced by working out the structure of tacit knowing. This structure shows that all thought contains components of which we are subsidiarily aware in the focal content of our thinking, and that all thought dwells in its subsidiaries, as if they were parts of our body. Hence thinking is not only necessarily intentional, as Brentano has taught: it is also necessarily fraught with the roots it embodies. It has a *from-to* structure.[18]

The art of knowing lies in the skill of bringing subsidiary awareness to bear on a meaningful focus of attention.

Like Newman, Polanyi offers no formal proof that tacit knowledge is the foundation of all knowing. He invites his readers to consider their own experiences of learning skills in order to recognize "the well-known fact *that the aim of a skillful performance is achieved by the observance of a set of rules which are not known as such to the person following them*."[19] Knowledge of a skill is demonstrated by performance rather than by listing the correct rules; his initial examples are things like riding a bicycle, operating a glass-blowing machine, building a violin, and assessing works of art.[20] From these examples, he proceeds to the claim in the next chapter that articulation itself is a skillful performance that builds on a foundation of "mute abilities."[21] No set of words on the page can transmit this insight; readers must recognize for themselves that knowledge depends on tacit foundations.

The Tacit, Personal Dimension of the Illative Sense

Newman adverted to two quite different kinds of tacit knowledge: that which is only accidentally tacit, because it may be converted into an assertion based on formal reasoning, and that which is irreducibly tacit. Simple assent, being *practically* unconscious, may upon inspection reveal itself as capable of formalization:

> A great many of our assents are merely expressions of our personal likings, tastes, principles, motives, and opinions, as dictated by nature, or resulting from habit; in other words, they are acts and manifestations of self: now what is more rare than self-knowledge? In proportion then to our ignorance of self, is our unconsciousness of those innumerable acts of assent, which we are incessantly making. And so again in what may be almost called the mechanical operation of our minds, in our continual acts of apprehension and inference, speculation, and resolve, propositions pass before us and receive our assent without our consciousness. Hence it is that we are so apt to confuse together acts of assent and acts of inference. Indeed, I may fairly say, that those assents which we give with a direct knowledge of what we are doing, are few compared with the multitude of like acts which pass through our minds in long succession without our observing them.[22]

In the unreflective state of simple assent, we may remain unconscious of the view from which our assents stem: "Each of us looks at the world in his own way, and does not know that perhaps it is characteristically his own."[23]

> When confronted with this fact of human experience, it is natural to embark on a conversion project to transform simple assent into complex assent.[24] There are some notable successes in this effort, as when we move from a hunch to certitude through a long process of finding or creating connections to verify the insight: "it not infrequently happens, that while the keenness of the ratiocinative faculty enables a man to see the ultimate result of a complicated problem in a moment, it takes years for him to embrace it as a truth, and to recognize it as an item in the circle of his knowledge."[25] Other fundamental presuppositions resist such illumination.

There are some kinds of knowledge that refuse to be cast into formal operations. Just as there are no rules that can replace genius,[26] so there are no rules that can take the place of real apprehension:

> This is the mode in which we ordinarily reason, dealing with things directly, and as they stand, one by one, in the concrete, with an intrinsic and personal power, not a conscious adoption of an artificial instrument or expedient; and it is especially exemplified both in uneducated men, and in men of genius,—in those who know nothing of intellectual aids and rules, and in those who care nothing for them,—in those who are either without or above mental discipline.[27]

It is clear that Newman recognizes insight as a skillful performance that integrates many subsidiarily known clues:

> [A peasant who can accurately predict the weather] does not proceed step by step, but he feels all at once and together the force of various combined phenomena, though he is not conscious of them. Again, there are physicians who excel in the *diagnosis* of complaints; though it does not follow from this, that they could defend their decision in a particular case against a brother physician who disputed it. They are guided by natural acuteness and varied experience; they have their own idiosyncratic modes of observing, generalizing, and concluding; when questioned, they can but rest on their own authority, or appeal to the future event.[28]

Polanyi's thesis that we always know more than we can tell seems to map perfectly over Newman's observations on the skill of sound judgment:

> What I have been saying of Ratiocination, may be said of Taste, and is confirmed by the obvious analogy between the two. Taste, skill, invention in the fine arts—and so, again, discretion or judgment in conduct—are exerted spontaneously, when once acquired, and could not give a clear account of themselves, or of their mode of proceeding. They do not go by rule, though to a certain point their exercise may be analyzed, and may take the shape of an art or method.[29]

Illative Sense and Tacit Knowledge

Both men agree that the mental experiment of translating all assents (commitments) into articulation breaks down in a philosophically significant fashion. If we cannot give a complete account of how we know what we know, we must revise our notions of knowledge and certitude.

Confronted with the fact of tacit knowledge, we face a choice between devaluing our certitudes against an objectivist standard, or else adopting the view that tacit, personal knowledge is real knowledge. In the latter model, the illative sense is what holds us to our self-set standards of judgment:

> Thus in concrete reasonings we are in great measure thrown back into that condition, from which logic proposed to rescue us. We judge for ourselves, by our own lights, and on our own principles; and our criterion of truth is not so much the manipulation of propositions, as the intellectual and moral character of the person maintaining them, and the ultimate silent effect of his argument or conclusions upon our minds.[30]

Even though words are used to communicate the argument or conclusions, the act of *weighing* the value of the propositions employed is a tacit act.

Like Polanyi, Newman saw that the tacit dimension of thought necessarily implies that knowledge remains personal:

> ... unless I am mistaken, they [certitudes known without formal reasoning] are to be found throughout the range of concrete matter, and that supra-logical judgment, which is the warrant for our certitude about them, is not mere commonsense, but the true healthy action of our ratiocinative powers, an action more subtle and more comprehensive than the mere appreciation of a syllogistic argument. It is often called the "judicium prudentis viri," a standard of certitude which holds good in all concrete matter, not only in those cases of practice and duty, in which we are more familiar with it, but in questions of truth and falsehood generally, or in what are called "speculative" questions, and that, not indeed to the exclusion, but as the supplement of logic. Thus a proof, except in abstract demonstration, has always in it, more or less, an

element of the personal, because "prudence" is not a constituent part of our nature, but a personal endowment.[31]

Personal knowledge is ultimately rooted in feelings—hence the appropriateness of the metaphor that this self-reflexive, subsidiary awareness is a "sense."[32] Newman noted that the "personal element" in proof is dependent on such intellectual passions:

> And the language in common use, when concrete conclusions are in question, implies the presence of this personal element in the proof of them. We are considered to feel, rather than to see, its cogency; and we decide, not that the conclusion must be, but that it cannot be otherwise. We say, that we do not see our way to doubt it, that it is impossible to doubt, that we are bound to believe it, that we should be idiots, if we did not believe.[33]

The passionate roots of our convictions cannot be brought wholly into the light of analysis. Even when we are able to dig them out for examination, they cease to function *as* roots so long as they are exhumed from the ground of personal knowledge that gave them life. When the mind is operating normally, without straining to catch itself in the act of understanding, it is the illative sense that draws upon the roots of knowledge implicitly, without seeing directly how it is that these lines of passion transmit what is necessary for thought and provide stable frameworks for growth.

Newman spoke of the illative sense as an instinctual operation of the mind. Though the term "instinct" may be fraught with difficulties, depending on the model used to interpret this term, Newman's primary concern was to call attention to the fact that the vital functions of our minds have a life of their own that we rely on tacitly:

> I commenced my remarks upon Inference by saying that reasoning ordinarily shows as a simple act, not as a process, as if there were no medium interposed between antecedent and consequent, and the transition from one to the other were of the nature of an instinct,--that is, the process is altogether unconscious and implicit. It is necessary, then, to take some notice of this natural or material Inference, as an existing phenomenon of the mind; and that the more, because I shall

thereby be illustrating and supporting what I have been saying of the characteristics of the inferential process as carried on in concrete matter, and especially of their being the action of the mind itself, that is, by its ratiocinative or illative faculty, not a mere operation as in the rules of arithmetic.[34]

Because it operates tacitly, the "existing phenomenon" of "unconscious and implicit" reason may easily be overlooked in theories of consciousness and knowledge. The subsidiaries of thought work precisely as subsidiaries only when they remain buried beneath the level of focal awareness. Newman noted that in proposing to call such resources "instincts," he did not mean to imply that the correct employment of intelligence is strictly determined by our nature, as might be supposed from the model of instincts employed by naturalists to explain animal behavior:

> It is difficult to avoid calling such clear presentiments by the name of instinct; and I think they may be so called, if by instinct be understood, not a natural sense, one and the same in all, and incapable of cultivation, but a perception of facts without assignable media of perceiving. There are those who can tell at once what is conducive or injurious to their welfare, who are their friends, who their enemies, what is to happen to them, and how they are to meet it. Presence of mind, fathoming of motives, talent for repartee, are instances of this gift.[35]

Where Polanyi used his distinctions between subsidiary and focal awareness and between tacit and explicit knowledge to call attention to this phenomenon, Newman distinguished between instinct and argument:

> It is assent, pure and simple, which is the motive cause of great achievements; it is a confidence, growing out of instincts rather than arguments, stayed upon a vivid apprehension, and animated by a transcendent logic, more concentrated in will and in deed for the very reason that it has not been subjected to any intellectual development.[36]

Even though we can integrate new subsidiaries in order to change the pattern of our focal awareness, the new perceptual framework nevertheless exhibits the quality of being given spontaneously to us by an action of the intellect that is as natural as the operation of any of the bodily senses:

> We proceed by a sort of instinctive perception, from premiss to conclusion. I call it instinctive, not as if the faculty were one and the same to all men in strength and quality (as we generally conceive of instinct), but because ordinarily, or at least often, it acts by a spontaneous impulse, as prompt and inevitable as the exercise of sense and memory. We perceive external objects, and we remember past events, without knowing how we do so; and in like manner we reason without effort and intention, or any necessary consciousness of the part which the mind takes in passing from antecedent to conclusion.[37]

It seems clear that in his discussion of the illative sense as an instinctive operation, Newman affirmed as a matter of fact that we know more than we can tell about how the mind moves itself to conclusions.

Even though Newman was primarily interested in establishing the tacit dimension of the illative sense as a matter of fact, he provided two substantive sets of observations that help us understand in some measure why we cannot formalize the whole of what we know: first, he held that the things grasped by thought remain fundamentally incommunicable; second, that thought itself is fundamentally non-verbal.

Newman, like Polanyi, believed that apprehension of a reality supplies a *contact* with, but not complete *control* over that reality. For Newman, a notion about a thing represents only one abstract aspect of a complex fact:

> This is true of other inferences besides mathematical. They come to no definite conclusions about matters of fact, except as they are made effectual for their purpose by the living intelligence which uses them. . . . universals are ever at war with each other; because what is called a universal is only a general; because what is only general does not lead to a necessary conclusion. . . . "*Latet dolus in generalibus*;" they are arbitrary and fallacious, if we take them for more than broad views and aspects of things, serving as our notes and

> indications for judging of the particular, but not absolutely touching and determining facts.
> Let units come first, and (so-called) universals second; let universals minister to units, not units be sacrificed to universals. John, Richard, and Robert are individual things, independent, incommunicable.[38]

The act of real apprehension does allow us to integrate these partial aspects into a tacit vision of the whole—in Polanyi's language, to develop a *Gestalt* that transforms and unifies our perceptions—but the thing remains something other than our view of it:

> We cannot see through any one of the myriad beings which make up the universe, or give the full catalogue of its belongings. We are accustomed, indeed, and rightly, to speak of the Creator Himself as incomprehensible; and, indeed, He is so by an incommunicable attribute; but in a certain sense each of His creatures is incomprehensible to us also, in the sense that no one has a perfect understanding of them but He. We recognize and appropriate aspects of them, and logic is useful to us in registering these aspects and what they imply; but it does not give us to know even one individual being.[39]

We know more than we can tell, then, because the things that we know are not purely rational constructs, but incommunicable realities.

Newman's second observation that helps to explain the tacit dimension shows that thought, like things, eludes articulation. This is a truth that may be confirmed by introspection, but cannot be proven to those who refuse to assent on "reasonings not demonstrative."[40] Newman was convinced that it is wrong to assume that "whatever can be thought can be adequately expressed in words."[41] Since we cannot inspect others' interior processes, we can only see for ourselves in our own patterns of consciousness that there are indeed "acts of the mind without the intervention of language."[42] Newman was conscious of the paradox of attempting to speak about that which language cannot adequately express, and he concedes that examples which confirm his position "are difficult to find, from the very circumstance that the process from first to last is carried on as much without words as with them."[43] Ironically, some of Newman's most beautiful and arresting rhetoric is devoted to the topic of the inadequacy of language to represent the free flow of thought:

> Science in all its departments has too much simplicity and exactness, from the nature of the case, to be the measure of fact. In its very perfection lies its incompetency to settle particulars and details. As to Logic, its chain of conclusions hangs loose at both ends; both the point from which proof should start, and the points at which it should arrive, are beyond its reach; it comes short both of first principles and concrete issues. Even its most elaborate exhibitions fail to represent adequately the sum-total of considerations by which an individual mind is determined in its judgment of things; even its most careful combinations made to bear on a conclusion want that steadiness of aim which is necessary for hitting it. As I said when I began, thought is too keen and manifold, its sources are too remote and hidden, its path too personal, delicate, and circuitous, its subject-matter too various and intricate, to admit of the trammels of any language, of whatever subtlety and of whatever compass.[44]

It is very appropriate that personal knowledge can only be recognized and accredited by "personal reasoning":

> Anyhow, there is a considerable "surplusage," as Locke calls it, of belief over proof, when I determine that I individually must die. But what logic cannot do, my own living personal reasoning, my good sense, which is the healthy condition of such personal reasoning, but which cannot adequately express itself in words, does for me, and I am possessed with the most precise, absolute, masterful certitude of my dying some day or other.[45]

It is the illative sense, employing the "more subtle and elastic language of thought,"[46] which tacitly governs such personal reasoning and which secures personal certitude about matters of fact:

> Great as are the services of language in enabling us to extend the compass of our inferences, to test their validity, and to communicate them to others, still the mind itself is more versatile and vigorous than any of its works, of which language is one, and it is only under its penetrating and subtle action that the margin disappears, which I have described as intervening between verbal argumentation and conclusions in

Illative Sense and Tacit Knowledge 201

> the concrete. It determines what science cannot determine, the limit of converging probabilities and the reasons sufficient for a proof. It is the ratiocinative mind itself, and no trick of art, however simple in its form and sure in operation, by which we are able to determine, and thereupon to be certain, that a moving body left to itself will never stop, and that no man can live without eating.[47]

When the mind turns in on itself to discover the principles of its own operation, it paradoxically takes on the character of a thing, and resists analysis: "As we cannot see ourselves, so we cannot well see intellectual motives which are so intimately ours, and which spring up from the very constitution of our minds..."[48] It seems clear that one reason it is appropriate to say we know more than we can tell is that we can think more than we can say.

The essential incommunicability of things and thought creates a situation in which even our words themselves may mean more than we can tell.[49] Articulation enables joint thought, but does not control it completely:

> It will be our wisdom to avail ourselves of language, as far as it will go, but to aim mainly by means of it to stimulate, in those to whom we address ourselves, a mode of thinking and trains of thought similar to our own, leading them on by their own independent action, not by any syllogistic compulsion. Hence it is that an intellectual school will always have something of an esoteric character; for it is an assemblage of minds that think; their bond is unity of thought, and their words become a sort of *tessera*, not expressing thought, but symbolizing it.[50]

Real apprehension, not notional apprehension, is the source of knowledge of realities. Since we may see more than we can say, there is room for development of understanding even while the language of a school is preserved:

> Nor is it possible to limit the depth of meaning, which at length he [one who has real apprehension] will attach to words, which to the many are but definitions and ideas.
>
> Here then again, as in the other instances, it seems clear, that methodical processes of inference, useful as they

are, as far as they go, are only instruments of the mind, and need, in order to their due exercise, that real ratiocination and present imagination which gives them a sense beyond their letter, and which, while acting through them, reaches to conclusions beyond and above them. Such a living *organon* is a personal gift, and not a mere method or calculus.[51]

Like Polanyi, Newman recognized that the tacit dimension maintains priority over articulation even in the act of speaking.

Since formal operations cannot govern the full range of assent, we proceed by means of the method of verisimilitude[52] or the cumulation of probabilities: in the modern idiom, if it walks like truth and talks like truth, it probably is truth:

It is plain that formal logical sequence is not in fact the method by which we are enabled to become certain of what is concrete; and it is equally plain, from what has been already suggested, what the real and necessary method is. It is the cumulation of probabilities, independent of each other, arising out of the nature and circumstances of the particular case which is under review; probabilities too fine to avail separately, too subtle and circuitous to be convertible into syllogisms, too numerous and various for such conversion, even were they convertible.[53]

Although Newman called this a "method," it is clear that there is very little that is methodical about it, since there are no rules about how many converging probabilities one must discover in order to make the decision that what *seems* like truth *is* truth. When a pioneer of thought is breaking away from the mainstream of opinion, there may be many more lines pointing away from the new position than point toward it. Polanyi's theory of how subsidiaries tacitly bear upon the focus of attention to form *Gestalten* parallels Newman's description of the informal reasoning that leads to certitude:

Next, from what has been said it is plain, that such a process of reasoning is more or less implicit, and without the direct and full advertence of the mind exercising it. As by the use of our eyesight we recognize two brothers, yet without being able to express what it is by which we distinguish them; as at first sight we perhaps confuse them together, but, on better

Illative Sense and Tacit Knowledge 203

> knowledge, we see no likeness between them at all; as it requires an artist's eye to determine what lines and shades make a countenance look young or old, amiable, thoughtful, angry or conceited, the principle of discrimination being in each case real, but implicit;—so is the mind unequal to complete analysis of the motives which carry it on to a particular conclusion, and is swayed and determined by a body of proof, which it recognizes only as a body, and not in its constituent parts.[54]

When the parts of the proof are brought out of the tacit dimension into focus, they lose the character of subsidiaries and cease to have the power of bearing on the conclusion—the seamless whole falls into pieces and seems incapable of being reassembled because the parts that constitute the whole seem so very different under analysis than they do when functioning as subsidiaries to real apprehension:

> If it is difficult to explain how a man knows that he shall die, it is not more difficult for him to satisfy himself how he knows that he was born. His knowledge about himself does not rest on memory, nor on distinct testimony, nor on circumstantial evidence. Can he bring into one focus of proof the reasons which make him so sure?[55]

When a subsidiary is put at the focus of attention, it is found to be wanting. It no longer draws strength from the tacit merger with other suggestive patterns of thought, and it is clear under the light of analysis that it does not arrive at the conclusion toward which it tends.

Newman's favorite visual image for the cumulation of probabilities is drawn from Newton's illustration of what he means by a "limit":

> This being the state of the case, the question arises, whether, granting that the personality (so to speak) of the parties reasoning is an important element in proving propositions in concrete matter, any account can be given of the ratiocinative method in such proofs, over and above that analysis into syllogism which is possible in each of the steps in detail. I think there can; though I fear, lest to some minds it may appear far-fetched or fanciful; however, I will hazard this

imputation. I consider, then, that the principle of concrete reasoning is parallel to the method of proof which is the foundation of modern mathematical science, as contained in the celebrated lemma with which Newton opens his "*Principia*." We know that a regular polygon, inscribed in a circle, its sides being continually diminished, tends to become that circle, as its limit; but it vanishes before it has coincided with the circle, so that its tendency to be the circle, though ever nearer fulfillment, never in fact gets beyond a tendency.[56]

In the same way, converging lines of thought approach the limit of becoming proofs without ever ceasing to be mere probabilities when examined in isolation from the rest of the picture, just as any segment of Newton's polygon will appear as a straight rather than a curved line under sufficient magnification. Newman continued:

In like manner, the conclusion in a real or concrete question is foreseen and predicted rather than actually attained; foreseen in the number and direction of accumulated premises, which all converge to it, and as the result of their combination, approach it more nearly than any assignable difference, yet do not touch it logically (though only not touching it,) on account of the nature of its subject-matter, and the delicate and implicit character of at least part of the reasonings on which it depends. It is by the strength, variety, or multiplicity of premises, which are only probable, not by invincible syllogisms,—by objections overcome, by adverse theories neutralized, by difficulties gradually clearing up, by exceptions proving the rule, by unlooked-for correlations found with received truths, by suspense and delay in the process issuing in triumphant reactions,—by all these ways, and many others, it is that the practiced and experienced mind is able to make a sure divination that a conclusion is inevitable, of which his lines of reasoning do not actually put him in possession.[57]

According to the rules of strict logic, it is clear that the two figures are not identical and never can be, given the original definitions of a circle and a regular polygon. From the standpoint of informal reasoning, one may decide that some differences make no difference

Illative Sense and Tacit Knowledge

for all practical purposes. A decision is required in order to cross the gap between what logic supplies and inference suggests, but it is a decision perfectly proportioned to the capacity of the mind to judge that the risks involved are negligible. To use the metaphor of an asymptote, one might say that the converging lines of belief never completely join the axis of reason, but the further one follows the convergence, the smaller the step is from the series of uncertainties to certitude.

In Newman's view, it is the illative sense that determines whether assent should be granted on the basis of the accumulation of probabilities: "It is by the strength, variety, or multiplicity of premisses, which are only probable, not by invincible syllogisms ... that the practiced and experienced mind is able to make a sure divination that a conclusion is inevitable, of which his lines of reasoning do not actually put him in possession."[58] Newman characterizes this process as "reasoning from wholes to wholes," all of which are apprehended tacitly and personally:

> I say, then, that our most natural mode of reasoning is, not from propositions to propositions, but from things to things, from concrete to concrete, from wholes to wholes. Whether the consequents, at which we arrive from the antecedents with which we start, lead us to assent or only towards assent, those antecedents commonly are not recognized by us as subjects for analysis; nay, often are only indirectly recognized as antecedents at all. Not only is the inference with its process ignored, but the antecedent also. To the mind itself the reasoning is a simple divination or prediction; as it literally is in the instance of enthusiasts, who mistake their own thoughts for inspirations.[59]

Each whole that is brought to bear upon another whole may reveal itself under analysis to be the fruit of an illation, so that the project of untangling the lines of thought becomes hopelessly snarled with interconnections. The mind tires of the effort, but every exploration of the phenomenon suggests that the same kind of difficulty of analyzing an integration will be found in every subsequent instance. "The mind is like a double mirror, in which reflections of self within self multiply themselves till they are undistinguishable, and the first reflection contains all the rest."[60] There is no point at which we may say that, at last, we have gotten clear of the obligation to rely on tacit integrations of apprehension. Personal knowledge—"personal certitude" in Newman's terms—depends on the illative sense:

> In the extract which I make from it [an argument about literary authorship], we may observe the same steady march of a proof towards a conclusion, which is (as it were) out of sight;—a reckoning, or a reasonable judgment, that the conclusion really is proved, and a personal certitude upon that judgment, joined with a confession that a logical argument could not well be made out for it, and that the various details in which the proof consisted were in no small measure implicit and impalpable.[61]

In the course of a heated argument, when one person continuously poses the question, "How do you know *that*?", the only honest answer is, "I just know it." Like Polanyi, Newman's grammar licenses us to believe what we cannot prove. The illative sense is that which marshals the resources of the tacit dimension so that we may obtain, correct, and develop personal knowledge.

Ian Ker brought together three key images that Newman used to illustrate how inadequate arguments bound together by an illative assessment take on a strength that no one of them possesses alone:

> The "proof of Religion," he wrote in a letter in 1861, using a striking analogy, "I liken ... to the mechanism of some triumph of skill ... where all display is carefully avoided, and the weight is ingeniously thrown in a variety of directions, upon supports which are distinct from, or independent of each other" [*LD* xix, 460]. Or, as he later explained by an even more compelling analogy, "The best illustration ... is that of a *cable* which is made up of a number of separate threads, each feeble, yet together as sufficient as an iron rod," which represents "mathematical or strict demonstration" [*LD* xxi, 146] The cable will certainly break if enough threads give way, but if the threads hold, then the cable is as strong as any metal bar. For, to use yet another image, a cumulation of probabilities is like a "bundle of sticks, each of which ... you could snap in two, if taken separately from the rest" [*LD* xxiv, 146].[62]

In other "grammars of assent," one begins with clear and distinct ideas and attempts to create "chains" of argument; in such formal systems, the argument is never any stronger than the weakest link in the chain. Newman begins with ideas that cannot be completely expressed in words and supposes that even those trains of thought which stop short of the goal nevertheless make a definite contribution to the final act of judgment. When the pieces of the intellectual mechanism are assembled, or the strands of thought woven into a cable, or the branches of probability gathered into a bundle, one can no longer see each component separately and cannot directly inspect its contribution to the function of the whole.

The Illative Dimension of Tacit Knowledge

Just as Newman took note of the tacit and personal dimension of knowledge while pursuing the theme of the illative sense, so Polanyi adverted to the power of illation while concentrating on tacit knowledge. Where the notion of the illative sense highlights the capacity of personal judgment, the notion of tacit knowledge emphasizes the product of using our judgment in a responsible fashion. Newman's metaphor that the power of the mind to come to judgment is a "sense" gives the impression of a singular reality, whereas Polanyi's remarks alternate between singular and plural expressions. The shifts from singular to plural images correspond to the elusive nature of subsidiary and focal awareness, in which many different intellectual inputs (memory, current awareness, hunches, partial proofs, conditional reasoning, testimony, suggestive analogies, etc.) are integrated. An illation often has the quality of an undivided whole even though many component parts subtend the integration.

In order to explore how Polanyi's map of the mind intersects with Newman's on the issue of the nature and scope of personal judgment, I will trace the same four themes discussed in the preceding section: knowledge of things, knowledge of thought, articulation, and the method of verisimilitude. This discussion is intended to show that tacit knowledge depends on the illative sense.

In assessing how people make contact with external reality, Polanyi implies that "the intuition of rationality in nature [has] to be acknowledged as a justifiable and indeed essential part of scientific theory."[63] Such "powers for recognizing rationality in nature"[64] give birth to the language of science:

> I suggest that we should be more frank in facing our situation and acknowledge our own faculties for recognizing real entities, the designation of which form a rational vocabulary. I believe that a classification made according to rational criteria should form groups of things which we may expect to have an indefinite number of properties in common, and that accordingly the terms designating such classes will have an intension referring to an indefinite range of uncovenanted common properties shared by the members of a class. The ampler the intensions of a key feature, the more rational should be as a rule the identification of things in its terms and the more truly should such a classification reveal the nature of the classified objects; while classifications made according to terms having no intension should be rejected as purely artificial, unreal, nonsensical; unless indeed they *are* designed purely for convenience, as e.g., an alphabetic register of words.[65]

After an intuitive formation of a vocabulary, there next comes the deployment of rules of operation, which are also managed by means of spontaneous judgment:

> Thus both the first active steps undertaken to solve a problem and the final garnering of the solution rely effectively on computations and other symbolic operations, while the more informal act by which the logical gap is crossed lies between these two formal procedures. However, the intuitive powers of the investigator are always dominant and decisive.[66]

Just as Newman saw formal reason "hanging loose at both ends," needing to be grasped by the informal reasoning of the illative sense in order to play its proper role in the life of the mind, so Polanyi described the relationship between tacit and formal reason:

> Moreover, a symbolic formalism is itself but an embodiment of our antecedent unformalized powers—an instrument skillfully contrived by our inarticulate selves for the purpose of relying on it as our external guide. The interpretation of primitive terms and axioms is therefore predominantly inarticulate, and so is the process of their expansion and reinterpretation which underlies the progress of mathematics.

Illative Sense and Tacit Knowledge

> The alternation between the intuitive and the formal depends on tacit affirmations, both at the beginning and at the end of each chain of formal reasoning.[67]

The intuitive regulation of "antecedent unformalized powers" of reason is one of the central features of the illative sense.

Polanyi knew well that the notion "intuition" is a philosophical can of worms: "I have watched many a university audience listening to my account of intuitive discoveries silently, with sullen distaste."[68] The language of "intellectual passions" that he develops to describe the orientating powers of the mind avoids some of the distasteful connotations of "intuition." It may be easier to gain a hearing among scientists by appealing to their sense of beauty rather than to confront them with a theory of intuition:

> Only a tiny fraction of all knowable facts are of interest to scientists, and scientific passion serves also as a guide in the assessment of what is higher and what of lesser interest; what is great in science, and what relatively slight. I want to show that his appreciation depends ultimately on a sense of intellectual beauty; that it is an emotional response which can never be dispassionately defined, any more than we can dispassionately define the beauty of a work of art or the excellence of a noble action.[69]

Polanyi, like Newman, examined other areas of life in which people are guided by taste. In these areas, it is the intellectual passions which enable us to "feel our way to success":[70]

> The unspecifiability of the process by which we thus feel our way forward accounts for the possession by humanity of an immense mental domain, not only of knowledge but of manners, of laws, and of the many different arts which man knows how to use, comply with, enjoy or live by, without specifiably knowing their contents. Each single step in acquiring this domain was due to an effort which went beyond the hitherto assured capacity of some person making it, and by his subsequent realization and maintenance of his success. It relied on an act of groping which originally passed the understanding of its agent and of which he has ever since

remained only subsidiarily aware, as part of a complex achievement.[71]

All of Polanyi's reflections on science as a skillful performance were modelled on this kind of unfolding of the intellectual passions—what Newman might have called the education of the illative sense. Note the paradox that, in the last analysis, science cannot be conducted scientifically; because it depends on skillful performances based on tacit integrations, science is ultimately an art.

When Polanyi addressed the issue of how we know what we think, he again had no single, pithy term to concentrate attention on the illative dimension of the mind. In his view, knowledge depends on tacit acts of self-appraisal:

> If, as it would seem, the meaning of all our utterances is determined to an important extent by a skillful act of our own—the act of knowing—then the acceptance of any of our own utterances as true involves our appraisal of our own skill. To affirm anything implies, then, to this extent an appraisal of our own art of knowing, and the establishment of truth becomes decisively dependent on a set of personal criteria of our own which cannot be formally defined.[72]

In discussing articulation as one instance in which such self-appraisal is required, Polanyi recognized that we have to trust the power of the mind for recognizing rationality in itself as well as in nature:

> I believe that we should accredit in ourselves the capacity for appraising our own articulation. Indeed, all our strivings towards precision imply our reliance on such a capacity. To deny or even doubt our possession of it would discredit any effort to express ourselves correctly, and the very conception of words as consistently used utterances would dissolve if we failed to accredit this capacity. This does not imply that this capacity is infallible, but merely that we are competent to exercise it and must ultimately rely on our exercise of it. This we must admit if we are to speak at all, which I believe to be incumbent on us to do.[73]

Illative Sense and Tacit Knowledge

In Newman's terms, the capacity for self-appraisal is the illative sense. Polanyi observed that we must rely on this power for sound judgment whenever we want to sum up our intellectual position:

> The assent which shapes knowledge is fully determined in both cases by competent mental efforts overruling arbitrariness. The result may be erroneous, but it is the best that can be done in the circumstances. Since every factual assertion is conceivably mistaken, it is also conceivably corrigible, but a competent judgment cannot be improved by the person who is making it at the moment of making it, since he is already doing his best in making it.[74]

Assessing for ourselves when our mental efforts are sufficient to warrant assent is precisely the task of the illative sense.

For Newman, the illative sense depends on views informally adopted, but also is responsible for affirming or rejecting those fundamental presuppositions of thought. Polanyi used the same metaphor in only slightly different language when considering the fact that our intellectual passions are dependent on our "vision of reality":

> Our vision of reality, to which our sense of scientific beauty responds, must suggest to us the kind of questions that it should be reasonable and interesting to explore. It should recommend the kind of conceptions and empirical relations that are intrinsically plausible and which should therefore be upheld, even when some evidence seems to contradict them, and tell us also, on the one hand, what empirical connections to reject as specious, even though there is evidence for them—evidence that we may as yet be unable to account for on any other assumptions. In fact, without a scale of interest and plausibility based on a vision of reality, nothing can be discovered that is of value to science; and only our grasp of scientific beauty, responding to the evidence of our senses, can evoke this vision.[75]

Both Newman and Polanyi agreed that the thought which takes a view cannot be adequately expressed in words, even though that thought underlies all of our speaking:

> I believe that by now three things have been established beyond reasonable doubt: the power of intellectual beauty to reveal truth about nature; the vital importance of distinguishing this beauty from merely formal attractiveness; and the delicacy of the test between them, so difficult that it may baffle the most penetrating scientific minds.[76]

For Newman, one's view of things is what establishes the antecedent probability of what will be found to be true. In addition to the visual metaphor, Polanyi used the structural image of an interpretative framework as the source of the scale of plausibility:

> Just as the eye sees details that are not there if they fit in with the sense of the picture, or overlooks them if they make no sense, so also very little inherent certainty will suffice to secure the highest scientific value to an alleged fact, if only it fits in with a great scientific generalization, while the most stubborn facts will be set aside if there is no place for them in the established framework of science.[77]

Just as Newman held that the presuppositions of thought are adopted informally by means of the illative sense, so Polanyi stressed the informal adoption of interpretative frameworks:

> The acceptance of such conceptual innovations is a self-modifying mental act in search of a truer intellectual life. . . . This can be true only because the acceptance of a new conception, even when it is specified by a definition, is ultimately an informal act: a transformation of the framework on which we rely in the process of formal reasoning. It is the crossing of a logical gap to another shore, where we shall never again see things as we did before. To the extent, therefore, to which mathematics is the accumulated product of past conceptual innovations, our affirmation of mathematics is likewise an irreversible, informal act.[78]

Our critical standards are built upon the foundation of "a-critical choices," that is, on the foundation of the operations of the illative sense:

Illative Sense and Tacit Knowledge

> Objectivism has totally falsified our conception of truth, by exalting what we can know and prove, while covering up with ambiguous utterances all that we know and *cannot* prove, even though the latter knowledge underlies, and must ultimately set its seal to, all that we *can* prove. In trying to restrict our minds to the few things that are demonstrable, and therefore explicitly dubitable, it has overlooked the a-critical choices which determine the whole being of our minds and has rendered us incapable of acknowledging these vital choices.[79]

As Newman said, "It is to the living mind that we must look for the means of using correctly principles of whatever kind, facts or doctrines, experiences or testimonies, true or probable, and of discerning what conclusion from these is necessary, suitable, or expedient, when they are taken for granted..."[80]

Like Newman, Polanyi recognized that there is a specific emotional quality to the act of assent: "It is by satisfying his intellectual passions that mathematics fascinates the mathematician and compels him to pursue it in his thoughts and give it his assent."[81] This sense of assurance and finality is not infallible, but it is based upon the supposition that truth is intrinsically beautiful:

> A symphony is obviously something new achieved by the human mind; but in calling it a symphony its composer demands recognition for it as something inherently excellent. The natural scientist and the engineer are not so free to satisfy themselves; no scientific theory is beautiful if it is false and no invention is truly ingenious if it is impracticable.[82]

For Newman, the illative sense is that which upholds our personal standards of excellence. Polanyi attributed the same function to a "tacit faculty":

> We may now begin to recognize the nature of *the tacit faculty* which accounts in the last resort for all the increase in knowledge achieved by articulation, and the nature of the urge to exercise it. We have seen this faculty revealed in somewhat different ways in all three characteristic relations between thought and speech. In the ineffable domain it made sense of the scanty clues conveyed by speech; in listening to a readily

intelligible text and remembering its message, the conception grasped by it formed the focus of our attention; and lastly, it was seen to be the center of operations for readjusting the tacit and the formal components of thought, which had fallen apart by a process of sophistication. The faculty on which we relied in all these situations was our power for comprehending a text and the things to which the text refers, within a conception which is the meaning of the text.[83]

If "illative sense" is substituted for "the tacit faculty" in this passage, it seems that no harm is done to the thought of either Newman or Polanyi.

Both Newman and Polanyi would agree that articulation comes from a wordless center. The illative sense may be understood as the tacit coefficient of thought that allows us to pass from thought to speech:

> There is a corresponding variation in the tacit coefficient of speech. In order to describe experience more fully language must be less precise. But greater imprecision brings more effectively into play the powers of inarticulate judgment required to resolve the ensuing indeterminacy of speech. So it is our personal participation that governs the richness of concrete experience to which our speech can refer. Only by the aid of this tacit coefficient could we ever say anything at all about experience—a conclusion I have reached already by showing that the process of denotation is itself unformalizable.[84]

Newman's notion of the illative sense implies the integration of all of the "powers of inarticulate judgment" that are at our disposal. Polanyi calls the cumulation of these various intellectual inputs a "sense of fitness":

> My own view admits this controlling principle by accrediting the speaker's sense of fitness for judging that his words express the reality he seeks to express. Without this, words having an open texture are totally meaningless, and any text written in such words is meaningless.[85]

Illative Sense and Tacit Knowledge

The reality that Polanyi wished to accredit is what Newman called the illative sense: "To accept the indeterminacy of knowledge requires, on the contrary, that we accredit a person entitled to shape his knowing according to his own judgment, unspecifiably."[86] Just as Newman saw the illative sense as the source of sound judgment about how and when we may assent, so Polanyi placed "personal judgment"[87] at the heart of his epistemology:

> While the logic of assent merely showed that assent is an a-critical act, 'commitment' was introduced from the start as a framework in which assent can be responsible, as distinct from merely egocentric or random. The center of tacit assent was elevated to the seat of responsible judgment. It was granted thereby the faculty of exercising discretion, subject to the obligations accepted and fulfilled by itself with universal intent. A responsible decision is reached, then, in the knowledge that we have overruled by it conceivable alternatives, for reasons that are not fully specifiable.[88]

If the integration of these two positions is correct, one may say that "the center of tacit assent" is the illative sense.

In the following summary of Polanyi's reflections on the knowledge of thought and of things, his notion of "a personal component" of thought seems to have the same character as Newman's notion of "an illative sense":

> To this extent, then, whether thought operates indwellingly within a universe of its own creation, or interprets and controls nature as given to it from outside, the same paradoxical structure prevails through the articulate systems so far surveyed. There is present a personal component, inarticulate and passionate, which declares our standards of values, drives us to fulfil them and judges our performance by these self-set standards.[89]

One need not do too much violence to Newman's texts to show that the illative sense shares all of the characteristics listed by Polanyi in the passage just quoted:

personal component	illative sense
inarticulate	non-verbal (217), supra-logical (251)
passionate	an instinct or inspiration (280)
declares standards of values	chooses its own authority (279)
drives us to fulfill them	binds us to believe (251)
judges by self-set standards	a rule to itself (283)

The two conceptual maps, though not identical, do appear to cover much the same territory in similar fashion.

Newman's "method of verisimilitude" may not appear very methodical in the modern world, since it proceeds by informal rather than formal reasoning. It is on the basis of the illative sense that one sums up all of the lines of thought at one's disposal and decides that the accumulated evidence is "close enough" to the truth to be taken as true. In Polanyi's view, this act of integrating disparate subsidiaries is one of the most important skills required by science:

> The perturbations of the planetary motions that were observed during 60 years preceding the discovery of Neptune, and which could not be explained by the mutual interaction of the planets, were rightly set aside at the time as anomalies by most astronomers, in the hope that something might eventually turn up to account for them without impairing—or at least not essentially impairing—Newtonian gravitation. Speaking more generally, we may say that there are always some conceivable scruples which scientists customarily set aside in the process of verifying an exact theory. Such acts of personal judgment form an essential part of science.[90]

As Newman said, one may assent on grounds that are not demonstrative. The scientist exercises "personal judgment" that it is wise to neglect certain strands of evidence in order to pull others together:

> It is the normal practice of scientists to ignore evidence which appears incompatible with the accepted system of scientific knowledge, in the hope that it will eventually prove false or irrelevant. The wise neglect of such evidence prevents scientific laboratories from being plunged forever into a turmoil of incoherent and futile efforts to verify false allegations. But there is, unfortunately, no rule by which to

Illative Sense and Tacit Knowledge 217

avoid the risk of occasionally disregarding thereby true evidence which conflicts (or seems to conflict) with the current teachings of science.[91]

Even mathematicians, unencumbered by the requirement that their speculations have any bearing on reality at all, must rely on the skill of deciding for themselves what evidence they will accept as persuasive:

> The inarticulate coefficient by which we understand and assent to mathematics is an active principle of this kind; it is a passion for intellectual beauty. It is on account of its intellectual beauty, which his own passion proclaims as revealing a universal truth, that the mathematician feels compelled to accept mathematics as true, even though he is today deprived of the belief in its logical necessity and doomed to admit forever the conceivable possibility that its whole fabric may suddenly collapse by revealing a decisive self-contradiction. And it is the same urge to see sense and make sense that supports his tacit bridging of the logical gaps internal to every formal proof.[92]

The Cartesian model of strict proof descending from self-evident principles does not work for science in general or mathematics in particular: "The alternative to this, which I am seeking to establish here is to restore to us once more the power for the deliberate holding of unproven beliefs."[93] The illative sense is just such a power to believe what we cannot prove.

Conclusion

This essay aims to show the convergence of Newman's and Polanyi's fundamental insights into the tacit and personal dimension of human judgment rather than to develop a complete harmonization of their terminology. Some of the similarities between the two positions are less surprising than others, given that both men wrote in English in England; there is no evidence, however, that Polanyi was in any way influenced by Newman's writings. An exhaustive catalogue of all points of contact will not necessarily improve our grasp of the central issues of illative sense and tacit knowledge—the list would be more exhausting than illuminating. If the latter two sections of this essay have not persuaded the reader that the two positions share the same fundamental insights, then it is doubtful that inspection of subsidiary similarities will make the case. If the substantial convergence of the positions is recognized, then many other connections might be explored: the role of conscience in knowledge; the freedom and responsibility to choose one's fundamental vision of reality; the hermeneutic circle between interpretative frameworks and interpretations; the imagination as the vehicle of contact with reality; the passions and emotions which support and accompany the operations of the intellect; the tacit creation and interpretation of symbols; and the affirmation of a post-critical philosophy as an alternative to the objectivist, critical philosophies descended from the Enlightenment.

In keeping with Polanyi's recognition that we know more than we can tell, there are many more connections between Newman and Polanyi than this essay can make explicit. Notions seem to be very much like neurons: they send out connections in every direction and in three dimensions. This analysis of the interconnections between Newman's and Polanyi's notions follows only a few of the contact points, and attempts to take them one-by-one, whereas living ideas, like neurons, constantly sum and re-sum the effects of many impulses wandering through the neural network. For epistemologies based on the dream of clear and distinct ideas, the inability to make all connections explicit is counted a failure; for epistemologies based on illative sense and tacit knowledge, the myriad of inarticulable links is a token that one has made contact with a profoundly important reality.

NOTES

1. This claim is patterned on John T. Ford's insight into the nature of Newman's *Essay on the Development of Doctrine*, which was developed in a course entitled, "Newman the Theologian."
2. Edited and with introduction by Nicholas Lash (Notre Dame: University of Notre Dame Press, 1979). "Illative sense" is etymologically related to "inference"—the fourth principal part of the Latin verb "infero" is "illatus."
3. Zeno, *John Henry Newman: Our Way to Certitude: An Introduction to Newman's Psychological Discovery: The Illative Sense and His "Grammar of Assent"* (Leiden: E.J. Brill, 1957), 2, 263: in a letter to Charles Meynell, November 17, 1869.
4. In the ninth chapter of the *Grammar*, Newman quotes from his 1837 work, *The Prophetical Office of the Church*, and then uses the term "illative sense" to sum up his reflections on informal reasoning and to demonstrate the continuity of this thought (*Grammar*, 296-7). Zeno notes that the "doctrine of the illative sense may be found in the University Sermons when [Newman] speaks about implicit and explicit reason" (*Certitude*, 13; cf. 168). In the *Grammar*, Newman makes a parallel distinction between informal and formal inference, and speaks of informal inference as one of the distinctive operations of the illative sense (*Grammar*, 283).
5. *Newman's University Sermons: Fifteen Sermons Preached before the University of Oxford, 1826-43*, with introduction by D.M. MacKinnon and J.D. Holmes (London: S.P.C.K., 1970; third edition, 1871), 257.
6. *Grammar*, 276-7; cf. 283, 321.
7. Lash, introduction to the *Grammar*, 12. The source of the Caswall quotation is C.S. Dessain, *John Henry Newman* (London: Adam and Charles Black, 1966), 148; Lash continues, "On these two propositions, cf. *Grammar*, 128, 209."
8. *Grammar*, 234-239.

9. Richard Gelwick, *The Way of Discovery: An Introduction to the Thought of Michael Polanyi* (New York: Oxford University Press, 1977), 4, 31-2.
10. Scott, "The Question of Religious Reality: Commentary on the Polanyi Papers," *Zygon* 17 (1982) 85-6.
11. *Ibid.*, 86.
12. Polanyi, *Knowing and Being*, edited by Marjorie Grene (Chicago: University of Chicago Press, 1969), 93, 97, 104.
13. *Knowing and Being*, 87.
14. Chicago: University of Chicago Press, 1958.
15. The phrase Polanyi used most often in *Personal Knowledge* is the "tacit coefficient" of knowing and speaking (86, 169, 250, 257, 259, 336). He also spoke of "tacit assent" (95, 260, 266, 312), "tacit affirmations" (131), "tacit judgments" (205, 206), "tacit endorsements" (207, 268) and "tacit commitments" (251). "Tacit knowledge" (169) or "tacit knowing" (264) serves in Polanyi's later writings and in this essay as a useful reminder of all that Polanyi had to say about the "ineffable domain" of knowledge (87). Marjorie Grene noted that tacit knowing is subsidiary to the notion of commitment in *Personal Knowledge* (introduction to *Knowing and Being*, xiv).
16. *Meaning*, 61; emphasis added. The same claim appears in nearly identical form in *Knowing and Being* (195). In 1964, Polanyi wrote a new introduction to *Science, Faith and Society* (Chicago: University of Chicago Press), which had originally been published in 1946 and which has no reference to "tacit knowledge" or the "tacit coefficient" or to any of the parallel expressions that appear in the 1958 *Personal Knowledge*. In this introduction, Polanyi observed that the word "intuition" plays the same role in the earlier work that "tacit coefficient" does in the later, and maintained that "This conception of reality and of the tacit knowing of reality underlies all my writings" (10). If so, the insight remains fundamentally the same although the language used to express it varies somewhat through Polanyi's philosophical career.
17. Polanyi, *The Tacit Dimension* (New York: Doubleday and Company, 1966), 4.
18. *Tacit Dimension*, x.
19. *Personal Knowledge*, 49.

Illative Sense and Tacit Knowledge

20. *Personal Knowledge*, 50, 52, 53, 55.
21. *Personal Knowledge*, 70.
22. *Grammar*, 157.
23. *Grammar*, 291.
24. This "conversion project" comes to us naturally as well as through the recommendations of critical philosophies: "Our inquiries spontaneously fall into scientific sequence, and we think in logic, as we talk in prose, without aiming at doing so. However sure we are of the accuracy of our instinctive conclusions, we as instinctively put them into words, as far as we can . . ." (*Grammar*, 228).
25. *Grammar*, 143.
26. "In saying this, I am not disposed to deny the presence in some men of an idiosyncratic sagacity, which really and rightly sees reasons in impressions which common men cannot see, and is secured from the peril of confusing truth with make-belief; but this is genius, and beyond rule" (*Grammar*, 81).
27. *Grammar*, 261.
28. *Grammar*, 261-2. Newman went on to discuss similar skills in lawyers, detectives, and similar experts, as well as in "reading" the character of those with whom we come in contact in our personal affairs.
29. *Grammar*, 266.
30. *Grammar*, 240.
31. *Grammar*, 251.
32. Newman did not directly use the (admittedly provocative and contemporary) term "feelings." Instead, he used various forms of the verb "to feel," in order to distinguish the quality of illation from that of formal argument, as in this passage: ". . . 'rational' is used in contradistinction to argumentative, and means 'resting on implicit reasons,' such as we feel, indeed, but which for some cause or other, because they are too subtle or too circuitous, we cannot put into words so as to satisfy logic" (*Grammar*, 256).
33. *Grammar*, 251.
34. *Grammar*, 260.
35. *Grammar*, 263.
36. *Grammar*, 177. Along similar lines, Newman distinguishes between tacit, "mental reasoning" and formal, "verbal reasoning" (*Grammar*, 212).

37. *Grammar*, 209.
38. *Grammar*, 223.
39. *Grammar*, 226.
40. *Grammar*, 150.
41. *Grammar*, 212.
42. *Grammar*, 220.
43. *Grammar*, 254-5.
44. *Grammar*, 227.
45. *Grammar*, 227.
46. *Grammar*, 281-2. This phrase was used in the first of four brief observations that Newman made about the exercise of the illative sense.
47. *Grammar*, 282-3.
48. *Grammar*, 264-5.
49. This is another favorite slogan of Polanyi's: "I can say nothing precisely. The words I have spoken and am yet to speak mean nothing: it is only *I* who mean something *by them*. And, as a rule, I do not focally know what I mean, and though I could explore my meaning up to a point, I believe that my words (descriptive words) must mean more than I shall ever know, if they are to mean anything at all" (*Personal Knowledge*, 252).
50. *Grammar*, 245.
51. *Grammar*, 250.
52. Newman used this phrase in his 1871 Preface to the third edition of the *University Sermons*: "Again: there are two methods of reasoning—*a priori*, and *a posteriori*; from antecedent probabilities or verisimilitudes, and from evidence, of which the method of verisimilitude more naturally belongs to implicit reasoning, and the method of evidence to explicit" (xii). "Faith, viewed in contrast with Reason in these three senses, is implicit in its acts, adopts the method of verisimilitude, and starts from religious first principles . . . The Author has lately pursued this whole subject at considerable length in his 'Essay in Aid of a Grammar of Assent.'" (xvi-xvii). In the *Grammar*, Newman correlates the notions of "inference" and "verisimilitude": "Inference is the conditional acceptance of a proposition, Assent is the unconditional; the object of Assent is a truth, the object of Inference is the truth-like or a verisimilitude. The problem which I have undertaken is that of

ascertaining how it comes to pass that a conditional act leads to an unconditional" (209).
53. *Grammar*, 230.
54. *Grammar*, 232.
55. *Grammar*, 239.
56. *Grammar*, 253.
57. *Grammar*, 253-4.
58. *Grammar*, 254.
59. *Grammar*, 260-1.
60. *Grammar*, 162.
61. *Grammar*, 259.
62. *The Achievement of John Henry Newman* (Notre Dame: University of Notre Dame Press, 1990), 50-1.
63. *Personal Knowledge*, 15-16.
64. *Personal Knowledge*, 13.
65. *Personal Knowledge*, 114-15.
66. *Personal Knowledge*, 130.
67. *Personal Knowledge*, 131; cf. 258.
68. *Personal Knowledge*, 149.
69. *Personal Knowledge*, 135.
70. *Personal Knowledge*, 62.
71. *Personal Knowledge*, 62-3.
72. *Personal Knowledge*, 70-1.
73. *Personal Knowledge*, 91.
74. *Personal Knowledge*, 314.
75. *Personal Knowledge*, 135.
76. *Personal Knowledge*, 149.
77. *Personal Knowledge*, 138.
78. *Personal Knowledge*, 189.
79. *Personal Knowledge*, 286.
80. *Grammar*, 282. The discussion of how the illative sense functions in the selection of first principles continues to the next page as well.
81. *Personal Knowledge*, 188.
82. *Personal Knowledge*, 195.
83. *Personal Knowledge*, 100. Emphasis added.
84. *Personal Knowledge*, 86-7.
85. *Personal Knowledge*, 113.
86. *Personal Knowledge*, 264.

87. This is an expression which occurs frequently in *Personal Knowledge*: 18-9, 20, 31, 79-80, 105-6, 119, 259, 307, 312, 367. For the most part, one may substitute Newman's phrase, "the illative sense" in these passages without altering Polanyi's meaning, e.g.: "I have given evidence before of the emotional upheaval which accompanies the mental reorganization necessary for crossing the logical gap that separates a problem from its solution. I have pointed out that the depth of this upheaval corresponds to the force of personal judgment [the illative sense] required to supplement the inadequate clues on which is a decision is being based" (*Personal Knowledge*, 367).
88. *Personal Knowledge*, 312. Polanyi's notion of a-critical assent in this passage strongly resembles Newman's understanding of "simple assent," while Polanyi's notion of commitment has the same qualities as Newman's reflections on "complex assent."
89. *Personal Knowledge*, 195.
90. *Personal Knowledge*, 20.
91. *Personal Knowledge*, 138.
92. *Personal Knowledge*, 189.
93. *Personal Knowledge*, 268.

NEWMAN ON THE CRITICIZABILITY OF CATHOLIC FAITH

John R. Connolly

Because of his statements on the incompatibility of faith and doubt Newman's notion of faith has often been criticized as being too narrow, too dogmatic and not sufficiently open to rational criticism. However, M. Jaime Ferreira correctly points out in her book, *Doubt and Religious Commitment: The Role of the Will in Newman's Thought*, that you cannot find an exact correspondence between a thinker's position on the relationship between faith and doubt and his/her understanding of the role of rational criticism within faith.[1] Ferreira argues that some thinkers, like Paul Tillich, see faith and doubt as compatible but devalue the need for rational criticism, while others, like Newman, hold that faith and doubt are incompatible, but affirm the need and importance of rational criticism.[2]

Therefore, in her analysis of Newman's notion of faith Ferreira transforms the discussion from one of the relationship between faith and doubt to a question of the role of rational criticism (which Ferreira refers to as "criticizability") in faith. On the one hand, the commitment of faith must be unconditional and immune to certain forms of rational criticism. On the other hand, in order to be rational the commitment of faith must be open to some forms of rational criticism. The question of the role of rational criticism in faith becomes a question of delineating in what areas faith is immune to rational criticism and in what areas it is susceptible to rational criticism.

The primary objective of this chapter will be to investigate the role which rational criticism plays in the assent of Catholic Divine

Faith. In "Papers in Preparation for *A Grammar of Assent*, 1865-1869" Newman defines Catholic Divine Faith, "*Fides Divina Catholica*," as the acceptance of public revelations on the basis of the authority of God revealing through the voice of the infallible Church.[3] In the same passage Newman describes another form of Divine Faith which he calls "*Fides Divina*" and defines as the acceptance of private divine revelations on the authority of God, but not of the Church.[4] Our concern here will be exclusively with what Newman calls Catholic Divine Faith. Furthermore, we will confine ourselves to a discussion of those forms of rational criticism which are either compatible or incompatible with the actual assent of Catholic Divine Faith. We will not discuss the role which rational criticism plays in the rational processes leading up to the act of Catholic Divine Faith, i.e., the practical and speculative judgments of credibility. The outline for this chapter will be based upon two conclusions which Ferreira makes regarding the nature of Divine Faith in her book, *Doubt and Religious Commitment*. The first section of this chapter will present a critical analysis of Ferreira's statement that Newman's analysis of certitude and doubt in the *Grammar of Assent* serves as a model for his understanding of Divine Faith.[5] In the second section the validity of Ferreira's conclusion that the certitude of Divine Faith does not require a rebellion against reason and is not a form of irrational dogmatism will be investigated.[6]

The Grammar of Assent as the Model for Divine Faith

Although Ferreira sees the treatment of certitude in the *Grammar of Assent* as the model for Divine Faith, she maintains that the discussion of Divine Faith itself is beyond the scope of the *Grammar of Assent*. Ferreira maintains that in the *Grammar of Assent* Newman is speaking about a natural human religious belief which is distinct from Divine Faith and that Newman disclaims any intention of treating Divine Faith as such in the *Grammar of Assent*.[7]

Ferreira's interpretation gives the impression that Newman holds that there are two forms of Christian Faith, or at least two ways of religiously adhering to the revealed doctrines of Christian Faith. One form is a natural religious belief and the other is Divine Faith. Drawing upon terminology which Newman uses in some of his other works Ferreira identifies this distinction with Newman's distinction between "fides acquisita," or "fides humana," and "fides divina."[8]

According to Ferreira both forms of adherence have the same material object, namely, the religious doctrines and dogmas of Christian Faith (i.e., the Trinity, the Incarnation etc.). However, the two differ according to their formal object. In "fides acquisita" the revealed doctrines are known and accepted on the basis of reason alone and, therefore, this adherence is purely natural. In "fides divina" the same truths are accepted on the basis of the authority of God revealing and, as such, this adherence is a gift of grace and, therefore, a supernatural act.[9]

Ferreira bases this distinction and her position that the primary subject matter of the *Grammar of Assent* is religious human belief, or "fides acquisita," on a statement that Newman makes in Part V of the *Grammar of Assent*,

> And secondly, I mean by belief, not precisely faith, because faith, in its theological sense, includes a belief, not only in the thing believed, but also in the ground of believing; that is, not only belief in certain doctrines, but belief in them expressly because God has revealed them; but here I am engaged only with what is called the material object of faith, with the thing believed, not with the formal.[10]

Since Divine Faith involves the discussion of belief in doctrines "expressly because God has revealed them" and Newman says that he is not going to treat this aspect of faith here, Ferreira concludes that the discussion of Divine Faith is beyond the scope of the *Grammar of Assent*, and, on this basis, makes her suggestion that the *Grammar of Assent* is only treating natural religious belief, or "fides acquisita."[11]

There are, however, a couple of problems with this interpretation. For one thing Newman's statement quoted above is made in Chapter V of Part I of the *Grammar of Assent* and not in an introduction to the whole book. In fact, there is no introduction to the *Grammar of Assent*, and it seems clear that Newman intends this statement to apply only to the section which follows, that is, a discussion of two *revealed* truths, "He is One" and "He is Three," and not to the entire *Grammar of Assent*. Futhermore, Newman, in this section, never explicitly makes reference to a natural religious belief which is distinct from Divine Faith. He simply refers to the distinction between the formal and material object of Divine Faith and states that in this section he is only concerned with the material object. Newman never states that he thinks there can be a natural religious assent, outside of grace, given to religious doctrines like the Trinity. This interpretation is corroborated by a statement which Newman makes in "Papers in Preparation for *A Grammar of Assent*, 1865-1869" to the effect that truths which are revealed are received by Divine Faith and truths which are not revealed are received by human faith.[12] Finally, neither in this section, nor anywhere else in the *Grammar of Assent*, does Newman refer to the distinction between *"fides acquisita"* and *"fides divina."*[13]

Not only is Ferreira's interpretation of Newman's distinction between human faith and Divine Faith not necessarily applicable to the *Grammar of Assent*, but its main corollary, that Divine Faith is beyond the scope of the *Grammar of Assent*, is also arguable. In fact, in the section of the *Grammar of Assent* mentioned above Newman goes on to discuss two doctrines, "He is One" and "He is Three," both of which are revealed truths and, as such, objects of Catholic Divine Faith. Also, toward the end of Chapter V Newman indirectly brings up the formal object of Divine Faith when he discusses Catholic Faith.[14] Futhermore, it seems quite feasible to suggest that when Newman wrote the *Grammar of Assent* he had as his goal not only the justification of human certitude, but also the rational justification of Catholic Divine Faith. One of the reasons Newman wrote the *Grammar of Assent* was to lay a rational foundation for the faith of the ordinary Catholic, whose faith, for Newman, was always the work of divine grace and, therefore, Catholic Divine Faith. Everything which Newman writes about apprehension, assent, inference, certitude, etc. has as its final objective the rational justification of Catholic Divine Faith. In fact, Fitzpatrick suggests that perhaps the reason Newman's analysis of certitude in the *Grammar of Assent* takes the direction it does, that is, with his particular descriptions of apprehension, assent, inference, certitude and the role of the illative sense, is because Newman ultimately has in mind the justification of divine faith which has the particular characteristic of being an assent which goes beyond the evidence.[15] Could it not be that Newman is involved in something similar to Paul Tillich's method of correlation? While he is investigating the human question, he is keeping the divine answers in mind. Perhaps Newman's statement in his 1860 paper on "The Evidences of Religion" is relevant here. "And this being the case, I hope no reader will misunderstand me, and think that I am forgetting its [religious faith] divine origin because I am investigating its human history."[16] Therefore, perhaps a more accurate way of describing the scope of the *Grammar of Assent* would be to say that it is an analysis of the human side of Catholic Divine Faith. This is quite different from saying that Newman is only discussing a natural human religious belief in the *Grammar of Assent* and that Divine Faith is beyond its scope.

Another problem which Ferreira raises regarding the relationship between Newman's analysis of certitude in the *Grammar of Assent* and the certitude of Divine Faith is the question of the nature of the affirmation involved in Divine Faith. According to Ferreira the affirmation of Divine Faith does not require an affirmation over and above the affirmation of human certitude, as outlined in the *Grammar of Assent*. Although she grants a certain distinctiveness to the certitude of Divine Faith, Ferreira does not think that it requires an affirmation over and above the affirmation of human certitude. Ferreira also bases this position on her interpretation of the relationship between human faith and Divine Faith which we have already discussed. According to Ferreira Newman distinguishes between human faith and Divine Faith in terms of the distinction between the formal and material objects. Employing this traditional distinction Newman, Ferreira maintains, holds that the material object of human faith and Divine Faith are identical and that the two are distinguished on the basis of their formal objects only.[17] As a result, Divine Faith, for Newman, can sufficiently maintain its distinctiveness on the grounds that it differs from human faith on the basis of its formal object, that is, that Divine Faith is an affirmation through grace based upon the Word of God revealing and human faith is not.[18] Based upon this Ferreira concludes that the higher certitude of Divine Faith can be explained on the basis of the added operation of grace and that its distinctiveness does not warrant maintaining that Divine Faith requires an affirmation over and above the affirmation of human faith.[19]

However, there are some real problems with Ferreira's interpretation of the nature of the affirmation of Divine Faith. For one thing the evidence which Ferreira presents in favor of Newman's identification of the material object of human faith and Divine Faith is weak. And secondly, Newman's writings on Catholic Divine Faith are filled with acclamations of the Pre-eminence of the certitude of Divine Faith. With regard to the first point nowhere in his writings does Newman explicitly state that human faith and Divine Faith have the same material object. The only evidence from Newman which Ferreira offers in support of this interpretation is the passage in the

Grammar of Assent which we have already cited.[20] However, as has also been demonstrated previously Ferreira's interpretation of this passage is not supported by the evidence.[21] In this passage Newman does not make a clear distinction between human faith and Divine Faith, nor does he state that the two have the same material object, while differing only according to their formal objects.

Regarding the second point Newman's statements in his writings on the Pre-eminence of Catholic Divine Faith demonstrate that the role of grace is so distinctive and unique that the adherence of Catholic Divine Faith does require an affirmation over and above the affirmation involved in the certitude of human faith. The preponderance of the evidence indicates that Newman held that Catholic Divine Faith possessed a certitude that was greater than and superior to all human certitudes. In the discourse on "Faith and Doubt" Newman describes the certainty of Catholic Divine Faith as greater than any other certainty.[22] Newman's *Theological Papers on Faith and Certainty* further support the view that he saw Catholic Divine Faith as having the highest degree of certainty.[23] In his *Thesis de Fide* Newman describes the certitude of Catholic Divine Faith as an "absolute and perfect" certitude.[24]

Now, what for Newman is the basis of this superior certitude of Catholic Divine Faith? Can the process of arriving at the certitude of Catholic Divine Faith be explained, according to Newman, simply on the basis of the human rational process of reaching certitude as outlined in the *Grammar of Assent*? Are the purely rational processes of assent, investigation, informal inference and the illative sense sufficient in themselves to lead the believer from the evidences of Christianity to the certitude of Catholic Divine Faith? Admittedly, it seems evident that Newman would see these processes as being operative in the human side of the psychological response of the act of Catholic Divine Faith. However, it seems equally evident that for Newman the certitude of Catholic Divine Faith cannot be completely explained as the result of these natural, human and rational processes.

The certitude of Catholic Divine Faith is not based exclusively upon rational processes. The certitude of Catholic Divine Faith is not based upon the intrinsic grounds of rational evidence nor upon the intellect's ability to prove and demonstrate the truths of Divine Faith.[25] In Catholic Divine Faith assent is not given because one sees with the eye or sees with reason.[26] Catholic Divine Faith is not a mere conviction of reason.[27] The assent of Catholic Divine Faith goes beyond the limitations and probability of the rational evidence available for faith. Although it shares this feature with human certitude, the certitude of Catholic Divine Faith cannot be solely explained on the basis of the human rational operations involved in the process of arriving at certitude. What enables Catholic Divine Faith to go beyond the probability of the evidence to an assent of certitude is the fact that the assent of Catholic Divine Faith is based upon the authority of the Word of God. As Newman states the certitude of Catholic Divine Faith is based ". . . solely on the fact that God, the Eternal Truth who cannot deceive nor be deceived, has spoken."[28] What enables the believer to accept the truths with the absolute certitude of faith is none other than that they have the guarantee that they have been revealed by the infallible Word of God. It is evident that for Newman Catholic Divine Faith is supernatural and cannot exist without its formal object, the authority of the Word of God revealing.[29] Furthermore, it is equally clear that what this is saying is that ultimately the certitude of Catholic Divine Faith is the result of the grace of God. As Newman points out in the discourse on "Faith and Doubt" Catholic Divine Faith is not a "mere act of our own which we are free to exert when we will," but is "quite distinct from an exercise of reason," and is, ". . . wrought in the mind by the grace of God, and by it alone."[30]

For the Catholic the Word of God, and along with it grace, is encountered and known in and through the mediation of the teaching authority of the Catholic Church which has the gift of infallibility. The teaching authority of the Catholic Church plays a central role in the certitude of Catholic Divine Faith. According to Newman what the Church declares is God's Word and is, therefore, true.[31] Newman often speaks of the Catholic Church as the "oracle of God."[32] However, the authority of the Catholic Church is even more commanding because it possesses the gift of infallibility. Consequently, Newman refers to the Catholic Church as the "sure oracle of truth," and the "messenger of heaven."[33] Newman strongly expresses this view of the role of the Catholic Church in the *Grammar of Assent*. " The word of the Church is the word of revelation. That the [Catholic] Church is the infallible oracle of truth is the fundamental dogma of the Catholic religion. . ."[34]

Perhaps Newman's most definitive statement on the Preeminence of the certitude of Catholic Divine Faith is found in the *Grammar of Assent*. Here Newman states that Divine Faith is superior to human faith not merely in degree of assent, but in nature and kind, so that the two do not admit of being compared to one another.[35] Newman continues by further explaining the nature of the superiority of the assent of Divine Faith: " . . . in the assent which follows on a divine announcement, and is vivified by a divine grace, there is, from the nature of the case, a distinctive difference." Newman's understanding of religious truth is rooted in what Miller refers to as the principle of disproportion.[36]

On the one hand, when applied to religious truth the principle of disproportion demonstrates that a religious doctrine, even through truthful, is only a partial truth.[37] An infallible statement defines only some partial aspect of a given religious truth. Infallibility only guarantees that the aspect of a religious truth which is explicitly defined will be free from error. Consequently, it is only that explicitly defined aspect of an infallible teaching which is immune to criticism. However, on the other hand the principle of disproportion demonstrates that there are many aspects of a religious truth, including an infallibly defined one, which are open to debate and offer areas in which there is legitimate freedom for speculation.[38] In an infallible doctrine the areas open to rational criticism would include such areas as the undefined aspects of the doctrine involved, its relation to other doctrines, the prefatory and introductory remarks which precede the definition, the reasons given for the definition, historical references and the interpretation of texts cited.[39] Therefore, even an infallible teaching has aspects which are open to rational criticism and so infallibility does not render Catholic Divine Faith absolutely immune to rational criticism.

Following Vatican Council I Newman holds that the domain of the Catholic Church's infallible teaching authority is limited to its teachings in the area of faith and morals.[40] This means that there are many areas in which the Catholic Church's teachings are not guaranteed by the gift of infallibility. From his works in the Uniform Edition it is evident that Newman made a distinction between the infallible and noninfallible teachings of the Church.[41] As a general rule when Newman makes the distinction between infallible and noninfallible teachings he insists that a Catholic has an obligation to obey the Church and the Pope even in matters which are not infallible.[42] However, in *The Letter to the Duke of Norfolk*, Newman makes a notable exception to the general rule. When, in certain extreme cases, there is a conflict between conscience and the teaching of the Pope in noninfallible matters, one should follow conscience even if it means disobeying the Pope.[43] Newman gives a classical statement of the priority of conscience in religious matters in the following remark.

> Certainly, if I am obliged to bring religion into after-dinner toasts, (which indeed does not seem quite the thing) I shall drink—to the Pope, if you please,—still, to Conscience first, and to the Pope afterwards.[44]

Newman cites a statement from the Fourth Lateran Council, "He who acts against his conscience loses his soul," and such authorities as St. Thomas Aquinas, St. Bonaventure and Cajetan in support of his position on the priority of conscience.[45]

Another aspect of Newman's view of infallibility which is significant for the role of rational criticism in Catholic Divine Faith is that Newman holds that the exercise of infallibility, either by a council or the Pope, must be subordinate to Revelation, the deposit of faith. In the *Apologia Pro Vita Sua* Newman insists that infallibility must be guided by Scripture and Tradition.[46] When discussing the limitations of infallibility in *The Letter to the Duke of Norfolk*, Newman argues that an infallible proposition will have no claim upon the Catholic believer unless it is referable to the Apostolic *depositum*, either through the channel of Scripture or Tradition.[47] Toward the end of *The Letter to the Duke of Norfolk* Newman cites a quotation from a Pastoral Letter of the Swiss Bishops (a Pastoral which has received the Pope's approbation, Newman adds) on the limitation of the power of the Papacy.

> He [the Pope] is tied up and limited to the divine revelation, and to the truths which that revelation contains. He is tied up and limited by the Creeds, already in existence, and by preceding definitions of the Church. He is tied up and limited by the divine law, and by the constitution of the Church.[48]

What the above statements suggest is that Newman does see a distinction between Revelation, the deposit of faith, and the Church's authoritative expressions of that revelation. The Church is the infallible oracle of God's Revelation, but it is not completely identified with the Word of God. The consequences of such a distinction for the place of rational criticism within Catholic Divine Faith are significant. For if one makes such a distinction, it cannot be claimed that one owes the same type of assent to the teachings of the

Church that one owes to the Word of God. The distinction provides a whole range of areas in which rational criticism can be applied to the concrete teachings of the Church, whether they are infallible or not.

Therefore, even though for Newman the assent of Catholic Divine Faith involves an unconditional commitment which of its nature makes it immune to certain forms of rational criticism, in no way has Newman reduced Catholic Divine Faith to a form of dogmatism which involves a rebellion against reason. On the contrary, it is evident that for Newman there are many areas in which Catholic Divine Faith is open to rational criticism. Without attempting to be exhaustive we will briefly examine some of the forms of rational criticism which Newman holds to be compatible with the assent of Catholic Divine Faith.

One of the main forms of rational criticism which Newman maintains is compatible with the assent of Catholic Divine Faith is investigation. Investigation, for Newman, is the rational process of examining the grounds for the truth of a proposition to which we are giving assent. It is the rational act of trying to prove what we already hold to be true.[49] We are moved to do this for various reasons: either to convince someone who disagrees with us on a given point, to ascertain the producible evidence in favor of a proposition, to fulfill what is due to ourselves and to the claims and responsibilities of our own education and social status.[50] What is distinctive about investigation is that throughout the whole process we continue to assent to the proposition we are investigating and never doubt its truth.[51] Since it does not involve doubt, or the suspension of assent, while the process of reasoning is being conducted, investigation is compatible with assent and certitude. The absence of doubt is what distinguishes investigation from inquiry. Inquiry implies doubt, investigation does not and it is for this reason that those who assent to a truth ". . . may without inconsistency investigate its credibility, though they cannot literally inquire about its truth."[52] Newman goes on to state that for the educated person investigation into the proof of things to which they give assent is ". . . an obligation, or rather, a necessity."[53]

In the *Grammar of Assent* Newman suggests that investigation is compatible with Catholic Divine Faith when he distinguishes between investigation, which does not imply doubt, and inquiry, which does imply doubt, and condemns inquiry as being incompatible with Catholic Faith, because it implies doubt.[54] When discussing Catholic

Divine Faith in the discourse on "Faith and Doubt, Newman admits that investigation is compatible with the faith of the Catholic believer. The reason being that since investigation does not involve doubt, as inquiry does, investigation is compatible with the certitude of Divine Faith.[55]

Theology itself is a form of investigation for Newman. In *The Development of Doctrine* Newman defines Theology as the scientific analysis of revealed truth.[56] Theology is a form of questioning which is compatible with the "fullest and most absolute faith."[57] In Theology reason serves faith by handling, examining, explaining, recording, cataloging, and defending the truths of faith. Reason also provides intellectual forms of expression for the truths of faith, elicits what is implicit, compares, measures and connects revealed truths with one another forming them into one theological system.[58] According to Newman scripture supports this form of investigation and Mary provides us with a model of this spirit of inquisitiveness in faith. She "kept these things and pondered them in her heart" (Luke 2:51). Newman adds that Jesus himself does not countenance a blind unthinking faith, what Newman calls "lightness of mind."[59] On the contrary, Jesus called upon his disciples to use reason and to submit to it.[60]

Another form of rational criticism which Newman held was central to Theology was historical criticism, particularly as a necessary element in the process of interpreting revealed truths. According to Thomas J. Norris, Newman could not conceive of revealed truth apart from the categories of history and, consequently, historical criticism was essential to Newman's theological method.[61] One of Newman's first objectives after becoming a Catholic was to establish a School of Theology at Maryvale. According to Wilfrid Ward the purpose of this school would have been to investigate the apparent conflicts of truth within history, truth would eventually win out. Newman had a ready formula to handle the apparent conflicts between human truths and the revealed truths of faith. According to Newman the believer can be certain that:

> "... nothing shall make him [her] doubt, that, if anything seems to be proved ... in contradiction to the dogmas of faith, that point will eventually turn out, first, *not* to be proved, or secondly, not *contradictory*, or thirdly, not contradictory to any thing *really revealed*, but to something which has been confused with revelation."[62]

In general, the findings of this criticism support the conclusion that within Catholic Divine Faith, there is room for freedom of thought. Miller presents a very convincing case supporting the thesis that Newman was a strong advocate of freedom of thought within the Church.[63] One of the factors which enabled Newman to be such a strong advocate of this freedom of thought was his trust in the power of truth. Newman felt that essentially truth could never contradict itself and that, in the apparent conflicts of truth within history, truth would eventually win out.

The conclusions of this chapter confirm Ferreira's view that the assent of Divine Faith, for Newman, is not an irrational form of dogmatism which requires a rebellion against reason in order to be maintained. However, the extent of the openness of Catholic Divine Faith to rational criticism as presented in this chapter does not go as far as, perhaps, Ferreira would like. Ferreira's acceptance of a strand of defectibility in Newman's notion of certitude and her identification of the affirmations of human faith and Divine Faith seem to open Divine Faith to forms of rational criticism which are not accepted as being compatible with Catholic Divine Faith.

NOTES

1. M. Jaime Ferreira, *Doubt and Religious Commitment: The Role of the Will in Newman's Thought* (Oxford: Clarendon Press, 1980), 4-5.
2. *Ibid.*
3. John Henry Newman, "Papers in Preparation for *A Grammar of Assent, 1865-1869*," ed., Achaval and Holmes, The Theological Papers of John Henry Newman on Faith and Certainty (Oxford: Clarendon Press, 1976), 132-33.
4. *Ibid.*, 132-34. These private revelations come through what Newman calls the private channels of revealed truth. He mentions three channels of private revelation (Visio, Scriptura, Traditio divina), and adds a possible fourth, the necessary conclusion from a defined premise. Although obligatory on the mind possessing them, the truths of Divine Faith cannot be imposed upon others and Catholics who do not accept them are not outside the Church.
5. Ferreira, *Doubt and Religious Commitment*, 141-42. Ferreira speaks only of Divine Faith and does not explicitly refer to the distinction between Catholic Divine Faith and Divine Faith.
6. *Ibid.*, 144.
7. *Ibid.*, 15. Ferreira states that in the *Grammar of Assent* Newman is only examining the assent which follows religious inquiry.
8. *Ibid.*, 131.
9. *Ibid.*
10. John Henry Newman, *An Essay in Aid of a Grammar of Assent* (London: Longmans, Green and Co., 1947), 76.
11. Ferreira, *Doubt and Religious Commitment*, 15. Although Pailin does not describe Newman's subject matter in the *Grammar of Assent* as a natural religious belief, he does state that Newman does not discuss the supernatural aspect of faith in this work, David A. Pailin, *The Way to Faith: An Examination of Newman's Grammar of Assent as a Response to the Search for Certainty in Faith* (London: Epworth Press, 1969), 263, note # 31. Jay Newman states that considerations of revelation do not enter into the scope of the *Grammar of Assent*, Jay Newman, *The Mental Philosophy of John Henry Newman* (Waterloo, Ontario,

Canada: Wilfrid Laurier University Press, 1986), 66-67. However, it must be pointed out that Newman does not say that revelation is beyond the scope of the present inquiry, but "because He says it," the formal object of faith, is beyond the scope of the present inquiry, Newman, *Grammar of Assent*, 76.

12. Newman, "Papers in Preparation of GA," 133-34.
13. Pailin, *Way to Faith*, 266, note # 22.
14. Newman, *Grammar of Assent*, 114-15.
15. P.J. Fitzpatrick, "A Study in the *Grammar of Assent*, II," *Irish Theological Quarterly*, 45,4 (1978), 230. Actually, Fitzpatrick offers this as limitation of Newman's analysis in the *Grammar of Assent*.
16. Newman, "The Evidences of Religion," January 12, 1860, *The Theological Papers on Faith and Certainty*, 86.
17. Ferreira, *Doubt and Religious Commitment*, 135.
18. *Ibid.*, 136.
19. *Ibid.*, 131-32, 134, 136.
20. See above, 4.
21. See above, 4-5.
22. John Henry Newman, *Discourses Addressed to Mixed Congregations* (London: Longmans, Green, and Co., 1906), 224. See also, William R. Fey, *Faith and Doubt: The Unfolding of Newman's Thought on Certainty* (Shepherdstown, WV: Patmos Press, 1976) 224.
23. Newman, "Papers of 1853 on the Certainty of Faith," *The Theological Papers on Faith and Certainty*, 4-5. Here Newman maintains that Catholic Divine Faith has the highest degree of certainty, one that excludes fear as well as doubt.
24. John Henry Newman, ed., by Henry Tristram, "Cardinal Newman's Thesis de Fide and his proposed Introduction to the French Translation of the University Sermons," (1847) *Gregorianum*, 18 (1927), Thesis # 110, 236.
25. Newman, *Grammar of Assent*, 237. Cf., Newman, "Faith and Private Judgment," *Mixed Congregations*, 194-95.
26. Newman, *Mixed Congregations*, 195-96.
27. *Ibid.*, 224.
28. Newman, *Thesis de Fide*, Thesis # 110, 236.
29. Newman, *The Theological Papers on Faith and Certainty*, 37, 38, 139.

30. Newman, *Mixed Congregations*, 224-25.
31. *Ibid.*, 215.
32. *Ibid.* Cf., John Henry Newman, *Apologia Pro Vita Sua; Being a History of His Religious Opinions* (Oxford: Clarendon Press, 1967), 215.
33. Newman, *Mixed Congregations*, 227.
34. Newman, *Grammar of Assent*, 115.
35. *Ibid.*, 140-41.
36. Edward Jeremy Miller, *John Henry Newman on the Idea of Church* (Shepherdstown, West Virginia: The Patmos Press, 1987), 83-84.
37. *Ibid.*, 84.
38. *Ibid.*
39. John Henry Newman, *A Letter Addressed to His Grace the Duke of Norfolk on Occasion of Mr. Gladstone's Recent Expostulation, Certain Difficulties felt by Anglicans in Catholic Teaching Considered* (London: Longmans, Green and Co., 1907) Vol. II, 324-31. Cf. Miller, *Newman on Idea of Church*, 112.
40. Newman, *Duke of Norfolk*, 325. Cf., *Apologia*, 227.
41. *Ibid.*, 224. See also, Newman, *Development of Doctrine*, 104 and *Apologia*, 230-31.
42. Newman, *Development of Doctrine*, 104, *Duke of Norfolk*, 224-26, 235-36, and *Apologia*, 225.
43. Newman, *Duke of Norfolk*, 246-58.
44. *Ibid.*, 261.
45. *Ibid.*, 259.
46. Newman, *Apologia*, 227, "It [infallibility] must refer to the particular Apostolic truth which it is enforcing, or (what is called) *defining*."
47. Newman, *Duke of Norfolk*, 229-30.
48. *Ibid.*, 339.
49. Newman, *Grammar of Assent*, 144.
50. *Ibid.*
51. *Ibid.*, "Therefore to set about concluding a proposition is not *ipso facto* to doubt its truth; we may aim at inferring a proposition, while all the time we assent to it."
52. *Ibid.*, 145.
53. *Ibid.*
54. *Ibid.*, 144.
55. Newman, *Mixed Congregations*, 226-27.

56. Newman, *Development of Doctrine*, 321.
57. *Ibid.*
58. *Ibid.*
59. *Ibid.*, 322.
60. *Ibid.*
61. Thomas J. Norris, *Newman and His Theological Method: A Guide for the Theologian Today* (Leiden: E.J. Brill, 1977), 158-59.
62. John Henry Newman, *The Idea of a University Defined and Illustrated: I. in Nine Discourses Delivered to the Catholics of Dublin, II. in Occasional Lectures and Essays Addressed to the Members of the Catholic University* (London: Longmans Green and Co., 1907), 446-47.
63. Miller, *Newman on Idea of Church*, 81-98.
64. John Henry Newman, *The Idea of a University Defined and Illustrated: I. in Nine Discourses Delivered to the Catholics of Dublin, II. in Occasional Lectures and Essays Addressed to the Members of the Catholic University* (London: Longmans Green and Co., 1907), 446-47.

IMAGINATIVE DISCERNMENT:
Newman's Safeguard of Faith and Morals

Gerard Magill

>Moral truth is gained by patient study,
>by calm reflection, silently as the dew falls . . .[1]

To appreciate the stature of John Henry Newman (1801-1890) in the centenary year of his death an essay on his view of catechesis can provide an unusual overview of many important elements in his writings.[2] Newman's dedication to teaching religion, both as a pastor and a scholar, resulted in a plethora of publications that remain challenging a century later. Although he never specifically studied catechesis at length, his understanding of its major features became apparent in the analysis of belief throughout his works. In particular, his interest in catechesis arose from his concern for safeguarding faith and morals. My essay will be restricted to Newman's writings because there appears to be no extensive study in the secondary literature of Newman's catechesis from the perspective of both Faith and Morals.[3] I will argue that Newman appealed to the Religious Imagination as the safeguard of Faith and Morals: the resulting insight into moral truth, the fruit of imaginative discernment, occurring only "slowly as the dew falls," as suggested in the citation which begins this essay.

Religious insight had occurred in Newman's two conversion experiences. As a teenager of fifteen, his first conversion was deeply emotional. Impressed by the Calvinistic and the Evangelical writings of his day, his lack of clear religious convictions shifted to an affective awareness of the divine presence in his life. But his second conversion, to Catholicism thirty years later in 1845, was discerned in a more rational way. He decided to take the path to Rome as a result of his historical analysis of doctrinal development down the Christian centuries. In October 1845 he published this work, still incomplete due to his conversion, as *An Essay on the Development of Christian Doctrine.*[4] He had resigned from his university fellowship at Oriel College, Oxford three days previously, a position he had held as an Anglican vicar since 1822. The entwining of emotion and reason in these two conversion experiences shaped his catechesis; he would navigate the journey of spiritual growth by integrating his finely attuned feelings with his acutely perceptive intellect.

However, Newman's contribution to catechesis is modest because he never focused upon the context and content of catechesis as we might now. But his interest in the method that underlies the formation of religious belief remains relevant and arguably[5] can provide a valuable basis for catechesis today. His view of catechesis embraced a threefold dialectic between his pastoral, educational, and theological concerns for safeguarding faith and morals. That is, he wanted to establish an intricate bond between the lifelong process of growing in faith (his pastoral concern), effective religious education (his educational concern), and dialogue between believers (his theological concern), in order to build a Christian community of ongoing conversion. This essay examines these three concerns to explain how they fit together as interdependent features of his catechesis by an appeal to the Religious Imagination.

1. *Pastoral Concern: Love and Faith*

Newman was very anxious to persuade his readers of the importance of living knowledge in faith and morals. He pointed out the dangers of a merely nominal allegiance to religion that proclaimed belief but did little to implement it in concrete action. In 1852 he identified this attitude in his discourses at the Catholic University of Dublin, where he had been appointed rector by the English Bishops. Recalling the biblical imagery of the sower he explained that a shallow profession of faith "springs up suddenly, it suddenly withers" (*Idea*, 202); this superficiality is the mark of a "Religion of Reason" (*Idea*, 182)[5] that undermines the fabric of Christianity as a religion of faith and morals, of proclamation and action.

While recognizing that abstract belief crosses denominational lines, to contrast it with genuine religious commitment he called upon his experience of Catholicism "as a system of pastoral instruction and moral duty" (*Idea*, 183). From a pastoral perspective he argued that we can have faith that involves the whole person, heart and mind. We can perceive concrete truth with a vigor that urges moral action. We can have an orthodoxy tied to orthopraxis. This constitutes a living knowledge that underlies religious teaching. In later lectures on the university, delivered in 1854, Newman identified this with catechesis.

> Religious teaching ... is the living voice, the breathing form, the expressive countenance, which preaches, which *catechises* (*H.S.* 3:14, my emphasis).[6]

To acquire such dynamic belief he prescribed a connection between learning in love and growing in holiness. This can be called his pastoral concern for safeguarding faith and morals. In his sermon, "Love the Safeguard of Faith against Superstition," preached at St. Mary's in 1839, he examined the borderline between legitimate faith and superstition.[7] Written just five years before his conversion, his homily manifested a greater sensitivity to the balance of emotion and reason than had been the case in his earlier, more evangelical conversion. Here he sought to avoid the extremes of nineteenth-century rationalism and romanticism by proposing love as the safeguard of faith.

Faith requires an act of the intellect, but it cannot be reduced to reason alone. Rather, he explained that faith "is itself an intellectual act, and it takes its character from the moral state of the agent" (*Sermons*, 249-250). He meant that faith is influenced by our subjective attitude: "right Faith is an intellectual act, done in a certain moral disposition" (*Sermons*, 239). This insight is central to his pastoral outlook: ethical virtue influences the intellectual perception of faith. Hence, love is crucial for faith.

However, for love to be the "illuminating principle of true faith" (*Sermons*, 234), moral disposition alone is insufficient; God's grace is also required, that is, "the Light of heaven which animates and guides it (faith)" (*Sermons*, 249). That is why growth in the moral disposition of love is lifelong, even though aided by God's light. Faith, then, always implies "a moving forward in the twilight, yet not without clue or direction" (*Sermons*, 249). While sailing in the Mediterranean in 1833 on his return from Italy he eloquently expressed this understanding of Divine love as illuminating faith: "Lead, Kindly Light, amid the encircling gloom."[8]

Despite Newman's appeal to the head and heart for the development of faith, his view hovers around a relativism that must be addressed carefully by catechesis today lest the complexity of religious belief is reduced to a naive moralism. Experience tells us that good people do not necessarily have the best religious insights. This poses the question whether love ought to have the priority over faith that Newman apparently suggests. The propensity for widespread diversity in religious belief based upon the subjective disposition of love is potentially, for the critical scholar, the most serious weakness in Newman's argument. Such questions arise because the title of Newman's sermon, "Love as the safeguard of Faith," is quite different from the ensuing discussion in the sermon that love is only one important aspect of faith. The sermon claims that God's grace interacts with the human intellect in religious belief, not that love alone is sufficient for faith.

However, close attention to his argument and its context diminishes the threat of relativism. The importance of the interaction between love and the intellect, between the heart and the head, becomes clearer in light of Newman's historical struggle. He resisted religious rationalism in the nineteenth century, which he described as "a time when love was cold" (*Sermons*, 197), as much as he rejected religious romanticism which he explained was "not a religion of . . . acts of faith and of direct devotion; but of sacred scenes and pious sentiments" (*Grammar*, 56).[9] By repudiating both extremes, certainly from his years at Oriel onwards, his sermon suggested that he was more interested in the parallel of love and faith with emotion and reason, than in creating a priority of love over reason.

As early as 1835, in the *Parochial and Plain Sermons*, which he preached to his parishioners in St. Mary's and which inspired the Oxford Movement so much, relativism clearly caused him alarm. For he recognized the danger of "making the test of our being religious, to consist in our having what is called a spiritual state of heart, to the comparative neglect of the Object from which it must arise" (*P.S.* 2:154).[10] Precisely to counter this he justified his theory of belief by appeal to reasoning and warranted judgement. The objective truth of faith and the subjective disposition of love (which he also called devotion) must complement one another. And thirty years later, in 1865, he reminded his readers of the complementarity in this tension:

"that distinction between faith and devotion on which I am insisting. It is like the distinction between objective and subjective truth" (*Diff.* 2:27-28).[11] Newman wanted to harness love and faith, emotion and reason, to encourage a subjective discernment of truth that eschewed relativism.

He also insisted that subjective holiness was indispensable for faith. By associating love with our moral disposition or state of heart in 1839, he was projecting spiritual growth as critical for the process of faith development: "holiness, . . . or love, however we word it, and not Reason, is the eye of Faith" (*Sermons*, 238). Developing faith is a matter of ongoing conversion both of the head and the heart. But the change of heart was the cornerstone of his spirituality: "(w)hen men change their religious opinions really and truly, it is not merely their opinions that they change, but their hearts" (*P.S.* 8:225). Love generates the momentum for the intellectual perception of faith insofar as it molds our subjective disposition. Here is the Christological basis of Newman's spirituality.

In 1838 he published his *Lectures on Justification* in which he sidestepped the Scholastic and Reformation debate on the meaning of justification by returning to the biblical teaching. He argued that justification is not primarily a matter of faith or works; rather, justification is "that one great gift of God, the indwelling Christ in the Christian soul" (*Justification*, 154).[12] God's indwelling, then, was the love that would become his illuminating principle of faith. Therefore, these lectures clarify his subsequent view of moral disposition (love), as referring both to virtue and to holiness: to virtue because "righteousness is nothing else than moral goodness" (*Justification*, 107); to holiness insofar as "(t)hat indwelling is ipso facto our justification and sanctification" (*Justification*, 154). In other words, in the year prior to his sermon on love and faith, when writing these lectures, he had described moral disposition as including virtue and devotion (holiness).

His pastoral concern was to portray personal holiness as concomitant with moral virtue, each arising from Christ's saving presence in our hearts. This represented the ideal of his Christological spirituality, an ideal that not only integrated personal morality with holiness but also one that would later symbolize his elevation to the College of Cardinals in May 1879. For his coat of arms Newman chose the words "Cor ad Cor Loquitur," that is, "Heart Speaks to Heart," a tribute to his zeal for truth in faith and morals.

In sum, Newman argued that learning faith in love cannot be separated from growing in holiness. These facets of his pastoral concern reined together the disparate forces of head and heart in seeking to safeguard faith and morals. But his pastoral concern did not explain the intellectual aspect of personal growth. As a second feature of his catechesis his educational concern addressed this question.

2. Educational Concern: Intellectual and Moral Character

Newman indicated the connection between his pastoral concern and his educational concern for religious truth in a letter written to W.G. Ward in November 1860: "the more a man is educated, . . . the holier he needs to be, if he would be saved" (*Letters*, xix:417). The parallel between education and piety was founded upon a deeper principle—that personal growth, like the development of doctrine, occurs slowly over a long period: "to live is to change, and to be perfect is to have changed often" (*Development*, 40). But change alone does not guarantee intellectual or spiritual maturity. Newman had to examine the sort of personal change that enhances religious commitment. This can be called his educational concern for safeguarding faith and morals.

Although he made a clear distinction between religion, virtue, and knowledge,[13] he was convinced of the significant influence of education upon personal character: "(b)ut education . . . implies an action upon our mental nature, and the formation of a character" (*Idea*, 114). Here Newman was referring not just to the moral character that was so important for his pastoral concern, but also to the intellectual formation of the individual that would embody his educational concern at his Catholic Dublin university.

Nearly two decades later he explicitly combined these concerns to form the basis of his theory of belief when writing the *Grammar* in 1870. Both the intellectual and moral aspects of personal growth influence the perception of religious truth:

> We judge for ourselves, by our own lights, and our own principles; and our criterion of truth is not so much the manipulation of propositions, as the intellectual and moral character of the person maintaining them" (*Grammar*, 302).

Here an interesting parallel appears between Newman's pastoral and educational concerns. Just as the relation between moral virtue and holiness specified the former, the latter is distinctive because of the interaction between moral virtue and wisdom. The force of this comparison emphasizes that both love and wisdom illumine faith.

Wisdom had a very specific meaning for Newman. He argued that education should never be reduced to accumulating or memorizing information. True learning results from relating diverse aspects of knowledge. As a result, wisdom represents our synthesis of knowledge. In the discourses on university education at Dublin in 1852 he explained that wisdom was not a static, encyclopedic summary of data, but rather a creative outlook of integrative learning in which each aspect of knowledge is "interpretative of one another in the unity of a whole" (*Idea*, 179). Wisdom interprets data within a broad vision. To describe this outlook he coined the term, the "enlargement of mind" (*Idea*, 130), suggesting a keen mental alertness. This constituted the cultivation of the intellect: "it is an acquired faculty of judgement, of clearsightedness, of sagacity, of wisdom, of philosophical reach of mind . . ." (*Idea*, 152). Another term to describe his ideal of education was "the expanding reason" which he associated with catechesis. After his installation as rector of the new Catholic University at Dublin in June 1854, he described the university in this way:

> It is the place where the *catechist* makes good his ground as he goes, treading in the truth day by day into the ready memory, and wedging and tightening it into *the expanding reason* (H.S. 3:16, my emphasis).

Catechesis requires "the expanding reason," or wisdom, as the educational basis for the development of religious belief. Therefore, faith is illuminated by wisdom as well as love. Insofar as wisdom and love (or holiness) are influenced by the moral character of the individual, Newman established an important bond between his educational and pastoral concerns, between wisdom and holiness, each inseparable from personal virtue. Based upon this rapport between holiness, virtue, and wisdom, he developed another major feature of his catechesis: his theology of history and the Christian community.

3. Theological Concern: History and Community

When Newman lectured on the identity of a university in 1854 his pastoral, educational, and theological concerns for religious truth were inseparable. He argued that "we must come to the teachers of wisdom to learn wisdom" (*H.S.* 3:9). Therefore, religious teaching can be perceived pastorally as ". . . the living voice . . . which catechizes" (*H.S.* 3:14), a catechesis based upon the illumination of faith by love and holiness. If this is to occur we must primarily rely upon tradition: "in theological language, Oral Tradition" (*H.S.* 3:14). Catechesis, or oral teaching, the living tradition of the Church, can illumine religious belief, just as love and wisdom do. This can be called his theological concern for safeguarding faith and morals.

Four years earlier in 1850 he had identified the urgency of promoting theology in the English Church. Monsignor George Talbot, the papal chamberlain to Pope Pius IX, had encouraged Newman to use his services to inform the Pope of the church's needs in England. Newman's response was stunning: ". . . our most crying want is the want of theology" (*Letters*, xiv:35). Such interest in promoting theology followed on the heels of the educational concern that he had expressed in the previous year when repudiating mistaken Protestant perceptions of Catholicism: "I want an intelligent, well-instructed laity . . . In all times the laity have been the measure of the Catholic spirit."[14] In the following decades the role of the educated laity became a significant feature of his theology, especially when examining how the Catholic Church should respond to its newfound religious freedom.

A vigorous revival of English Catholicism in the middle of the nineteenth century was the direct result of Catholic Emancipation in 1829 and the restoration of the English hierarchy in 1850. Newman, five years after his own conversion, eloquently celebrated this renewal in his moving sermon, "The Second Spring," which he preached on the occasion of the first provincial synod of the new hierarchy at Oscott in July 1852. He qualified his exhilaration and optimism by a wise caution to the Bishops: should we be surprised, he asked, if ". . . the spring-time of the Church should turn out to be an English spring, . . . of keen blasts, and cold showers, and sudden storms?"[15] His warning was well founded as a chilling controversy over authority began to cloud the Catholic revival.

A tempest loomed between Ultramontanism, led by Archbishop Manning and W.G. Ward, and Liberal Catholicism, championed by Wilfred Ward under the leadership of Sir John Acton and also Richard Simpson. Although Newman sided with neither group, his moderate views were more sympathetic with the latter. This became more apparent as the years passed. In July 1859 his article "On Consulting the Faithful in Matters of Doctrine" was published in the *Rambler*, the journal of Liberal Catholics, edited by Richard Simpson. Newman made a claim that shocked the Bishops and alienated the Ultramontanists. He argued that the historical judgments of the Christian community, which he called the subjective conscience of the Church, should be consulted before the definition of doctrine.[16]

The two crucial elements of his article on consulting, the role both of historical discernment and of the Christian community in the perception of religious truth, had already appeared in his essay on doctrinal development which had spurred his conversion in 1845. First, he had argued that development ". . . is carried on through and by means of communities of men and their leaders and guides" (*Development*, 38); and second that the legitimacy of such change "imparts to the history" of religion an unavoidable polemic (*Development*, 39). But his 1859 article in the *Rambler* brought these concepts of history and community much more closely together. As a result his confidence in the role of history and community for discerning religious truth provided an interpretative principle for his later thought, especially when explaining his religious convictions in the *Apologia*: "the principle of dogma" is ". . . the fundamental principle of my religion" (*Apologia*, 54).

Newman's defence of dogma can be easily misconstrued as an outright appeal to ecclesial authority. But his unhesitating defence of Catholic dogma cannot be separated from an increasing reliance in his later writings upon the historical judgments of the believing community. The authoritarian rigor of Ultramontane dogmatism had no place in his thought. And the restrictive discipline of the Vatican's *Syllabus of Errors* in 1864 and the First Vatican Council's declaration of Infallibility in 1870 caused Newman little hesitation in continuing to defend the historical judgments of the community. That is why, with prophetic boldness, in 1875 he defended ". . . the supreme authority of Conscience" (*Diff.* 2:246), and attempted to explain away the papal reservations about the primacy of conscience.[17] Almost a century later, the Second Vatican Council would stand with Newman to defend the supremacy and dignity of conscience.[18]

Newman's respect for conscience was an expression of his theological concern to uphold the historical judgments of the Christian community in the perception of religious truth. Conscience, then, accompanies the flourishing of holiness, virtue, and wisdom, features of his pastoral and educational concerns. Although he made no systematic connection between these concerns, they constitute separate but intertwined facets of his catechesis, his quest for moral truth needing the combined insights of each. The cohesion between these insights required the imagination.

> Truth, a subtle, invisible, manifold spirit, is poured into the mind of the scholar . . . through his affections, *imagination*, and reason; . . . by all those ways which are implied in the word *"catechising"* (*H.S.* 3:14-15, my emphasis).

4. *Imaginative Discernment*

In these words Newman indicated that the imagination is separate from affection and reason. Although there were many uses of the imagination in his thought, the dominant one appears as a link between the heart and the head. His appeal to the imagination included both emotion and intellect, and represented the complex interaction of the pastoral, educational, and theological concerns of his catechesis. In this sense the imaginative discernment of religious truth was the safeguard of faith and morals. To understand what this meant requires a brief review of the imagination in his thought.

First, the imagination enables us to grasp truth in an experiential way. This was crucial for the effective teaching of church dogmas which are expressed in propositions that are all too often mere abstractions, though they can express truth in a concrete and real way:

> A dogma is a proposition; . . . It is discerned, rested in, and appropriated as a reality, by the religious imagination (*Grammar*, 98).

Analogously, our belief in marriage as an abstract doctrine is transformed when we decide to marry. Through experience our imagination makes concrete and enlivens our abstract belief in marriage.

Second, this experiential function of the imagination is inseparable from its holistic role. For example, when we decide to marry we hold all the relevant arguments together, in a comprehensive whole to justify our commitment. It is the imagination that maintains this synthesis. Newman likened this function to ". . . mounting some high hill or church tower, by way of reconnoitring its neighbourhood" (*Idea*, 140). At root, the imagination can grasp complex knowledge in an experiential way, relating its many aspects coherently together. Hence, in 1857 he explained that "(r)eason in the imagination holds views at once per modum unius . . ."[19] as a whole, comprehensively.

Each of these functions of the imagination reflects Newman's pastoral and educational concerns. First, the experiential character of the imagination yields a living knowledge of truth. For example nuptial commitment represents a qualitatively different perception of marriage than that of abstract doctrine. Dynamic allegiance like this was central to his pastoral concern. Second, the comprehensive nature of the imagination discerns how each part of knowledge fits with the others, for example the decision to marry accumulates the available advantages and disadvantages into a meaningful whole. Integrative learning of this type was central to his educational concern. Finally, in 1870 Newman put the experiential and comprehensive functions of the imagination, each of which expressed his pastoral and educational concern for truth, at the service of theological insight:

> . . . the theology of a religious imagination . . . It has a living hold on truths . . . It is able to pronounce by anticipation, what it takes a long argument to prove . . . It interprets what it sees around it (*Grammar*, 117).

In other words, the imagination's living hold on truth (his pastoral concern), and its interpretation of surrounding knowledge (his educational concern), justify religious insight by anticipating a conclusion that cannot be rigorously proven. For example a complex decision to marry transcends a logical list of the available arguments. This anticipation of truth, reaching forward to grasp the appropriate conclusion, implements his theological concern to respect the historical judgments of the believing community even though they cannot be analytically demonstrated. Twenty-five years earlier, in 1845, he had placed this understanding of imaginative discernment at the core of doctrinal development and at the root of his catechesis. Religious insight results when we put our knowledge ". . . into a number of statements, strengthening, interpreting, correcting each other, and with more or less exactness approximating, as they accumulate, to a perfect image. There is *no other way of learning or of teaching*" (*Development*, 55, my emphasis).

Conclusion

Newman's understanding of the imagination encompassed his pastoral, educational, and theological concerns for religious truth. Each concern received its depth of meaning from the others while contributing distinctively to his view of catechesis. My argument that imaginative discernment is the safeguard of faith and morals in Newman's thought articulates the role of imagination in his catechesis, implied in his study of doctrinal development in 1845, explicitly stated in his lectures on the university in 1854, and theologically refined in his justification of religious belief in 1870. Despite the lack of any systematic study of catechesis by Newman, he nonetheless presented an interesting theological view. That is, beyond the inconsistencies that arise due to the occasional nature and style of his writings, there appears a coherent approach to religious teaching and learning in which imaginative discernment is the safeguard of faith and morals.

If my argument is plausible, Newman's achievement lies in comprehending catechesis as a holistic process in which spirituality and belief are developed as communal responsibilities. Above all, his appeal to the imagination entails a dynamic reciprocity between handing on the tradition, both in faith and morals, and the flourishing of personal experience, especially within the ecclesial community. Recalling my first citation, perhaps that is why he encouraged us to undertake a life pilgrimage of religious teaching and learning in which moral truth dawns upon us "silently as the dew falls."

NOTES

1. Newman wrote these words in a letter to his mother, Harriett Newman, in March 1829, *The Letters and Diaries of John Henry Newman*, 2:131. Edited by C.S. Dessain et al., vols. 1-6 (Oxford: Clarendon Press, 1978-84); vols. 11-22 (London: Oxford University Press, 1961-72); vols. 23-31 (Oxford: Clarendon Press, 1973-77). Hereafter referred to as *Letters*.
2. A version of the first three parts of my essay appears in "A View of Newman's Catechesis," *The Living Light* 27:2 (Winter 1991).
3. For some articles on Newman's catechesis: John R. Griffin, *Newman: A Bibliography of Secondary Studies* (Front Royal, Virginia: Christendom Publications, 1980), 44-45, 55. For a recent theological study of Newman's catechesis as a contribution to theory of religious education see Gunter Biemer, "Religious Education—a Task Between Divergent Plausibilities," *John Henry Newman and Modernism*, edited by Arthur Hilary Jenkins, Newman-Studien, vol. XIV (Sigmaringendorf, Germany: Verlag Glock und Lutz, 1990), 15-28.
4. See John Henry Newman, *An Essay on the Development of Christian Doctrine*, foreword by Ian Ker (Notre Dame, IN: University of Notre Dame Press, 1989), x. Hereafter referred to as *Development*.
5. John Henry Newman, *The Idea of a University, Defined and Illustrated*, edited, introduction, and notes by I.T. Ker (Oxford: Clarendon Press, 1976). The first part collects Newman's 1852 university discourses, originally collated with the title, *Discourses on the Scope and Nature of University Education. Addressed to the Catholics at Dublin*, only published in 1873.
   The second part contains his *Lectures and Essays on University Subjects* (1858). Page references are to the final (ninth) edition (1889). Hereafter referred to as *Idea*.
6. John Henry Newman, *Historical Sketches* (1872), vol. 3 (London: Longmans, Green, and Co., 1891). These lectures were first published separately in 1854 in the *Catholic University Gazette*, a journal of the new Catholic university in Dublin, then in 1856 in one volume, *Office and Work of Universities*, and finally in 1872 with a new title, *Rise and*

Progress of Universities, in volume 3 of *Historical Sketches*. Page references are to the 1872 edition. Hereafter referred to as *H.S.*

7. John Henry Newman, *Newman's University Sermons. Fifteen Sermons Preached before the University of Oxford 1826-43*, first published in 1842, 3rd. edition in 1871, introductions by D.M. McKinnon and J.D. Holmes (London: SPCK, 1970). Hereafter referred to as *Sermons*.

8. John Henry Newman, "The Pillar of the Cloud," (1833), *Verses on Various Occasions* (London: Burns and Oates, 1883), 152.

9. John Henry Newman, *An Essay in Aid of a Grammar of Assent* (1870), edited, introduction, and notes by I.T. Ker (Oxford: Clarendon Press, 1985), pagination of Newman's 1881 edition. Hereafter referred to as *Grammar*.

10. John Henry Newman, *Parochial and Plain Sermons* (from 1834), eight volumes (London: Longmans, Green, and Co., 1891). Hereafter referred to as *P.S.*

11. John Henry Newman, "A Letter Addressed to the Rev. E. B. Pusey, D.D., on Occasion of his Eirenicon" (1864), in *Certain Difficulties Felt by Anglicans in Catholic Teaching*, vol. 2 (London: Longmans, Green, and Co., 1898). Hereafter referred to as *Diff. 2.*

12. John Henry Newman, *Lectures on the Doctrine of Justification* (London: Rivingtons, 1885). These lectures were delivered from 13 April until 1 June, 1837 at St. Mary's, and were published in March 1838. Hereafter referred to as *Justification*.

13. See Discourse V111 in the *Idea*, especially 211, and also John Henry Newman, *Apologia Pro Vita Sua* (1864), 26, edited, introduction and notes by M.J. Svaglic (Oxford: Clarendon Press, 1967). Hereafter referred to as *Apologia*.

14. John Henry Newman, *Lectures on the Present Position of Catholics in England*, 390 (London: Longmans, Green, and Co., 1899). These lectures were originally addressed in 1851 to the "Brothers of the Oratory," which was a confraternity of laity attached to Newman's Oratory.

15. John Henry Newman, *Sermons Preached on Various Occasions*, 1857 (London: Longmans, Green, and Co., 1892), 179-180.

16. See John Henry Newman, *On Consulting the Faithful in Matters of Doctrine*, edited with an introduction by John Coulson (London: Geoffrey Chapman, 1961), 55, 73. Originally published in the *Rambler* 1 (July 1859): 198-230, and reprinted in 1871 in the third edition of *The Arians of the Fourth Century* as an appendix with significant revisions.
17. John Henry Newman, "A Letter Addressed to His Grace the Duke of Norfolk on Occasion of Mr. Gladstone's Recent Expostulation," (1874), in *Diff.* 2. Specifically, Newman discussed Pope Pius IX's reservation about the liberty of conscience in his Encyclical *Quanta Cura*, 1864 (*ibid.*, 251).
18. The "Pastoral Constitution on the Church in the Modern World" (1965), number 16, and the "Declaration on Religious Liberty" (1965), number 3, in *Vatican Council 11*, Austin Flannery, general editor (Wilmington, Delaware: Scholarly Resources Inc., 1975).
19. *The Theological Papers of John Henry Newman on Faith and Certainty*, edited by Hugo M. de Achaval and J. Derek Holmes (Oxford: Clarendon Press, 1976), 46.

CONTRIBUTORS

Madeleine Kisner, A.S.C., Professor of English/Communications, Kansas Newman College, Wichita, Kansas, has written on Eliot in *The Midwest Quarterly*, as well as writing the Appreciation and Poetry in *Newman at Oxford*. Her poems have appeared in anthologies of the American Poetry Association.

Ronald Burke, Professor and Chair, Philosophy and Religion, University of Nebraska at Omaha, was schooled at Notre Dame, Yale, and under the tutelage of Ninian Smart. In 1976, he founded the ongoing Roman Catholic Modernist Group in the AAR. He has published regarding Modernists in the *Journal of Religion*, *Religious Studies Review*, *Theological Studies*, and Eliade's *Encyclopedia of Religion*.

Edward E. Kelly, Professor of English, St. Louis University, co-edited Volume XXI of Newman's *Letters and Diaries* and has published many articles on Newman and other modern literary figures. He has read papers at international Newman conferences in Europe and America.

David G. Schultenover, S.J., Associate Professor of Theology, Creighton University, Omaha, is the author of *George Tyrrell: In Search of Catholicism* (1981), an intellectual history. His recently completed study on the background to the modernist crisis, *A View from Rome: On the Eve of the Modernist Crisis*, is in press, and he is currently writing a book on Tyrrell's ecclesiastico-political history.

Philip C. Rule, S.J., Professor of English, College of the Holy Cross, has written on Newman, Coleridge, and other aspects of nineteenth-century British religious thought in *Harvard Theological Review*, *Nineteenth-Century Prose*, *Faith and Reason*, and *Christianity and Literature*. He is currently preparing a book-length study of Coleridge and Newman.

Paul Crowley, S.J., Assistant Professor, Religious Studies Department, Santa Clara University, received his Ph.D. from the Graduate Theological Union in 1984. His areas of specialization are philosophic theology and hermeneutics.

Bernard J. Mahoney, Professor of Philosophy at Houston Community College, a Fulbright Scholar, wrote his Ph.D. thesis on *Newman and Aristotle: The Concept of the Conscience*, using materials from the Birmingham Oratory.

Francesco Turvasi, a professor at the Pontifical College Josephinum, Columbus, is a specialist on Modernism and on the Italian biblical scholar Giovanni Genocchi who is known as the "Italian Newman." He has published widely on these subjects.

Martin X. Moleski, S.J., is an Associate Professor of Religious Studies at Canisius College, Buffalo, New York. He is currently preparing to defend his doctoral dissertation, *Illative Sense and Tacit Knowledge*, at the Catholic University of America.

John R. Connolly, Professor of Theology and former Chair of the Department, 1982-90, Loyola Marymount University, Los Angeles, is the author of *Dimensions of Belief and Unbelief* (1980), and has published a number of articles on theology and ethics. His most recent study, "The Morality of Nuclear Deterrence: Conditional or Unconditional," appeared in the *Irish Theological Quarterly* (1988).

Gerard Magill, Assistant Professor of Theological Studies at St. Louis University, teaches Moral Theology and Newman Studies. He has published several articles on religious epistemology and morality in Newman's thought. Previously, he taught in the Theology Department at Loyola University, Chicago.

INDEX

Acton, John 25, 249
Analogy of Religion 47, 59, 108
Anton, Gunther xv
Apologia pro Vita Sua xxviii, 3-5, 18, 55, 82-86, 106, 107, 109, 173, 233, 246
Aquinas, Thomas xix, 25, 69, 85, 121, 134, 233
Arians of the Fourth Century 21, 24, 94, 95, 114-116, 249
Aristotle xxviii, 91, 134, 141
Arnold, Matthew 47, 82
Augustine xxviii, 62, 65, 76, 109

Browning, Robert 53
Butler, Joseph 47, 59-61, 108

Callista 47, 55, 137, 142
Carlyle, Thomas 46, 47
Cather, Willa 15
Cicero 46, 102
Coleridge, Samuel Taylor 108
Contemporary Review 49
Copeland, William 4
Cowper, William 101, 106

Darwin, Charles 24, 88
Descartes, Rene xvi
Dolling, Robert 64-66
Dollinger, Ignaz von xv
Drey, J.S. xv, xxxvi

Duke of Norfolk xxxi, 141, 233, 249

Eliot, George 100
Essay in Aid of a Grammar of Assent xxvii, 16, 18, 27, 55, 82, 106, 143, 145, 146, 189, 202, 244
Essay on the Development of Doctrine xxvi, 74, 189

Frohschammer, Jakob xv

Gadamer, Hans-Georg 111, 119, 120
Gallicanism xx
Gout, Raoul 58, 59
Greene, Graham 54, 55
Gregory XVI xvii

Hermes, George xv, xvii
Hopkins, Gerard Manley 52, 53, 55
Houtin, Albert 70, 84, 85, 145
Hugel, Friedrich von xxxiii, xxxix, 69, 77, 84, 86, 149, 152, 164
Hume, David 48, 91, 135, 139, 140, 143
Huxley, Thomas 53

Idea of a University xxii, 55, 87, 89, 101, 106, 107, 137, 138, 143, 146, 147, 168, 242, 246-247, 251

259

Index of Forbidden Books
xv, xvii, xxiii
Inquisition xvii

John Paul II xxxiii, 19
Joyce, James 53, 55
Jung, Carl 54, 55

Kant, Immanuel xvi,
xvii, 30, 72, 73
Keble, John 9, 10, 61
Kierkegaard, Soren 47
Kingsley, Charles 3-6, 11

Lamennais, Felicite de xv
Leo XIII xix, xxxii, xxxiii,
xxxvii, 148
Letters and Diaries
xxxviii, xxxix, 55, 89,
106, 107, 147, 241
Liberal Spirit xiv, xvii
Lindbeck, George 20,
29-33, 35-38, 41-43,
87
Locke, John 135, 143,
200
Loisy, Alfred 70, 81, 82,
145, 147-149, 152-173
Loss and Gain xxii, 47,
55, 66, 94

Manning, Henry Edward
xxxi, 11, 52, 55, 249
Mirari vos xvii

Newman, John Henry
xiii, xx, xxi, xxii, xxiii,
xxiv, xxv, xxvi, xxvii,
xxviii, xxix, xxx, xxxi,
xxxii, xxxiii, xxxiv,
xxxvii, xxxviii, xxxix,

xl, 3-29, 36, 37,
45-119, 121, 122,
123, 131-143,
145-153, 155,
158-171, 173-175,
189-200, 202-218,
225-236, 241-252
Novatianism xxxiv

*On Consulting the
Faithful in Matters
of Doctrine* xxix, 19,
77, 86, 111, 249
Oxford Movement xxii,
xxv, 9, 21, 46, 244

Pascal, Blaise xxviii, 82
Pascendi dominici gregis
57, 70, 71, 145
Pius IX xvii, xviii, xix,
xxxvii, 248, 249
Pius VII xvii
Poe, Edgar Allan 96,
107
Polanyi, Michael 189,
191, 192, 194, 195,
197-199, 201, 202,
206-218
*Prophetical Office of the
Church* 22, 95, 111,
189
Pusey, Edward 51, 245

Quanta Cura xviii, 249

Rahner, Karl xxxiv, 32,
110, 111
Ratzinger, Joseph xxxiv
Rickaby, Joseph 69
Rosmini, Antonio xv,
xvii

Schell, Herman xv
Schlegel, Frederich xv
Scholasticism xiii, xv, xvi,
    xvii, xxiii, xxvii, xxviii,
    xxxiv, 59, 69-71, 81
Scott, Thomas 25, 92,
    94, 191
Syllabus of Errors xviii,
    xxi, 249

Tennyson, Alfred 132,
    144
Tillich, Paul 31, 225, 228
Tyrrell, George Henry
    xxxii, xxxix, 19, 54,
    56-84, 86, 145, 152

Ultramontanism xiii, xix,
    xx, xxxvii, 249
University Sermons 24,
    26, 50, 58, 113, 134,
    146, 189, 190, 202,
    243
Vatican Council, First
    xxxi
Vatican Council, Second
    xxxiii
Vincent of Lerins 109,
    163

Ward, W.G. xxxviii, 11,
    18, 19, 25, 53, 56, 58,
    70, 73, 82-86, 88,
    106, 107, 135, 151,
    164, 235, 246, 249
Wiseman, Nicholas 7,
    11, 151
Wordsworth, William
    103, 104

For Product Safety Concerns and Information please contact our EU representative GPSR@taylorandfrancis.com
Taylor & Francis Verlag GmbH, Kaufingerstraße 24, 80331 München, Germany